*Mind Over Matter*

# MIND OVER MATTER

## PSYCHOKINESIS

BY

## LOUISA · E · RHINE

The Macmillan Company

Collier-Macmillan Ltd. / LONDON

The Macmillan Company
866 Third Avenue, New York, N.Y. 10022
Collier-Macmillan Canada Ltd., Toronto, Ontario

Library of Congress Catalog Card Number: 70-90224

First Printing

*To the many PK experimenters and
their subjects whose work
is reviewed herein, in the hope
that I have done it justice by reporting it
fairly, clearly, and accurately, even
though necessarily briefly.*

# ACKNOWLEDGMENTS

I gratefully acknowledge the help I have received in the preparation of this book, first of all from JBR, whose firsthand contact with the material has made him a critic *par excellence*. My thanks, too, to those others—including especially Mr. W. E. Cox—who have read parts of it and made useful suggestions; also to Carol Schaber, who made the drawings, and Mrs. Dorothy Pope, who helped to proof the manuscript.

L. E. R.

# Contents

❦

[ ix ]

STRANGER (SOCRATES): I do seem to myself to see one very large and bad sort of ignorance which is quite separate, and may be weighed in the scale against all other sorts of ignorance put together.

THEATITUS: What is that?

STRANGER: When a person supposes that he knows, and does not know; this appears to be the great source of all the errors of the intellect.

—*Dialogues of Plato*

*Mind Over Matter*

CHAPTER 1

# Background of the Research

⁂

"MIND over matter" is a familiar and self-explanatory phrase, but to most people, it is an idea without reality, a science fiction concept, not something that really happens.

However, if a mental ability to influence matter directly really existed—if it were definitely proven that a human being could influence matter by immaterial mind alone, it would be difficult to envisage quickly all the effects it would have on the thought and outlook of the present. One of the first viewpoints to be affected by it would be the current psychological one which holds that the brain rather than the mind of man is his governing system. This change alone would deeply affect philosophy and religion. But proof of such a mental power is necessary before conjecture can be profitable.

The modern mind has little reason to believe that a mental force to move physical objects exists, and is, in effect, educated against it. In the past the spontaneous occurrences that at times suggested that mind had influenced matter directly were too obscure, too "wild," too widely open to question to have kept the issue open in any general way. Instead, reports of such occurrences have generally been relegated to the realm of superstition. Nevertheless the issue has been raised even in this modern age, though only by a comparatively few persons. Not only has it been raised, but even tested seriously by careful experimental methods. This testing has produced a weight of evidence which seems to indicate that the mind does have a force that can affect physical matter directly. It appears to be a natural mental capacity, although a hidden and thus far an undeveloped one.

[ 1 ]

This experimental evidence has been accumulating in the field of parapsychology, under the heading of psychokinesis, or "PK." It is the result of the research of many people and covers more than a third of a century. But the human endeavor involved, as well as the weight of evidence that has been obtained, are virtually unknown to the general public. No complete and connected account for the layman of the whole development has ever been written, and even from the professional angle only one general review, and that one much condensed, has been available.[1]

To try to fill this void, the following presentation is made. It is an attempt to describe the main contribution of practically all of the PK experiments that have been reported in scientific journals. The objective is to provide an over-all view of the research to enable each person to judge for himself the weight of the evidence that now exists and seems to show that the phenomenon is real. With this evidence in mind the reader should be able to form an opinion about the nature of PK and its probable meaning.

Systematic research on PK can be said to have had its beginning one day in early 1934 when a young instructor in the Psychology Department of Duke University in North Carolina, J. B. Rhine, had a caller in his office who seated himself on the corner of the instructor's desk and said, "Hey, doc, I've got something to tell you I think you ought to know."

Duke students frequented that office, but they were usually at least a shade more decorous than this young man. They came because the instructor was known on campus as friendly to student visitors and because of the extracurricular experiments he had for several years been conducting with volunteers from his classes.

Rhine's experiments were on the topic that had generally been known as telepathy, but which he now called extrasensory per-

[1] Pratt, J. G., "The Case for Psychokinesis." *J. Parapsychol.*, 1960, 24, pp. 171–188.

ception or ESP. The students who had been subjects in that research had been asked to try to guess the symbols on cards they could not see or of which another person was thinking. A number of these subjects had succeeded at a rate of success much higher than coincidence alone would likely give. Some of those who had discovered this unsuspected ability in themselves had become so interested that they had made experiments of their own, and a few of them came to Rhine's office regularly to assist in the ESP research either as subjects in further tests or as student assistants to help in the experiments.

The young caller, however, was not a Duke student. Although he was still in college at a neighboring institution, he announced his main occupation: gambling. And it was in the course of pursuing his "profession" that he had learned the something he thought the instructor should know. It was a discovery, he said, that he was certain ought to be studied scientifically. He had heard of the research on ESP and that was the reason he brought his discovery here. He did not know just what the connection between it and ESP might be, or if there was any, but he thought the man who was interested in the one would certainly be interested in the other. Besides, he did not know of anyone else who would listen to what he had to say and take his discovery seriously, as he hoped Rhine would do.

The discovery was this. He had found that he could control the fall of dice—*by will power*. At times, he said earnestly, when throwing dice in gambling, he could get the faces of the dice to come up as he wanted them to. He was certain of it. He said he could not do it all the time, but only when in a special highly confident mental state and desperately needing to have specific faces of the die come up. The instructor asked if he could demonstrate the claim. With only a bit of hesitation because, he said, he had never done it for a professor, he agreed to try.

In a matter of minutes, the gambler and the instructor were hunched down in a corner of the office, the gambler throwing his dice on the floor. His actual success is not on record, but it was great enough to impress the observer and to arrest his interest and attention so much that it led him to start a new line of inquiry immediately.

The reason the instructor was so quickly interested in this claim of his young visitor was not only, or even mainly, because of the conviction the young man had about his own experience. The dice-throwing demonstration would scarcely have "taken" had not the instructor's mind been prepared for it. There was a reason why this research began at this particular time and place.

As to time, it had had to await a stage in the development of the statistical method of evaluating experimental results that introduced a level of reliability not known before. The method had begun to be used in the sciences generally in the latter part of the nineteenth century. During the following decades, it was coming into general use in all areas of scientific investigation, including that of psychical research, or parapsychology as it is usually called today. However, the application of the statistical method was not general practice in this field until the end of the 1920s when research on telepathy began at Duke University. By 1934 it was routine.

In 1927 J. B. Rhine (henceforth, here, JBR) and his wife (myself), both young Ph.D.'s recently from the University of Chicago, had come to the newly established Duke University because of an interest in psychical research, to work under the British psychologist, Professor William McDougall, F.R.S., who was the new head of the Duke Psychology Department. Unlike the majority of American psychologists, McDougall was much interested in that field. In this he was quite exceptional since psychical research was then, as now, far from being an orthodox field of inquiry. Scientists ignored it. Universities were not investigating its problems. Psychical research societies usually included in their membership a few university scholars who had done so, but not within university walls, although earlier a few had allowed experiments to be carried out on the campus. Such ventures, however, had been of short duration.

The problem that had preoccupied the psychical research societies mainly was the one they called the "survival problem." It was the question whether any part of the human being survives when the body dies. From mediums and sometimes from the spontaneous "psychic" experiences of individuals came reports that purported to be communications from the deceased. If that was what they were, they must have been communicated to the living persons by telepathy. But the question of whether telepathy really occurred even among the living was still an unsettled one. Often over the centuries it had been reported that a person had known the unexpressed thought of another when he had had no obvious way of doing so. A few laboratory tests too had been carried out indicating that some kind of telepathic transfer had occurred. One of these experiments had been made at Harvard in the twenties by Dr. G. H. Estabrooks and another at the University of Grönigan in Holland under Professor H. J. F. W. Brugmanns. These reports added credence to the idea that telepathy might be a real kind of communication. But its occurrence had not been firmly established, and the idea of it was unorthodox, too suggestive of superstition, it ran too strongly counter to established lines of thought, which said that the mind cannot "know without the testimony of the senses," for research on such a topic to be thought of within the respectable confines of university investigation.

McDougall, however, as mentioned, thought the problems of psychical research were so important that they should be investigated by universities and especially by psychology departments. The time was right for such a development just then, for a new school of psychology called behaviorism had recently arisen in which the viewpoint stressed was that the legitimate basis of study in psychology should include only objective facts of behavior that could be observed without any recourse to introspection. It thus emphasized the physical side of the human organism while entirely ignoring all subjective experience that could not be objectively measured.

The behavioristic viewpoint led psychologists to ignore questions about the nature of mind, will, or consciousness that earlier had been considered central topics in psychology. It was a viewpoint which was practically to banish even the words themselves from strictly "scientific" psychology.

McDougall's psychological thinking had led him to consider that living organisms and certainly man himself are not merely physical systems but that both conscious and unconscious aspects of mind are activated by purpose that guides and determines the behavior that results. Thus his psychology could scarcely have been in more direct conflict with the new behaviorism and with the mechanistic trend of the scientific world in general. Naturally he wanted to see if any evidence against that trend could be found.

Telepathy and clairvoyance, if they actually occurred, appeared to be evidence against mechanism because almost by definition they would be independent of physical barriers. Accordingly, both the head of the department and the instructor under him were interested in an experimental attempt to find out if they really occur, and, as it happened, even the founding head of the new university (Duke), Dr. William Preston Few, was in sympathy with the idea. They all wanted to answer the question by the most approved and reliable methods possible, so that the result, whether for or against, would be an objective and decisive one. It was this combination of men then that made the specific reason why the research on ESP began about 1930, but the time was not quite ripe for research on the question of the ability of the mind to affect matter directly. A later stage in thinking was still to be reached, one dependent on the outcome of the telepathy investigation. From 1930 to 1934 the research instituted by JBR and the colleagues and students whom he interested in it was devoted single-mindedly to discovering whether or not telepathy at least occurs.

Before long, however, as the research progressed it became clear that its objective would have to be broader than that of simply showing that one mind can get information about the thought of another person. The idea of telepathy alone was too narrow for the phenomenon that was shown to be involved here. Just as Columbus did not discover only San Salvador when he landed in the New World, the research that began as a search for telepathy showed that the mind's ability to get information without the use of the senses was much greater than had been anticipated. For it was soon clear that it could get information, too, where no man's thought was involved. It could get it about *things*, by the ability now known as clairvoyance just as readily. In fact the two seemed to be actually only different phases of one general one. It was an ability to perceive or know directly about the external world whether animate or inanimate.

True, no single individual showed the ability over the whole range of nature. In a given person the evidence of this general kind of extrasensory perception, or ESP, was fragmentary, minimal, obscure, and unpredictable. But the research results showed that the potentiality was there.

With the discovery of ESP and its confirmation by reliable statistical evaluation over and over again by different persons in different places, both McDougall and JBR, by 1934, knew they were on the trail of the answer they had been seeking. Somehow the human mind is not completely limited to its little brain case and to the sense impressions that reach it there. Somehow it can reach out directly and make a wider contact. The first publication about it, a monograph called *Extrasensory Perception* (1934), was then on the press.

With this broadened concept of inherent mental ability the time had come to raise the next question: If the mind can know without the senses can it also affect the external world without muscular or other material contact.

The question did not arise only because of the verification of ESP, however. Along with the age-old reports of personal "psychic" experiences that suggested telepathy were others that involved physical effects. Most of the experiences reported were entirely spontaneous, but a few others were semiexperimental.

Not long before the visit of the gambler, JBR had been reminded of the spontaneous kind when one of his students had
told a story that still stayed in his mind. The class had been
sitting around a camp fire one evening after a hike and a picnic
in the woods. The conversation had become more and more serious as the ESP research and its possible bearings were discussed.
Then one of the girls asked JBR if he could explain an odd thing
that had happened the night her father died. Her father's clock
had stopped at the exact time he died, she said, and it was not
run down or out of order. Of course, it could have been just a
coincidence, she realized, but she and her mother felt it might
have had a meaning. It might somehow have been connected with
the death. Did JBR think it could have been?

The question, which he could not answer, was only a reminder
of all the similar ones on record in which clocks were reported
to stop, pictures to have fallen from the wall, dishes to have
cracked, and other similar effects noted that in all cases seemed
to be in conjunction with human crises. In addition there was the
age-old claim of mysterious happenings commonly known as
"poltergeist." They ranged over reports of dishes being unex-
plainably smashed, door bells rung, sleepers being disturbed by
bed clothes being pulled off, and so on. Strange things were told
too about less sophisticated peoples. Anthropologists returning
from studies of the American Indian, or of the inhabitants of the
South Seas, or Africa often told of mysterious happenings like
rock throwing, tent shaking, and so on when no person apparently
could be found to have caused them. For reasons of policy however these accounts were usually only verbal, and omitted from
published reports that included mainly effects that could be laid
to magic, like the reputation for "rainmaking," in certain tribes
of American Indians. No one could be certain whether any of
these happenings were "real" or not. But if they were, then presumably some hidden mental power caused them.

Somewhat better attested than such spontaneous effects, but
still quite undetermined as to origin, were the semiexperimental

reports of the movement of physical objects in mediumistic séance rooms. In these, tables and other articles were reported to move without contact. Though many persons alleged they did, the evidence still was indecisive.

All of these seemingly bizarre effects were physical ones, yet no physical force seemed to have caused them. The clock as in the student's case was said not to have been run down, the table not to have been touched by anyone. The question of course was, if any of these things happened as reported, what caused them?

The general naive assumption through the ages has been that these were supernatural manifestations. Even in 1922 the French astronomer Camille Flammarion[2] making a general study of experiences of apparitions and premonitions (all of which now are classified as ESP), and of physical effects that occurred under comparable circumstances arrived at a spiritualistic explanation. One of the cases he cites is the following:

One night the bell—the cord which went from the alcove where my parents slept, to the nurse's room on the first floor—began to ring loudly.

In all haste my sister, whose room was next to that of the nurse, went to look for the latter, and both went down to learn if Mother were ill, and why the bell had rung.

My father and mother told them that they had been dreaming, and that no one had rung.

At that very moment they heard the bell ring again. My father sprang from his bed. The bell cord and clapper were still in motion.

There were thus four witnesses fully awake, and nothing could set the bell in motion save someone in the alcove.—Before going back to bed, my father looked at the clock; it was half past two. The night following the next he got a letter from Paris telling him of the death of a relative.—It had happened (the bell ringing) at the very night and the very hour his relative had died.[3]

[2] Flammarion, Camille, *Death and Its Mystery, V. II: At the Moment of Death.* trans. Latrobe Carroll (New York: The Century Company, 1922).
[3] *Ibid.,* 244–45.

Flammarion emphasized that "we knew absolutely nothing of the nature of this force," but by the end of his three-volume study he decided that the only explanation for the "manifestations" he analyzed is that they prove "there is no death." These all are evidence "that intelligent forces exist around us."

However, writing about the same time as Flammarion, another French scientist, a physiologist and later Nobel Prize winner, Dr. Charles Richet,[4] surveyed the "metaphysical" field of manifestations. More of an experimentalist than Flammarion, he studied phenomena in the séance room, including physical ones. The latter were manifested particularly but by no means exclusively by the medium Eusapia Palladino, whom he studied especially. He became convinced that at times in her presence, genuine telekinesis (movement at a distance) occurred and he reported that not tables only, but many other objects were displaced and sometimes moved from one place to another. This occurred, he believed, when Palladino, who was known to play tricks when possible, was completely controlled so that normal contact with the objects moved was impossible.

After his long analysis of metaphysical phenomena of all kinds, Richet, unlike Flammarion, concluded: "I cannot adopt the inference that there are spirits—intelligences outside of human intelligence. My inference is a different one; it is that *the human personality has both material and psychological powers that we do not know.* In our present state of knowledge, we are not in a position to know."[5]

While these two French authors are only a small sample of those thinkers who in the 1920s were trying to puzzle out an explanation for the reports of inexplicable occurrences in the field of psychic research, they fairly well represent the differing attitudes toward the mysteries involved held by thoughtful people

[4] Richet, Charles, *Thirty Years of Psychical Research*. trans. Stanley De-Brath (New York: The Macmillan Company, 1923).

[5] *Ibid.*, p. 596.

sufficiently interested and sufficiently open-minded to examine the evidence and try to understand it.

Of course, when the research on telepathy began at Duke, both McDougall and JBR were well aware of the long history of reports of physical effects and of the dearth of adequate proof as to whether they actually occurred as reported. Also they knew no explanation for them. But it was only after the realization that the mind has the potential of knowing the external world directly that it seemed logical to ask the question whether it also has the capacity to move or influence objective matter directly. If such should be the case, it might be the kernel of truth in all the old reports of unexplained physical effects that had made them persist and recur over the centuries and the globe. It might also be a key to a greater understanding of another long unanswered question, the question of the relationship of mind and body.

The prevailing wave of behavioristic thinking, by 1934 had swept the mind-body problem off the deck for many thinkers, but not for McDougall. He, and JBR as well, were still concerned to find an explanation for the interaction of two such seemingly different systems as the body and the mind.

With his now heightened interest in the possibility that the mind may have the power to affect objects directly, JBR for some time had been puzzling over a way to test the question. What kind of technique could be used? It would have to be one that could be adapted to the laboratory and, like the tests for ESP, easily amenable to statistical evaluation. To fill this need, the gambler's claim and the gambler's technique fitted in like a missing piece in a puzzle. If there was anything to the claim, then mind had affected matter directly.

But was the boy's conviction, and that of all the other gamblers who over the years had thought they controlled their dice, anything more than a false impression? The idea had usually been written off as nothing but the overreading of a chance effect. The only way to find out would be to keep records of the results of attempts to exert influence on the dice and to see if they were actually higher than would be produced by chance alone.

The young gambler, having told his story and made his demonstration, went on his way. He had discharged his obligation to science, but the project his visit launched went on and on. Initially, it was JBR's alone, but in time it spread more broadly, and in time, too, the ramifications and possible significance of the phenomenon have become a little clearer, and the promise of greater meaning they give adds much to the significance of the research.

The following account of the experiments to date shows the development of the necessary controls and techniques of testing by which reliable results have been achieved. It shows unspectacular laborious laboratory methods slowly dissecting out a vein of truth that may have lain hidden, even in spooky dark-room séances.

# CHAPTER 2

# The First Experiment

❧

THE technique of throwing dice to test the possible direct influence of mind on matter proved to be an excellent one. It was quick, easy, and took almost no equipment (the dime store sold the dice). The statistical evaluation of results was relatively simple, for, other things being equal, a six-sided cube had one chance in six of falling with any given face up, thus providing a ready-made basis for the estimation of the results to be expected by chance alone.

Another circumstance, too, helped to increase the likelihood that the experiment might show the effect in question. This fact was that the experiment was not based on a speculative theory only but on a familiar belief of gamblers that they can "influence" the dice by will power. As JBR well knew, the gambler in his office was not the only one who believed it. He was just the immediate reminder, the catalyst that precipitated the reaction at this particular place and time and to this particular person.

It was in a very exploratory way at first that JBR began to test the idea. Probably if he had been less experimentally minded, and had first asked himself *how* mind could affect matter, he would not have considered the idea even worth a trial, for, of course, on the face of it, no answer to that question was known. The science of physics only takes account of physical movement by physical causes, and the point here was that by definition no such causes would be involved.

But it was easy to give the gambler's idea a little test. The results were sufficiently encouraging that the antecedent doubt that falling dice would show the effect of will was soon converted into an incredulous "maybe." As a matter of fact, the technique, perhaps because of the fascination that has preserved it through the ages, caught on easily. Almost at once dice-throwing became something of a fad, as instructor and students alike informally tested out their ability to get the results they wished. Unlike many fads, however, this one did not quickly die out. The reason was that some of those who tried succeeded well enough to get the *feeling*, at least, that they had exercised a degree of control on the dice; and soon, too, in some cases, the figures showed that the feeling was not without reason.

It was not only an entertaining game-like procedure, but one that *appeared* to be giving evidence on an important and revolutionary principle.

If the PK research had started out in the big way that the size and import of the thesis under investigation might have deserved, no doubt a near-perfect plan or blueprint of procedure would have been worked out soon after the first die-fall. The necessary controls and an approved schedule for the investigation of each logically developing angle would have been worked out at the start by a highly paid director and as many helpers as he needed. If so, no one can say for sure whether the results would have been the same. It is just possible that the initial encouragement of extra-chance scores would not have been obtained, for other ingredients now known to be necessary for the success of this particular kind of process might have been lacking. One of these ingredients is strong, enthusiastic, and open-minded interest in the test and even a degree of excitement about the outcome. It is now known that such factors add up to a special mental attitude that seems to be necessary to initiate or "release" this particular mental process in a test situation.

At any rate, this was no grand level of research project. It was only a spontaneous experimental effort by a young instructor who was deeply interested to know the answer to his question and who had some students who soon caught his enthusiasm. From his ESP research, JBR had already learned that when the subjects are human beings, and when the effect to be elicited is an obscure, seemingly unstable, and sporadic phenomenon of the mind, other elements besides the mechanical type of precision used in testing the processes of the physical world are necessary. He knew this was true, first of all because the several years of research he had spent studying the way ESP works had shown that whether or not the mental process involved in it is brought into operation depends very much on the psychological state and attitude of the subject. He had found that it seemed to be influenced by the mental climate of the test much more than by factors in the physical situation. It could well be expected then that PK, if an actuality and if in any way related to ESP, would likely be similarly affected. Even the gambler did not profess to control his dice all the time. Only when he was sufficiently excited and in the peculiar state he called "hot" did he even suspect he could do so. With too much premeditation and the installation of formidable controls, the possibility was that an effect like PK—which must certainly be elusive, since it had not been discovered long ago—would be suppressed.

The important thing in a research like this, was first of all to keep on the trail of results that *looked* encouraging and later by carefully measured steps that would not risk the loss of the effect under study, to introduce the necessary precautions. Like the hunter of an elusive animal, to have a fancy or very efficient trap would be of small use unless it was placed along the proper trail. Thus the reports of the early experiments show the effect of an attempt not to change procedures abruptly, but to follow the trail carefully, and only gradually and slowly introduce the modifications and improvements needed by better design and more certain controls.

In his first dice tests, beginning spontaneously even before the gambler left, JBR used the same procedure the gambler had used. First of all he wanted to see if he himself could get a result that even *appeared* to be anything but a chance one.

The gambler simply shook the dice in cupped hands in the time-honored way and threw them on the floor in the corner of the office. Accordingly, at first this same practice was followed by JBR, the only difference being that a record of the uppermost faces of the dice as they lay was made before they were picked up and thrown again. From this record the value of the results was later computed by methods described briefly in the final section of this chapter.

At first JBR used the same kind of target the gambler used, which was a combination of faces. The gambler had thrown a pair of the cubes for "high dice," which meant, of course, for all combinations of faces totaling more than seven. Accordingly, in this early series of tests and in some of those that followed immediately after, the dice were thrown for the high combinations.

The expectation of a chance hit in throwing for high combinations is based on the fact that 15 of the 36 possible combinations of faces of the two will be eight or above. The chance of a hit in high-dice tests, therefore, is 15 in 36, or five in 12 throws of a pair. Twelve throws of a pair of dice was also a convenient unit turn for subjects to take or for sections of a project, and soon came to be called a "run," a standard unit in most dice experiments. In a run of 12 throws of a pair of dice (24 die falls) the expectation on the average for high dice is five; it is the same for low dice (six and below) and that leaves two as the number of sevens to be expected by chance in 12 throws.

In the first tests recorded and later written up by JBR, and published jointly,[1] beginning early in 1934 and covering several months of testing, various students, family members, and friends of ours—a total of 25 individuals—acted as subjects. Spontaneously, in tests with no equipment except a pair of white plastic commercial dice about $1\frac{1}{16}$ of an inch in size, the subjects threw them into a corner of the floor or onto a table, bouncing them against the side wall to ensure considerable random movement. JBR himself kept the record.

[1] Rhine, Louisa E., and Rhine, J. B., "The Psychokinetic Effect: I. The First Experiment." *J. Parapsychol.*, 1943, 7, pp. 20–43.

One point understood from the beginning was that the subject would have in mind the specified target as he threw and would genuinely will it to come up. Of course, everyone was naturally curious, interested, and prepared to give the test a good try or he would not have gotten caught up in it in the first place.

In this initial stage of the work some subjects got higher scores than others; and the scores of everyone, too, fluctuated from time to time. Most of these variations were not at the time explainable. However, a total of 562 runs (of 24 die falls each) were thrown in this exploratory unstructured series of tests, and the total number of hits (3,110) gave a positive deviation of 300 from chance (which was five times 562 or 2,810). This figure is so far from chance coincidence that it would not occur once in well over a billion such cases.[2] Even though the average rate of scoring per run was only 5.5 instead of the 5.0 that would be expected by chance, the extra-chance value it gave over *so great a number of runs,* left no doubt that part of the gambler's claim had been substantiated. At least the targets wished for had come up more often than would have been expected on the basis of chance. The next problem was to account for this deviation. Even though the gambler had been convinced he "did it," when his dice came up according to his wish, there were counter possibilities, of course, that would have to be ruled out before any such conclusion could be drawn.

One of the counter possibilities was that skilled throwing of the dice might have produced the positive results. Even though none of these subjects had been known to be adept at dice throwing, it had to be regarded as not impossible that some of them at least might have acquired a degree of skill. A different way of "throwing" than simply from the hand was needed.

The impromptu nature of the whole inquiry at this stage is shown by the device that was introduced. A 10-inch-wide board with corrugated cardboard tacked on it was inclined at about a 45-degree angle onto the seat of a large cushioned chair. Near

[2] This value and the rest given later in this chapter are derived by a formula given in the last section of this chapter.

the upper end of the board, two nails supported a small ruler which made a little shelf on which the pair of dice was placed. When the subject was ready, he lifted the ruler and released the dice and allowed them to roll down the board to tumble over the rough cardboard surface onto the cushion below. With this new setup, 108 more runs were made. The rate of hitting was just as high as before. It did not look as if skill in throwing the cubes could have produced the above-chance scores.

At the same time that JBR was making his tests, some of his students made tests by themselves and reported rates of hitting comparable to those he was getting. This work, however, was classified as "unwitnessed," and therefore, only suggestive regardless of the size of deviation above chance that was secured. This was but one of the precautions against possible error introduced early in the research. It was held to be necessary if results of experiments were to be considered acceptable, that they be validated by the observation and concurrence of at least two mature responsible persons. An attempt to set extra high standards in all aspects had been made in the ESP research and was continued as a matter of course in the PK investigations.

The problem of biased dice and their effect on scores was recognized from the beginning. The dice used were too cheap to have been intentionally "loaded," but could not be regarded as perfect. In fact, it seemed unlikely that even precision-made cubes could ever be fully relied upon to retain their quality throughout a long experiment. Instead, the decision was made to control for bias by the design of the test. In this case, it should be by changing the target from high dice to low dice at times and also to sevens. If the dice were biased in favor of one face, the bias would have to disfavor the opposite one. Accordingly, such tests were made, although in the exploratory situation in which this initial work was done the times and numbers of these other tests were not balanced off equally.

A sufficient number of runs was made for sevens, however, to give reassurance that bias would not account for the high-dice scores. In the same period during which the results with high combinations had been secured, using the same pair of dice, 91.3 runs were made, with sevens as target.[3] The expectation from chance alone in this case was two per run. The average score secured was only 2.49 per run, but even at that rate, in this number of runs, it yielded a value so high it would not occur by chance once in thousands of such experiments (p = .0003).

During this same period, and still with the same pair of dice, a series of runs for low combinations was also made. The low-dice series consisted of a total of 104 runs, made at various times in the course of the tests for high combinations. In these, of course, the subjects had to try to avoid the high faces on which they had earlier been concentrating and attend instead to the low ones which heretofore they had been trying to avoid. The result was unexpected. The scores for both the low combinations and the high combinations were insignificantly different from chance expectation and even slightly negative. But the *sevens* were significantly positive, the odds against chance being better than a thousand to one (p = .001).

How could such a result be interpreted? With odds as high as that, it could not be considered to be the result of chance. From a psychological viewpoint, however, it could make sense, for it could mean that the subjects succeeded in blocking their former mental "set" in favor of high combinations, but did not succeed in removing the inhibition they had developed against low ones. With both inhibitions prevailing the faces that came up had to come out as an excess of sevens. Such an interpretation was at least tenable.

Thus at the same time that the scores of the experiment were not a chance concidence, neither could they be considered to be the result of dice bias. The low scores for high dice when low combinations were the target served as controls against dice bias when high dice were the target. While controls of this kind did not

[3] Rhine, J. B., "Early PK Tests: Sevens and Low-Dice Series." *J. Parapsychol.*, 1945, 9, pp. 106–115.

prove that the dice were unbiased, they did show that bias would not produce this kind of result. And so it seemed to mean that the subject was having an effect on the way the dice fell, although not necessarily in the way he was consciously trying to affect them.

Another and perhaps even stronger indication of a psychological effect on the dice was hidden in these results. It had to do with the fact, given little attention at the time, that subjects usually scored best in the first runs they made in a session. This effect was pronounced enough that it led the experimenter to favor short sessions. But it was not until much later that the tendency for a decline in the rate of scoring in the session was recognized as a meaningful psychological one. As a matter of fact, the point did not get full emphasis until nearly nine years later when, in the summer of 1942, an analysis was made that brought out the full meaning of the effect. It was then revealed as a very definite type of evidence to show that something besides simple chance coincidence was present in these scores. It was all the stronger evidence of PK for having been unexpected by the experimenters at the time and consequently overlooked until long after much of their data had been collected and filed away.

Because this analysis turned out to be a landmark study and because it threw light on the beginning high-dice work, as well as that which followed, it can best be reviewed in the next chapter, even though to do so is to draw it considerably out of its chronological order. However, before going on to a discussion of the definitive analyses of 1942, it needs to be said that all of the early dice research, especially that already described and that which followed in the years immediately after, was rated by those concerned as only *exploratory*. Neither JBR, nor those who worked with him, considered it conclusive at the time. At the beginning, of course, there was no way to know that anything would come out of the almost impromptu dice throwing sessions. When extrachance scores were secured it only meant that like a glimmer of light in a tunnel, this *might* be evidence of a genuine phenomenon. These first experiments thus were necessarily groping efforts, and at the time not actually recognized even by those most involved as stepping stones to the discovery of a new principle.

As mentioned in Chapter 1 a new day dawned in the study of psychical phenomena when statistical methods of evaluation were introduced. Before that, for instance, if a person seemed to get someone else's thought when it had not been expressed he might think it was a case of telepathy. But others might say it was "just chance coincidence." Or if a gambler had a run of "high dice" when trying for high combinations, he might think as did the young man in JBR's office, that he had influenced the dice by will power, but others could say it was "just a chance coincidence." No one could tell in either case which explanation was correct, because no one had a way to estimate the range of event that could be laid to chance.

The statistical method is, in essence, one that defines chance occurrences and so, as it were, limits the areas that can reasonably be ascribed to "coincidence." Now, with a properly arranged experiment, decisions can be reached that were impossible before. The main need is that the possibilities like the number of faces of the die be known beforehand. The fact that a die was a six-sided cube thus made possible experiments that could be statistically evaluated, because the value that chance alone would give could be fairly accurately ascertained. If the experimental result was higher than the value to be expected by chance, it was easy to determine how much higher it was. Then scientists could agree at what level of increase over "chance" they would consider the result to be statistically significant.

The specific method of statistical evaluation that was used generally throughout most of the early PK research was that of finding the critical ratio (CR) yielded by the test, and it is the measure used in most of the published reports.

The CR measures how much the results differ from those that would be produced by chance alone, that is, from mean chance expectation (MCE). Readers not interested in statistics can very well skip the methods by which the CRs are computed, just as they skip the details of method by which life insurance tables, opinion polls, and the like are calculated. However, for those who are interested in a sketch of those methods, a final section is appended.

For nonmathematical readers only three statistical items need be remembered and they will soon become familiar and offer no difficulty. The three items are the CR, the *p-value*, and the *level of significance*.

The CR tells how much larger or smaller than a chance result the one obtained in the test is; thus a CR of 2.5 means the result is 2.5 times the standard deviation (see next page). The result could have been given instead as "odds" against chance, which, with a CR of 2.5 for instance would be approximately one hundred to one. Another way of expressing the same thing, one that can be given as a decimal, is the probability (p-value) of such a value, and in the above example it would be stated, $p = .01$ (strictly $p = .012$). Both of these terms will be used in giving the results of most of the experimental reports of the following chapters.

The third point to remember is that the criterion of significance has been set at a CR of approximately 2.5, or $p = .01$. Values at that level or above will be spoken of as "significant," meaning that they are to be considered as meaningfully beyond the range of chance. Those, however, lower than that such as 2.0 ($p. = .04$) for instance may be cited as "suggestive" but not as significant. At the other extreme, any p-values so highly significant that they require more than six ciphers will be described simply as having a probability against chance (a p-value) of "less than one in a million."

A point that may need a bit of explanation here concerns the material to be reviewed. As already mentioned the intention has been to include all of the reports of PK research that have been published. The "cut-off" date is the end of 1968.

The published material involved consists mainly of experiments that gave evidence of PK. As a matter of fact, most of them were published in the *Journal of Parapsychology* and the policy of that journal has been to accept only research reports that yield significant results, or that introduce methods or ideas that would be helpful to other research workers.

The reason for the policy is that in so unexplored a field many unprofitable researches might be undertaken (often by those who are not prepared for them) which would be entire failures and would contribute nothing, not even a sure reason for the failure. The point was that reasons for success needed to be established before reasons for failure could be considered "news." It seemed more efficient therefore for the progress of the research to fill the pages of the *Journal* with material that would be of some benefit to research workers as well as giving an idea of the progress of experimentation to general readers. Other journals have differed on policy regarding unsuccessful results. The argument has been that something can be learned even from unsuccessful results, if only what *not* to do—an argument, however, as already suggested, that only holds in areas in which reasons for failure can be established.

However, a special safeguard has been followed rather generally in recent years, which is to consider as a pilot investigation a first experiment on a given topic that yields results that are only suggestive. The author is then advised to repeat the experiment and see if the pilot finding can be confirmed by results that give a significantly large CR. If so, the point can be considered as relatively conclusive and a report of it will be published. Of course, it is important as in any other science to have independent confirmations too. On this account confirmations from other experimenters at other places are especially valuable.

To find the CR of the total score of a given test, the method is based on the procedure of throwing dice for a specified face for a given number of standard runs. Each run includes 24 die falls and the number of hits expected by chance per run is

$24 \div 6 = 4$. The first step of the evaluation is to find the "deviation" of the test score total, from the total expected by chance in the given number of runs. For instance, in 20 runs the number expected by chance on the average would be 20 times the chance average of a single run, or $20 \times 4 = 80$.

But if the actual score had been five per run instead of four, the actual score average for the 20 runs, would be $20 \times 5 = 100$. The deviation secured in the test then, would be $100 - 80 = 20$. The next step is to find the standard chance deviation, or SD. The SD is the accepted "yardstick" used to measure the variance from the expected chance mean or average, the MCE, which in this example is 80. This standard measure of variance has been worked out and is available in statistical tables as in the text book, *Parapsychology*[4] or it can be computed. If computed, since it varies with the number of trials $(n)$ the SD is found by the formula $/npq$ in which $p$ equals the probability of a hit per trial ($\frac{1}{6}$) and the $q$ the probability of a miss ($\frac{5}{6}$). In the example given the SD is 8.16. But the experimental deviation was $+20$. This, divided by 8.16 gives a CR of 2.45, and means that the result of the experiment was almost two and a half times that which chance would have been likely to produce. A score as high as $CR = 2.45$ therefore would be "marginally" significant.

CR values can be converted into p-values and standard statistical tables giving them are available. As the CR values increase, the p-values decrease (while the odds increase) so that a CR of 3.0 would have a p-value of about .003 and CRs still higher would have smaller p-values. However, the p-values cited for CRs in the following presentation are only half as small as those listed in statistical tables. This is for a reason that will be clear later (Chapter 5). It again is a more conservative measure than the one generally used in other sciences.

The standard of significance used in PK research was set at $p = .01$ or one in a hundred early in the ESP research. It is a

4 Rhine, J. B., and Pratt, J. G., *Parapsychology* (Charles C. Thomas, Springfield, Ill. 1957).

lower level than is customarily required in other sciences. They generally consider a value of about .05 or one in 20 as adequate. However, ESP and PK too are new and controversial topics and therefore it seemed necessary to use extra precautions in statistics as well as in experimental methods.

CHAPTER 3

# The Decisive Analysis

ALTHOUGH research on PK began early in 1934, no publication about it was made until more than nine years later. The reason for this long delay is of interest here, as is the special type of analysis made on the accumulated data of the PK research. The result of this analysis was the immediate reason why the long silence was broken.

After JBR made his series of tests that encouraged the idea that a mental effect might be involved, and even while those tests were still in progress, similar experiments were being carried out by other persons. Before long, at least after a year or two during which results continued to be encouraging and the suggestion that a PK factor had been shown was increasingly strong, the natural impulse was to publish an account of the work. Seldom do experimenters delay reporting new effects for which impressive experimental data are at hand. Along with the natural personal satisfaction of publication, there is also the need to get their results before their colleagues for the benefit of criticism, suggestion, and especially for confirmation if they are correct. One of the prime necessities in research, after an experimenter gets results that are significant, is for other experimenters also to get similar results under similar conditions.

In the case of the early PK experiments, however, publication did not follow discovery immediately. The main reason it was delayed was because of the situation that had developed in connection with the research on ESP. The first published report of that, the monograph *Extrasensory Perception*, had appeared in

1934.[1] The public was at once interested and seemed to accept the idea that ESP was real readily enough, but the scientific community showed only a little interest at first and before long what it did show was mainly negative. The report that experimental tests had indicated a human ability to get information without the senses was in fact met with considerable skepticism and even some hostility. The reaction seemed to be based, however (and this was unexpected), not so much on a criticism of the validity of the data or methods of getting them, as on an *a priori* assumption that extrasensory perception just cannot occur, and, therefore, that the reported results could not possibly be valid. This point of view was advanced again and again even though the critics could not say by what flaw the findings were invalidated. One of the repeated objections also was that the data of an extrasensory way of perceiving did not "square with existing knowledge," and, therefore, the results reported must be wrong. Just how any new and different discovery could ever be accepted on the criterion that it must square with the old was not explained. But because of opposition often on no more valid a basis than this, it was obvious that general scientific circles would not quickly consider the evidence for ESP on its merits.

At the same time, those persons who did take the trouble to judge the ESP research impartially found no basically devastating weakness in it. It looked, therefore, as if the claims of the discovery of ESP would stand and eventually, if not immediately, be accepted. But if now another revolutionary concept like PK were to be announced, coming as it would from the same laboratory, it might even tend to slow up whatever measure of recognition of ESP might be coming with the passing of time and the accumulating of more experimental data.

A second but minor consideration against publication existed, too. In spite of the increasing evidence for PK that each new

[1] Rhine, J. B., *Extrasensory Perception.* Boston Society for Psychic Research, Boston, Mass. Mar. 1934 (Reprinted, Bruce Humphries, 1964).

project added, JBR and all those experimenting with him were
only slowly themselves being persuaded that the effect was sufficiently well established that it could be defended successfully.
As each research over the next few years after 1934 had been
completed, they knew its weakness as well as its strength. The
earliest experiments, like JBR's initial high-dice tests (Chapter 2),
were frankly exploratory, and though most of the later ones were
somewhat better planned and executed, still not only did the
experimenter's own doubts about the reality of PK die slowly,
but also he knew the difficulty that well might be encountered
in trying to defend pioneer research on more than one front at
the same time.

For both these reasons, then, the decision was to put off publication for a more propitious time. In this situation, more time
it seemed could only be an asset. Research would continue and
the case, if as firm as the experimenters were coming to think
it was, would only be strengthened by each added confirmation.

News about the PK research quickly spread among JBR's friends
around the campus and to a few interested persons at other
places. Some of them undertook PK tests, too, and reported their
results to him. Most of them were positive. Thus, data kept piling
up in his files. This continued for more than eight years. It was
not until the summer of 1942 that an analysis and survey of all
the accumulated data as a unit was undertaken. It was the result
of this study that led at last to the decision to publish the results
of the PK experiments.

That summer World War II was absorbing much of the
thought and attention of the country. It had also taken all but
one of the graduate students who had been working in the Parapsychology Laboratory.[2] Active research was consequently practically at a standstill.

It was thus a suitable time to reexamine all of the PK experimental records and to try to evaluate their strength. Especially,

2 For establishment of Parapsychology Laboratory see Chap. 5.

a search could be made for "position effects" in the data to see if any were present similar to those that JBR had recently found in records of ESP experiments. In standard ESP tests he had noted a tendency for hits to occur more frequently in the first half of a column of trial records than in the second half. Sometimes the first few and the last few calls of runs of the 25 ESP card deck showed the highest scoring rate of all. This kind of distribution of hits produced a generally U-shaped curve in graphs of the frequency of hits in the run. This U-curve had been found to occur so often that it was a "position effect" that came to be taken as something of a mark of ESP. It was a second line of evidence that ESP had occurred and one quite distinct from the first one, which was the actual above-chance rate of scoring.

Similar curves of performance have been found in many other areas of psychological measurements in which tasks of the form of these of ESP are involved. The form is, of course, that in which a person is required to make a long series of similar responses in a structured column. For instance, in studies of recall using a series of words or syllables, a drop in rate of success is practically always obtained as the subject proceeds down the list. Gradients and declines are long familiar in reports of learning experiments, too, in that the beginnings and sometimes endings, as well, stand out more sharply than do the intermediate sections.

The position effects in ESP tests not only gave one more indication that ESP was a reality, but showed as well that it operated the same as somewhat comparable psychological processes. It was a logical question, then, whether PK hits also tended to fall into patterns that could only be accounted for by psychological principles. If so, this finding would be built-in evidence that they were the result of mental processes rather than of physical causes. It would be evidence over and above that of the statistical significance of the results of the individual experiments.

Accordingly, all the records of PK projects that had accumulated over the years since the beginning ones in 1934 were assembled and examined in turn to see if the hits recorded in them showed a characteristic patterning of position.[3] The direct objective was to see if there might be a definite tendency for the first part of the runs to yield higher rates of hitting than the final, or at least the middle ones, and also whether the scoring in the first runs of a session was higher on the average than on the later ones.

For the task, JBR had the help of the remaining graduate assistant, Miss Elizabeth (Betty) Humphrey. Fortunately for their examination, the records of PK experiments had been kept in a fairly uniform fashion. Generally the runs of a session or of an individual unit of a session had been recorded in vertical columns, one beside the other, across the successive pages of a bound record book. Each page with its series of columns was thus a record of the session in the chronological order in which the tests had been made. In other words, the page was usually the record of a unit task which began with the left-hand column of entries and ended with the one on the right.

The record itself could therefore now be used as a unit to be analyzed. The number of runs per page was not important as long as it was more than one, so there could be a first and last run to compare. Since as many as 10 runs could be recorded on a page, and since few experimental sessions had been longer than that, most of the sessions had required no more than a single record page. The few pages on which the session ran over onto a second were treated as a single page, since the objective was to observe the hitting pattern of a unit task.

It was necessary, of course, to include all data which were comparable in order to give the analysis the widest possible meaning. The records of 24 separate PK-test projects based on dice-throwing procedures were on hand, and although they had varied widely in specific techniques and conditions, 18 of them had been so recorded that the pages of their record books were adequately comparable. From them a total of 27,000 runs (of 24 single-die

[3] Rhine, J. B., and Humphrey, Betty M., 'The PK Effect: Special Evidence from Hit Patterns. I. Quarter Distribution of the Page." *J. Parapsychol.*, 1944, 8, pp. 18–60.

Subject   Chas. Brown     Observer   J. Smith

Date   7/28/37

Kind of Expt.   PK 6 dice for sixes

Use other side for remarks     Tot. score   60 runs: +31

*1st quarter, runs, hits, 8* (left margin)     *3rd quarter, 15 runs, 70 hits, +10* (right margin)

| 1 | 2 | 3 | 4 | 5 | 6 | 7 | 8 | 9 | 10 |
|---|---|---|---|---|---|---|---|---|----|
|   |   |   |   |   |   |   |   |   |    |
| 1 | 2 | 3 | 3 | 1 | 1 | 2 | 1 | 1 | 0 |
| 0 | 2 | 2 | 1 | 1 | 0 | 1 | 2 | 3 | 1 |
| 1 | 1 | 2 | 0 | 2 | 2 | 0 | 1 | 2 | 1 |
| 2 | 1 | 2 | 0 | 2 | 1 | 0 | 3 | 2 | 2 |
| 1 | 0 | 0 | 1 | 2 | 1 | 0 | 0 | 1 | 1 |
| 0 | 3 | 1 | 1 | 1 | 0 | 4 | 2 | 3 | 1 |
| 2 | 2 | 1 | 1 | 1 | 0 | 0 | 0 | 2 | 2 |
| 2 | 1 | 0 | 3 | 2 | 0 | 0 | 3 | 0 | 0 |
| 1 | 3 | 1 | 1 | 1 | 2 | 1 | 0 | 0 | 3 |
| 2 | 2 | 0 | 1 | 0 | 2 | 1 | 1 | 0 | 2 |
| 0 | 0 | 1 | 0 | 0 | 0 | 1 | 1 | 2 | 2 |
| 2 | 3 | 1 | 3 | 2 | 0 | 1 | 3 | 1 | 1 |
| 0 | 2 | 1 | 1 | 0 | 0 | 0 | 0 | 2 | 2 |
| 2 | 0 | 0 | 0 | 0 | 0 | 2 | 1 | 1 | 0 |
| 2 | 3 | 2 | 0 | 0 | 1 | 2 | 0 | 1 | 2 |
| 0 | 3 | 1 | 0 | 0 | 1 | 1 | 1 | 1 | 1 |
| 0 | 1 | 0 | 1 | 2 | 0 | 0 | 1 | 0 | 0 |
| 3 | 0 | 1 | 2 | 1 | 1 | 3 | 2 | 1 | 0 |
| 0 | 2 | 1 | 2 | 2 | 2 | 1 | 1 | 0 | 2 |
| 1 | 1 | 3 | 0 | 2 | 1 | 2 | 0 | 2 | 2 |
| 1 | 0 | 0 | 1 | 1 | 2 | 1 | 1 | 1 | 0 |
| 1 | 2 | 1 | 1 | 1 | 1 | 0 | 1 | 1 | 2 |
| 2 | 1 | 0 | 1 | 2 | 3 | 0 | 0 | 1 | 0 |
| 0 | 0 | 3 | 1 | 2 | 2 | 1 | 2 | 1 | 0 |
| 26 | 35 | 27 | 25 | 28 | 23 | 24 | 27 | 29 | 27 |
| +2 | +11 | +3 | +1 | +4 | -1 | 0 | +3 | +5 | +3 |

*2nd quarter, runs, hits, 3* (left bottom margin)     *4th quarter, 15 runs, 60 hits, 0* (right bottom margin)

FIGURE 1. Representative record sheet (with 10 columns of 24 throws of 6 dice) showing quarter distribution of hits.

falls each) were such that they could be analyzed for position effects.

To compare the average rate of scoring both down the run and in the successive runs as the task progressed, the record pages were in effect quartered by dividing them first into left and right halves and then dividing these into upper and lower parts (Figure 1). This meant that each run was divided into an upper and lower half, and the successive upper halves were divided into a left and right part, as were the lower halves. The number of hits in each quarter of the page was then determined (the quarter distribution, or QD as it came to be called), and a record made of the hits in the successive quarters, the first to the fourth.

When these totals were obtained not only was a decline in hitting shown between the beginning and the end of the task, but also from quarter to quarter. That of the first quarter was highest, and usually but not always that of the bottom left, next; then the top right; with the lower right, the lowest (Figure 2). The subjects thus had shown in their QDs a score decline in their individual runs, and also in the succession of runs across the page.

These declines not only occurred, but were often very pronounced, the difference between the score totals for the first and fourth quarters of all 18 experimental projects being so great as to have an extra-chance value of about 100,000,000 to one. The magnitude of this effect was unexpected, even though in individual experiments it had sometimes been noticed that the best results came early in the test. In others, however, the difference often had been slight and had gone unremarked by the individual experimenter at the time. But now when the records were taken all together, the trends were generally the same, and so their value was compounded.

For it was found that the trend had been general, and the result not something that had been caused by one or two exceptions. In fact, nearly all of the 18 separate projects which had been included contributed to it. Even the results of JBR's exploratory high-dice project gave strong evidence of it.

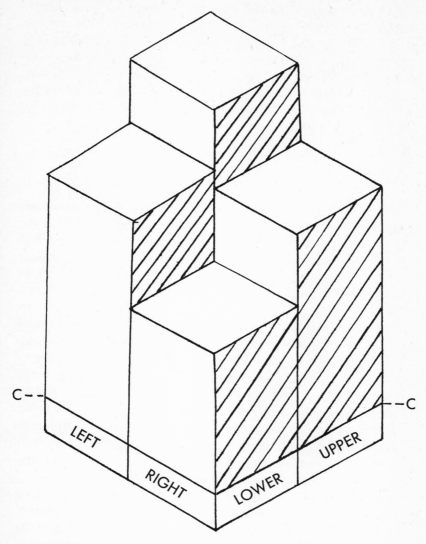

FIGURE 2. Typical quarter distribution graph showing decline in rate of hitting from first to last quarter of record pages. C is base line— i.e., chance expectation.

However, once the analysis was made, and the old 1934 high-dice data of JBR's initial experiment was evaluated for position effects, an interesting finding resulted. Of that data, 321 runs had been made in short sessions of two or three runs each. When the average scores for each of the first, second, and third runs were found (five hits in each run, expected by chance), they showed a very marked decline from first to third, the figures for which were respectively:

| | | | | |
|---|---|---|---|---|
| First Run | 123 runs | Average Score | 6.09 | CR = 7.07 |
| Second Run | 123 runs | Average Score | 5.15 | CR = 1.00 |
| Third Run | 75 runs | Average Score | 5.05 | CR = .27 |

This breakdown thus showed that the significance of the series came mainly from the first runs of the sessions and that the tendency to score best in the first run was general, not an effect that would occur by chance or because of any of the obvious counter explanations like skillful throwing or dice bias, recording errors, selection of or loss of records. No such artifact would produce regular patterns in the position of hits. Any or all of such causes would tend to produce a "chance" distribution of hits. Even the wild idea that the experimenters might have fraudulently manipulated their data could not be suggested in connection with these patterns, for at the time when the experiments were carried out, some even eight years earlier, none of the experimenters had anticipated that such an effect would be found or realized the significance it would have if it were. In the individual experimenter's experience, a subject's tendency to fail to score well toward the end of, or anywhere in, a session was only a frustration, not a result to be desired.

When it was realized that the scoring trends on the record pages were so marked that the differences between quarters were highly significant, no further effort at confirmation seemed actually called for. But like a Chinese toy with one design concealed within another, the question was then raised, what about position effects in smaller units than the page?

The record pages had represented units sessions of effort for the subjects, and in some of the experiments, as already mentioned, the sessions had been broken up into sets of only a few (usually three) runs each. At the end of such a set a pause had been made to score the runs or change the target before the session continued. In such cases, each set was in the nature of a subunit of the task of the session (or page) as a whole.

And so, to see if these smaller units, too, showed the psychological effect of "starting and stopping" all the records that were amenable were reanalyzed by set.[4]

Nine of the 18 experiments in the original analysis had been structured into sets, and when these sets were analyzed, their QDs were found to show a U-curve strikingly similar to that of the page. It meant that even in these smaller units, the likelihood of a hit varied with the position of the throw in the set.

This finding of position effects even in the set not only confirmed all over again the PK hypothesis, but added a bit to the understanding of the way PK works. It had earlier been suggested that declines in the ESP data, and now in those of PK, might be the result of fatigue. But if that had been the reason, no "pick-up" should occur on the upper part of the next run or at the end of a session. Instead of a U-curve a straight diagonal line across the page should result. This new finding showed that the decline in rate of hitting was not caused by fatigue, but rather was a psychological effect related to the subjects innate tendency to structure his test experience.

This meant that the PK phenomenon was not just an anomalous ability sometimes to hit the target but a process connected with and expressed according to deep unconscious motivating patterns, just as ESP had been found to be. Even if all the PK test series had yielded only a chance total, if they had shown internal position effects as striking as these, they would have shown that

[4] Rhine, J. B., and Humphrey, Betty M., "The PK Effect: Special Evidence from Hit Patterns. II. Quarter Distribution of the Set." *J. Parapsychol.*, 1944, 8, pp. 254–271.

*something* had drastically interfered with the kind of distribution
of hits on the record page that could be ascribed to chance alone.
Significant position effects on the page even more than significant
total scores were evidence of psychological influences because no
purely physical cause and no mistake in procedure would cause
them.

And so now the similarity of ESP and PK, as far as these internal effects were concerned, was emphasized. Now it was shown
that in PK, too, the likelihood of a hit was affected by the position of the individual trial in the run. Even though in ESP the
phenomenon was an idea and in PK it was a physical effect, it was
indicated now that they both were subject to the same kind of
psychological influences.

In ESP, as in the learning of a string of nonsense syllables for
instance, one can well suppose that the beginning of the task
would stand out. The end of it might too if the person knew when
he was coming to the end, like a gardener hoeing long rows, who
would find the end of a row endowed with added interest just
because it was the end.

All such effects are probably the result of changes in the strength
of attention and motivation that come in over the course of such
tasks. Those of the end show the satisfaction of completion, which
is real even though another row, or another run of ESP test cards,
is to be begun immediately. Position effects thus, in PK, too,
seemed now to show evidence of the rise and fall of motivation as
it fluctuated over the structured task.

When such evidence was found even in the "sub-tasks" of the
sets, it seemed that about the last point in the confirmation of
the actuality of a PK effect had been reached. Like strata of rock,
one area after another had been exposed and found to show the
mark of PK. The only possible alternative to it that could be
thought of was the long chance that some kind of error of checking hits or making computations could have been made in the QD
analyses. It was, therefore, decided to "go the last mile" and to call

in someone who had had no connection with those analyses, to make a recheck and an independent analysis.

It happened that available just then (1943) was an earlier student of JBR's and a former colleague at the laboratory, Lieutenant J. C. Pratt. On leave from the Navy for a few months, he was called in to do the job, and also incidentally to conduct a recheck of the analyses already made. He did both by making a separate analysis and correlating it with them.

In the first task Pratt checked all the available records to see if the 18 that had been analyzed by JBR and Betty Humphrey had correctly included all the records that could have been used. He found no others.[5]

In rechecking the statistical work he found several minor errors which when duly corrected did not change any of the conclusions that had been drawn relative to the significance of the QD distributions.

Pratt's independent analysis made on the data amenable to it used an arbitrary unit, the half-set. In this he divided the sets into their upper and lower and right and left halves to test the QD effect as had been done before on the pages as a whole and analyzed the quarters.[6] The result was a difference between the first and the fourth that yielded a significant $QD_d = 3.52$; $p = .004$. The analysis thus not only confirmed the general correctness of the earlier findings, but also added the information that even in these smaller units, there were pronounced position effects in line with those already found.[7]

[5] Pratt, J. G., "A Reinvestigation of the Quarter Distribution of the (PK) Page." *J. Parapsychol.*, 1944, 8, pp. 61–63.

[6] Rhine, J. B., Humphrey, Betty M., and Pratt, Lt. J. G., USNR., "The PK Effect: Special Evidence from Hit Patterns. III. Quarter Distribution of the Half-Set." *J. Parapsychol.*, 1945, 9, pp. 150–168.

[7] The $CR_d$ between two values is obtained by computation somewhat more involved than a CR of a given value. This is true particularly if the two groups are of unequal size. A formula for it can be found in the book, *Parapsychology*, already referred to, and also in standard statistics texts.

Now at last all shreds of doubt about the reality of PK were erased from the minds of those who were immediately involved and knew the weight of the total evidence. The question that now remained was not about the validity of the findings, but how best to get them before a wider public and to get the research examined by the scientific world. The Duke Parapsychology Laboratory (Chapter 5) then issued an invitation to anyone who cared to do so to come and examine the evidence at first-hand. It was an invitation, however, that yielded no acceptances. But many years later a critical review came out, the author of which denigrated the QD analyses by emphasizing the possibility of dice bias and unequal numbers of target faces.[8]

But whether or not anyone accepted the invitation to come and see the evidence, the time to publish the results had now arrived. The nine-year-long hesitation was removed for now the researchers themselves felt that they would be able to defend the work against all the criticisms that could be made against it.

However, the situation regarding even the reception of the ESP results by the scientific world was not yet favorable. Although it was nearly 10 years since the first account of them had been published and in spite of a fairly steady stream of subsequent research reports also confirming the occurrence of ESP, the indications still were that the work was receiving little impartial attention in the scholarly centers in which it should have had a pertinent bearing. These were, first of all, the academic departments of psychology, some of which had been in the forefront of resistance to the work on ESP. However, by 1942, most of the more strident criticism and objection to the very idea of ESP had died down. And so it was finally decided that the PK work would be published regardless of the way it might be received.

Accordingly, the initial high-dice work reported in Chapter 2 was published in the *Journal of Parapsychology* in March 1943. It was preceded by an editorial intended to help in clearing the

[8] Girden, E. "A Review of Psychokinesis (PK)." *Psychol. Bull.*, Vol. LIX (Sept., 1962).

way for the introduction of the topic of "physical phenomena," for no experimental reports on the topic had ever appeared before.[9] In spite of the many reports of the occurrence of unexplained physical effects in various mediumistic circles which had been published in journals of psychical research, no lasting impression on the western scientific world had been made to the effect that such reports might involve a valid principle. But now the editor, JBR, said that a number of experimental reports would be coming up in the *Journal* on the topic of direct mental action on physical objects, and it was hoped that these would stimulate a new epoch of investigation.

Two more editorials on PK followed in successive issues of the *Journal*. In them, an attempt was made to show that the idea of mind affecting physical matter directly is not as alien as at first thought it would appear to be. The probable relation between ESP and PK was enlarged on, also, and the importance of the discovery that "the mind has real force" was stressed.

In spite of these attempts to "naturalize" the concept of PK, however, the publication of the research on the topic did not produce the general effect which had been both anticipated and feared. Over the next three years the material of the 18 reports that had been included in the QD analysis and also the results of new researches that continued to come in were published in fairly regular order. All reports pointed to the fact that a psychological effect had been discovered in connection with the "willed" fall of dice that could not be accounted for except as a direct influence of mind on matter. Thus in an article in September 1945, JBR could say that henceforth, "merely to repeat PK tests with the simple objective of finding more evidence of the PK effect itself should be an unthinkable waste of time for all those who could achieve a higher purpose." But even so, scarcely any reaction favorable or unfavorable to the idea of PK was aroused. The world was preoccupied and absorbed by the war in its then

[9] Rhine, J. B., " 'Physical Phenomena' in Parapsychology." *J. Parapsychol.*, 1943, 7, pp. 1–4.

critical and unpredictable stage. Possibly, too, those sections of the scholarly world that had taken issue with the ESP reports were tired now and unready to take on a wider battle. Possibly the idea seemed just too fantastic to take seriously. At any rate, the PK results and their significance are even yet quite unknown generally and certainly have not been taken seriously in any but a very limited circle.

Within the field of parapsychology itself, work on PK has never been carried on as widely as on ESP, nor have as many experimenters engaged in it. But nevertheless, research did continue steadily but more slowly after the interruption of the war. Although the flurry of activity in the years between 1934 and 1942 has hardly been equaled since, even so, the accumulation of experimental data up to the present has continued. It is, however, scattered mostly in the pages of the *Journal of Parapsychology* and, as already mentioned, even reviews of it are few and incomplete.

In the published accounts of these early experiments, the major emphasis is on the exclusion of counter hypotheses, rather than on the bearing and implications of PK. That emphasis was because it was necessary to show the extent to which individual projects could be taken as unexplainable by counter hypotheses and not because the experimenters were not aware of the implications of their discoveries. By 1945 JBR at least was convinced that not only psychologists, but physicists, too, would eventually have to face the fact that "dice can be influenced by what is not as yet and perhaps never will be recognized as a physical factor." He continued, "To recognize an extra physical determiner as intruding upon a physical system would . . . open new frontiers of physics. . . ."

From this, it is clear that the researches conducted up to the time of that writing (1945) had convinced that writer that the effect did not conform to ordinary physical principles. But before his conviction can be widely shared, a general familiarity with the evidence on which it was based is necessary. The presentation of the following chapters, much abbreviated from the published reports, is an attempt to facilitate that familiarity. However, in attempting to present this material a curious dilemma arises. The strength of the case depends on the accumulated testimony of many separate research projects. In the actual establishing of a point like the one at issue here, one positive result is not enough, and perhaps not even a dozen. For every experiment that turns out well, others are needed to confirm it. No authority can say exactly when enough is enough. Each person must decide that for himself.

But, and this is the other horn of the dilemma, when an attempt is made like this one to present the evidence somewhat as it accumulated, it is easy to get the feeling in reading it that enough is enough long before the full story has been told. For the account of one research after another inevitably involves a certain sameness, if not actual repetition. The evidence against counter explanations must be given again and again in individual experiments and the point made repeatedly that the results show the operation of psychological influences "intruding upon a physical system." Time and again, too, some experimenter sets out to prove over again some point that another had already proven— or thought he had. All this is a record of the thorny path of discovery. But thorny as it may seem to others, to those who make such paths the excitement of the adventure and the lure of discovery lightens the load of monotony in the actual doing, if it does not entirely obliterate it. The really dedicated researcher can scarcely eat or sleep until he has checked up on his results to see how meaningful they may be. However, following the trail by proxy, as readers of exploratory accounts must do, may take a larger investment of patience than the researchers themselves were conscious of making.

It is necessary here, therefore, to make a long story shorter and as readable as the reality permits. This research, however, is like a wall built brick by brick whose strength comes from the individual items that compose it as well as from the total structure. No fairy wand waved this one into being, and no honest account of all the individual items in it can make it short and easy. But only by mentioning practically all of them, at least in essence, can the basis for judgment be given.

The accounts of the various experiments within chapters are given in something of the order in which they were made. In certain instances, however, a *logical* sequence of chapters rather than a simple chronological one has been followed.

CHAPTER 4

# Early Explorations

❧

THE news that JBR's experiments with dice-throwing were giving better than chance results spread quickly and considerable excitement was created among his students and acquaintances around the Duke Psychology Department. Was it really "mind-over-matter?" Could will power alone actually affect the movement of physical objects? It seemed unbelievable. The natural reaction of practically everyone who heard of it was one of skepticism. Still the results of those tests *could* mean that something like a force of will was involved.

Fortunately it was so easy to try out the suggestion that quite a few persons did so. All that was needed was a pair of dice and a corner of floor or a corner of books on a table into which to throw and bounce them. It can now be seen that the principal ingredient of a successful PK experiment was so built-in in these spontaneous and impromptu tests, that the inquirers at this stage were as unmindful of it as of the air they breathed. Their "spirit" was what they brought to it, one made of strong personal interest in the outcome of the tests.

The result was that before long practically everyone in JBR's circle in class and at home was throwing dice. To many of the students, it was a temporary enthusiasm that passed away after some encouraging or discouraging results satisfied their curiosity. But for a few of the more serious it did not stop there. To these few, their results meant something more than just the satisfaction of a passing curiosity. They were not content merely to get "encouraging" results, but wanted to be sure their scores were not simply random fluctuations. They wanted to convince themselves that their above-chance scores meant that the effect was real, that it was something that had to be explained, and that it just could be the result of their own will power affecting the dice they threw. And so they kept careful records and turned in reports of their work to JBR. The exploratory projects thus carried out by various students and others, even by Dr. McDougall himself, made up a first exploratory stage of the research on PK.

### MARGARET PEGRAM AND HER EXPERIMENTS

The first person after JBR himself who began and finished a unit of research was a student, Margaret Pegram. But she was not at Duke, and JBR did not even know she was doing it.[1] She was a senior at Guilford College, an undergraduate school about 50 miles from Duke. She was acquainted with JBR, however, and for some time had been interested in his ESP research. She had been a subject in some of the ESP tests and was looking forward to taking part in parapsychological research when she entered the Duke University graduate school in the fall after her graduation at Guilford.

When she heard about the tests with dice she at once began an experiment. By the end of the summer she had a record number of die throws to report. She had made them in the course of two separate experiments. In the first one she had thrown a pair of dice for doubles, willing both to come up for the same specified face more often than would be expected by chance. Before the college year ended she succeeded in doing so. Then, after her graduation in June, she started the second experiment and this occupied her spare time while at home during the summer vacation.

In the "doubles" project, she used two ordinary commercial white plastic dice with black spots, shaking them in cupped hands

[1] Reeves, Margaret Pegram, and Rhine, J. B., "The PK Effect: The First Doubles Experiment." 1945, 9, pp. 42–51.

and throwing them for the specified face onto a blanketed surface with backstop.

Using a bound composition book for her records, thus insuring that none would be lost or only the best selected, she recorded the total of the spots turned up on each throw. She threw first for double sixes and recorded the results in the upper half of the pages, then as a counterbalance she threw for double ones and recorded the results in columns in the lower half of the pages. A double, $6 + 6$, thus indicated a hit above, a double, $1 + 1$, a hit below.

The record of individual throws was made in a column of twelve throws each, a standard run of twenty-four die falls. Three such columns were bracketed together as a "set" on the page, because on the average one specific double should be expected to occur by chance in each thirty-six throws. Each page included six or seven sets. She tried to throw as many times for ones as for sixes, but in a few instances she was interrupted. Still she threw in all 369 runs for sixes and 364 for ones, making a total of 733 runs. The result on the sixes was an excess of twenty-eight, a CR of 2.56, p = .01; and on the ones of 10.67, CR = .98, p = .3—a significant outcome on the sixes but not on the ones.

This distribution of faces did not look like a purely chance effect but the higher score on sixes raised a problem to which several answers were possible. The main one, of course, was that the dice were biased for sixes. However, such possible bias would not explain the positive deviation when throwing for ones, or the negative deviations of both faces when the opposite was being thrown for. Something more than bias appeared to be involved. Possibly throwing for sixes was more interesting. At least Margaret P. noted that she felt a preference for them. Also, the ones always came second when the first freshness of the session had already been expended on sixes. This freshness effect, akin to that of novelty of any kind, as is known now, but of course was not realized then, would also have worked against a score on ones.

However, at the time, psychological aspects like these, though suggested, could not yet be given the weight which they would be given today. The main point was that when doubles were desired significant results had been secured, not all of which could be laid to dice bias.

Margaret P.'s second experiment began as soon as she finished the one on doubles. This was one to test whether she could get results with high-dice combinations as opposed to low-dice targets, as was then being done at Duke.[2]

Again she used a pair of dice, the same pair she had used for her doubles test. Again she kept her records neatly in a bound composition book. This time she threw until she had a record of nearly 1,000 12-throw runs.

In this experiment as before, she divided the record page by a horizontal line across the middle. She recorded the uppermost fall of each die for each throw for high combinations of dice faces in the upper half, those for low combination targets in the lower (Figure 3). In each upper half, three sets of three columns were recorded; the same in the lower. As before, the results were very significantly above chance. Those for high combinations were higher than those for the lower ones, but even so the scores for the low combinations yielded a significant CR of 2.58 or $p = .0098$.

When Margaret P. came to Duke in the fall, she must have felt considerable satisfaction when she gave her notebooks to JBR. She knew the total statistical value of the results was highly significant.

Naturally the notebooks were of much interest to all of those at Duke who had been involved in throwing for high- versus low-dice combinations, especially because this was the first experiment in which each target combination had been used at each session. In spite of the interest these results aroused, however, the work was not at the time considered as constituting a first-class experi-

    [2] Reeves, Margaret Pegram, and Rhine, J. B., "The Psychokinetic Effect: II. A Study in Declines." *J. Parapsychol.*, 1943, 7, pp. 76–93.

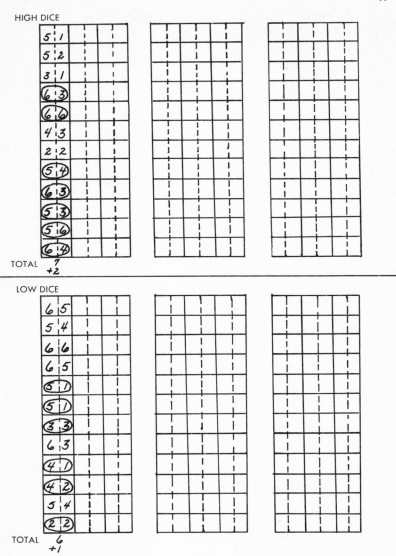

FIGURE 3.  Margaret F.'s Notebook record sheet, in experiment using "high-dice" and "low-dice" at targets.

ment, for the plan of the experiment had in it no control against possible skill in throwing, and even though Margaret P. was scarcely an experienced thrower of dice, this was a serious weakness in it. But an even greater one was then considered to lie in the fact that it was unwitnessed work. She might have made errors; and those who did not know her well might not even trust her honesty. On that account, the notebooks were stored away, and no further attention given them at the time. The work was considered suggestive, however, in showing that a subject primed to throw for one kind of target, could, if he wished, switch to another and succeed. From both experiments it looked as if he might succeed better with the target he liked best and used first, than with the second choice, but that he would not necessarily fail with the second and practically opposite choice. However, in the following years, the notebooks were, to all intents, forgotten.

But then in 1942, when material was being assembled for the analysis for position effects, Margaret P.'s old notebooks with the records of the original data of her two experiments were included with the rest, even though Margaret P. had long since left Duke. Since in the experiment with high-low combinations as target, the data had been recorded in uniform sets of three runs or columns each, this work was particularly amenable to the analysis. It was found that here, just as in JBR's experiment (Chapter 2), there was a general decline in the rate of scoring within the three runs of the sets. The hits in the first runs of the three were so much more frequent than in the last that the CR of the difference ($CR_d$) was 3.86; which gives the very significant p of .0001, a value much higher than any of those that had been recognized at the time this experiment was made. This decline within the set was present, too, in both the high- and the low-combination sections. In both sections there was also a slight upturn in rate of scoring at the end of the run.

And so the work recorded in these old notebooks now showed that even though no one had watched Margaret P. as she threw her dice, her records were essentially reliable. By no stretch of imagination could effects such as these lawful and significant hit distributions have been produced intentionally, or by skillful throwing. If they had been the result of any such factor, an incline rather than a decline would have been produced, for she would have improved with practice. And, of course, no effect like a decline in rate of hitting within the set could have been on her mind as she threw, for she was always hoping to obtain as high a score as possible. But here in the position effects of the hits on her pages, she had even shown by the upturn in rate at the lower part of her pages the "end value" that other comparable psychological tests have shown, thus confirming both the honesty of her pages and the psychological influences operating in her results.

But what about Margaret P.'s experiment with doubles? When the data in this part of the notebook were analyzed for a decline within the set (it will be recalled that results were recorded in groups of three runs, too), it was found that an *incline* instead of a decline had occurred. The runs thrown first gave fewer hits than those thrown third, with a difference decidedly significant; the $CR_d = 2.88$; $p = .003$. This result was one of the two instances in the eighteen separate experiments involved in the analysis in which the declines were not from the first to the last run of the set.

If this reversal in the direction of the hit patterns in Margaret P.'s first experiment had been discovered when the work was done in 1934 long before all the other experiments showing declines had been made, it would have been puzzling and confusing. But coming when these analyses did in 1942, when they showed the 16-to-two prevalence of declines over inclines in the data of the eighteen projects studied, the tentative interpretation of the effect here in the experiment with doubles was quite different.

Now the psychological attitudes of the two kinds of tasks Margaret P. had undertaken were contrasted, and it was easy to see that they differed. In this one she knew very well that the expectation of a hit just by chance was much lower (only one in thirty-six throws) than it was when she threw for face combinations (five in twelve throws). This knowledge could well have had a psychological effect on her. It could have meant that it took a larger number of trials in the early part of the runs for her to concentrate with strong determination, and only after she had achieved this did she actually exercise her PK ability more effectively. Another factor could well have been that in the first experiment, where the chance of a hit was five in twelve throws, she got the *feeling* of success much quicker by simply seeing her target appear frequently while here it was only one in thirty-six. And so, in 1942, this reversal of declines could be seen as probably lawful, too, in a psychological way and the result of a difference in the attitude of the subject in the two very different tasks.

This was, by the way, the only such experiment with specified doubles as targets. Therefore no confirmation for this oddity of incline can be cited.

### THE HOMER HILTON EXPERIMENTS

In the spring of 1934 after the news of JBR's dice-throwing experiments had circulated among his students, two of them from his psychology class wanted to see for themselves if they could get scores that would not be explainable as simply due to chance. These were two senior students, Homer Hilton, Jr., and George Baer.[3] Hilton was in the prelaw program, Baer in premedicine; each later became an active practitioner in his respective field.

These two young men discussed their project with JBR, but they did all of the actual testing themselves in their dormitory room. While they wanted first of all to see if they could get higher scores than chance would give, they recognized that if they

[3] Hilton, Homer, Jr., Baer, George, and Rhine, J. B., "A Comparison of Three Sizes of Dice in PK Tests." *J. Parapsychol.*, 1943, 7, pp. 172–190.

were able to do so, they needed to be sure that the results were not caused by biased dice. They, therefore, obtained some ordinary commercial dice and asked two other students who did not know about the PK experiment to "verify the laws of chance" by throwing the dice to see if all faces came up the proper number of times. They did so for 128 runs without discovering any significant imbalance of faces, and so the two student experimenters decided that with these dice, the "laws of chance" could be relied upon. They also arranged a device with a "mechanical release," something like the one JBR had used, for throwing the dice so that there would be no danger that they would get their results by skill. As it turned out after 128 runs with this, their scores were just as good as those they got when they threw by hand. And so since the hand-throwing was just as safe against criticism and because the release method was slower, they threw the rest by hand.

These young men also decided at the start that if they did get interesting scores, they might as well try to find out something about the way PK worked in relation to the size of the dice. They planned to throw for high combinations just as JBR had done in his experiment, but instead of using just one size of die, they decided to use three different sizes and see if their results would be in proportion to dice size. If so, it seemed reasonable to anticipate that the smaller the die the easier it should be to influence it and, therefore, they should get higher scores with the small dice than with the larger ones. Of the three pairs, the smallest measured $\frac{7}{16}$ of an inch; the medium, $1\frac{1}{16}$; and the largest, one inch. The medium size was the one which they had checked for imperfect balance.

In their main experiment the two students took turns acting as subject and recorder. They carried out 484 runs and secured 130 hits above what chance would have given, which meant they had a CR of 3.46; p = .0005. Beyond a doubt, they had extra-chance scores.

However, the results on the three different sizes of dice did not come out according to expectation. Somewhat better scores were obtained with the small dice, but the difference between sizes was not at all in proportion to the mass of the different sizes. The mass of the large dice was nearly 12 times that of the small ones, but the scores were only slightly higher. The scores can be most meaningfully expressed in this case as averages per run. Of course, throwing for the high combinations as they did, five hits would be expected by chance alone on each run. But with the small dice, the average they obtained was 5.36 per run; with the medium, 5.24; and with the large, 5.20. Accordingly, the average scores were not proportional to size, although they differed in that direction. This did not look as if the mass of the dice was controlling the rate of scoring appreciably.

As the dice were thrown both subjects had preferred the medium-sized dice. They seemed to be "just right" for handling, and consequently they had thrown them more often than either of the other sizes, even though the final results showed they had had a few more hits with the small ones. The large ones had seemed a little inconvenient for hand-throwing and had been liked the least.

Another innovation besides the several sizes of dice was introduced in part of the experiment. This variation was an attempt to see if the subject could do better if he threw one die at a time and put all his energy into that, instead of into a pair thrown together. (To score these single die throws for high combinations, they added the faces of each pair of successive throws.) This test was suggested by the same kind of reasoning they had used in trying the different dice sizes. The energy expended should have a greater affect on one die than on two.

The results here were even more distinctly against their hypothesis than in the case of the sizes, for when throwing one die at a time they failed to get a significant deviation. Practically all of their hits were made when throwing two dice at a time. Both subjects found throwing the single die slow and tiresome and they much preferred the pair. The outcome appeared to be the result of this preference. It was one that certainly would not have been expected on physical principles.

Later that year, after Hilton left college, he carried out a total of 824 more runs at his home, using his sister and her husband as well as himself as subjects.[4] In this work, too, the subjects threw for high combinations, but instead of throwing mainly by hand, they made an advance in method by using a small cup in which to shake and from which to throw the dice. The three sizes were used again, and again the medium size was preferred. In fact, they found the cup they were using a bit small for convenient handling of the large dice.

The total results again were highly significant, yielding a CR of 4.95, which would not occur by chance in 1,000,000 such experiments. This time, the deviations of the three sizes of dice showed the medium highest, and small next. But the score on the large was lower even than chance alone should give. It was suspected that this low score could have been caused by the frustration felt when trying to shake the large dice in a small cup. At any rate, the medium size was again preferred and again the differences were in no way proportional to the size of the dice.

On the whole, then, the work of Hilton and his collaborators, like that of Margaret P., raised the suggestion that the likes and dislikes of the subjects, rather than the physical relations of the dice had caused the difference in the deviations.

### THE FRANK SMITH EXPERIMENT

Another of JBR's students, Frank Smith, also started a PK project in the spring of 1934, about the same time Hilton and Baer began theirs.[5] Smith had been one of the subjects JBR had used

[4] Hilton, Homer, Jr., and Rhine, J. B., "A Second Comparison of Three Sizes of Dice in PK Tests." *J. Parapsychol.*, 1943, 7, 191–206.
[5] Rhine, J. B., "The PK Effect: Early Singles Tests." *J. Parapsychol.*, 1944, 8, pp. 287–303.

in his own experiment. He was a senior and graduated from Duke University that spring, then went on to Yale to the School of Forestry. He planned his experiment and discussed it with JBR before he left Duke and then continued it after he was at Yale.

Smith, like Margaret P., was his own subject throughout his experiment. Thus his work, too, fell into the "unwitnessed" category. Also, his introduction to the PK research was at its earliest stage before controls against dice bias and skilled throwing had been routinely introduced. And so because of lack of controls the results he reported, like Margaret P.'s, were then considered as only tentative. It was long after, in 1942, when marked position effects were found in his data that his work could be reclaimed and considered as giving evidence beyond counter explanations.

But even if Smith's work could not be given full weight until long after, it did play a suggestive part in the development of experimental procedures. The principal departure in his work, new at the time, soon after became routine. It was that he took a single die face for his target. Before that, only combinations of faces, high, low, sevens, and doubles, had been targets. The idea was to see if better results might be secured with a simpler target. It seemed that in order to secure a high-dice hit it would be necessar to influence two dice simultaneously, but if the target were only a single face, like three or six, then a hit could be made by influencing only one die. Smith accordingly, used the single face as a target and he, like many subjects after him, who, if given a choice, decided to throw for the six face.

In Smith's experiment he also carried farther than Hilton had the question of the effect of different numbers of dice per throw. He used a pair in one series of tests and then six in the other. The supposition again was that a greater number of hits should be made when the number of dice was small than when it was larger. As a matter of routine, all throws were made by shaking the dice in cupped hands, and then throwing and bouncing them against a back wall.

In both series together a total of 629 standard runs of 24 die falls each was thrown. A total of 201 hits above chance expectation was secured, giving a CR of 4.39, a decidedly extra-chance result, the probability of which is less than .00001. However, since there was no provision against imperfections in the dice, the value of the result lies mainly in the relative rate of hitting in the two series, which was practically the same whether two or six dice were thrown at a time. (The average rate per run, four being expected, was 4.33 in series 1 and 4.31 in series 2.) It was obvious that the rate of hitting had not been significantly reduced by increasing the number of dice per throw from two to six. Also, the results using the single-face target seemed not to be appreciably better or worse than those that had been secured with combination targets. The experiment as a whole then was another in which it seemed that the expectation on a physical analogy was not borne out.

Later, after the 1942 analysis, not only were decline effects found similar in some aspects to those of Margaret P., who also had worked alone as both subject and experimenter, but certain unique position effects also were found that seemed to be the mark of the individual personality and, therefore, a subjective one rather than one caused by physical circumstances. At the time Smith reported his experiment, his results were an encouragement to the introduction of further variations in physical relations, such as numbers of dice per throw.

Smith's work also illustrates a principle in what one might call the strategy of discovery. Any individual experiment in the development of a scientific investigation can serve a purpose even if it is not itself strong enough to stand alone. If it *gives a suggestion* that leads to other investigations, it has a place in the line of ongoing discovery. Only by repetitions and confirmations, anyway, is an individual research, even if yielding unquestionably strong results, finally woven into the fabric of reliable data. Thus it is that the early exploratory investigations of pioneers in any field have value that may be much greater when judged by the results of the long lines of research to which they were the stepping stones than their still exploratory methods would seem to make them.

## THE HARVEY FRICK EXPERIMENTS

Another former student of JBR's, Harvey L. Frick, who with his wife visited JBR in the summer of 1934, still further attested to the contagious character of the dice experiments. Frick was then a young psychologist at the Wayne School of Medicine, Detroit. The young couple was introduced to the PK research while at Duke. On their return home they undertook an experiment on their own using each other alternately as subject and recorder.[6]

The Fricks carried out three series of experiments without geting deviations on any of them that were significantly different from chance although each was slightly positive. In the first they used six dice per throw; in the second they added six smaller dice to the ones they used before. In the third series they tried to avoid the target, but still the results could be attributed to chance.

However, although that record might well have discouraged further attempts, they started a fourth series of tests. This time they doubled the number of both sizes of dice. They recorded the two sizes separately. All the faces of the die were used as targets at one time or another, but they allowed the subject to select the target face so that in the end, the six faces were unequally represented, each of the three higher faces having been the target much more often than the rest. With these 24 dice, they had completed 2,292 runs by the time the experiment was interrupted.

When the results for all four series (the three insignificant ones, and this one, too) were totaled, a deviation of 279 hits had been

[6] Rhine, J. B., and Humphrey, Betty M., "PK Tests with Six, Twelve and Twenty-Four Dice per Throw." *J. Parapsychol.*, 1944, 8, pp. 139–157.

obtained, which, in spite of the low average per run it represented (4.09 with 4.0 expected), still yielded a significant CR of 2.82; p = .0048. This extra-chance value had been contributed largely by the data of their fourth series.

However, the most interesting feature of the experiment lay in the contrasting totals of hits contributed by the two sizes of dice. The medium-sized dice gave significant results, a CR of 2.99; p = .0027, but the small ones did not. The CR on them was only 1.76; p = .078. This was contrary to what might have been expected had the matter of size been the effective factor, for on physical principles the smaller ones should have been the easier to influence.

When the position effects of hits on the record pages were determined, a still more unexpected contrast between the scoring of the two dice sizes was disclosed. With the medium dice typical declines were found, both vertically and horizontally. The $CR_d$ between the first and fourth quarter of the pages of all the data of the medium-sized dice pooled was a nearly significant 2.12; p = .034. But the trend on the small dice was the reverse, the fourth quarter being higher than the first. The $CR_d = 1.77$; p = .076. The $CR_d$s are not significant, but they suggested a tendency for the hits on the small dice to increase as those on the medium size decreased.

The general verdict for the four series, even without the careful balancing of target faces, which was the most serious weakness, was that results like this team of experimenters secured were giving glimpses of the PK principle in action. Dice bias would not explain contrasts like that of the reverse direction of deviation yielded by the two dice sizes, or the fact that the best results of all were secured in the series (the fourth) when 24 dice, instead of 12, were thrown each time.

It was suggested that perhaps the latter effect was secured because throwing 24 dice at a time was a novelty. In ESP tests, and now in those for PK, novelty had been found to be a potent factor. No one before the Fricks had thrown so many; and they also apparently preferred the medium size over the small, for the results on them were always counted and entered on the record first. These dice thus apparently had a psychological "edge" on the small dice, and so it was possible that they yielded better results for a psychological reason. At the same time, it could well have been that in the reverse effect noticeable on the smaller dice, causing their hits to increase as the others decreased, a kind of unconscious displacement of effect occurred. It could mean that in the progression of throwing through the individual run the PK effect tended to shift from the dice uppermost in attention to those less consciously so.

At the end of this experiment, Frick was still only partly convinced of the reality of PK, and so in the summer of 1937 he undertook another experiment.[7] In this one he worked alone, at the Detroit Institute for Parapsychological Research, (an organization no longer in existence). His plan of procedure was a departure from earlier projects mainly in the number of dice he used per throw. Since in the earlier work, he had found that 24 dice per throw seemed to yield results as good or better than smaller numbers, this time he increased the number to 60. As before, he shook and threw them from a cylindrical container onto a padded table top. He was himself both subject and recorder, throwing and recording in uniform fashion throughout.

The experiment was made in two series, A and B. Series A was the experimental series, and B was intended as a control on dice bias, but it was a novel one and gave a novel effect, which was much less interpretable then than later.

In series A Frick threw the 60 dice for the six face for the equivalent of 2,172 regular runs of 24 throws. He secured a positive deviation of 582, an average run score of 4.27, which yielded a very significant CR of 6.84, with an anti-chance value in the millions.

7 Rhine, J. B., and Humphrey, Betty M., "The PK Effect with Sixty Dice per Throw." *J. Parapsychol.*, 1945, 9, pp. 203–218.

The surprise came in with series B, his intended control on sixes. In this he decided to throw for ones to see how many sixes would come up and for the score he counted the sixes and the sixes only. But his intention to throw for ones was only "skin-deep," because his actual interest and attention, too, was still on sixes. He had been throwing for them just before and was still counting and recording them so that even though he did not realize it, he was still interested in them mainly.

Of course today the effect of unconscious "set" or motivation is recognized much more than it was when Frick was making this test so that it is easier to see now than it was then that in planning the control this way, when he himself was the subject, he was defeating his own intention. The result showed it, for it was not a comfortable chance number of sixes, but it was practically the same as that of series A. The deviation was 576, the average run score also 4.27, and the CR, 6.77, again an anti-chance value of millions to one. This result raised the question whether the dice were not merely so strongly biased that the bias probably produced the deviation in both A and B series, and it was an outcome that did not bolster Frick's wavering belief in PK. His verdict, when he gave his report to the laboratory, was a simple one. "The dice are crooked." Yet they had been made up of an assortment of sizes which had been used in other experiments with no such outstanding evidence of bias.

That is where the matter rested—until 1942. The records then were analyzed for position effects along with the rest of the accumulation. The outstanding result was that series A showed all the typical effects of position and was atypical only in that a slight chronological incline instead of decline was shown. And series B did, too, even including the chronological incline. In some instances, the declines in B were more distinct than in the A series. In both series the top halves of the record pages showed more hits than the bottom halves. In both series the four columns across the page (all of those of series A and the first four of series B) showed a decline from the first to the third with a slight rise on the fourth, and this trend, of course, meant that in both series the left half of the page showed more hits than the right. When these variations were summed up into quarter distributions, or QDs, the CR of the difference between the first and fourth quarters of the record pages was 1.20 for series A and for series B a practically significant 2.48; p = .013. Distributions like this are quite unlikely to be the result of chance, or of dice bias. The only explanation, besides PK, for such results would be that some unknown combination of factors of motivation and dice bias in conjunction operated just the same in both series. Pages are given in the *Journal* report to consideration of whether or not this could happen, but at the end of them, the possibility is concluded to be an impossibility when all facts, many of which cannot be reproduced here, are taken into consideration.

The analysis for position effects thus retrieved this work and showed, too, that a large number of dice per throw could succeed and that extra-chance score averages could be secured with them just as well as with smaller numbers per throw. The PK effect on dice, it appeared, was not limited to small numbers of dice per throw nor to any number yet tried. In fact, even earlier, in 1936, a still larger number per throw had been successfully used in several other experiments. In those, 96 dice were used and positive results achieved. But they were made in conjunction with tests on the effect of alcohol, caffeine, and the hypnotic state, and they will be discussed from those various viewpoints later (Chapter 7). Here, it is sufficient to note that tests were made that gave evidence that PK can be obtained with 96 dice thrown at a time and that the rate of success per run was not appreciably different from that yielded by smaller numbers per throw.

The analysis of Frick's data for position effects not only retrieved it as evidence on the use of a large number of dice per throw, but it did more than that. It called attention to the probable operation in PK of unconscious mental processes, along with conscious ones. In ESP it had been well established that unconscious processes very strongly affected the operation of that ability. Here, now the realization that series B was showing PK just as well as series A gave one of the earliest object lessons in the effect of unconscious mental processes on PK. By switching his conscious attention to the one face, but still remaining sufficiently aware of sixes to count and record them, Frick apparently convinced only his conscious self that he was actually interested in ones. Unconsciously the sixes were still in focus. PK was still invoved in them, apparently, and did not switch when the change was made on the conscious level.

And so, as it turned out, the series was not a loss. It was a showcase example of what can occur unconsciously when the subject is quite unaware of unconscious mental processes, as in 1937 practically everyone still was. The field of psychology itself was only slowly coming to take seriously the fact of unconscious mentality, although the rise of psychiatry and the Freudian doctrine of "the unconscious" were pushing the psychologists that way. It was not surprising therefore that Frick (he had been a philosophy and not a psychology major in college) was unaware of the extent to which his conscious motivation could, as it were, go underground.

Even in 1942, when the suggestive declines were found in Frick's data, it is doubtful if their full implications were appreciated. However, it was realized then that a subject to be successful must enter into a test like that of Frick's in his series B without unconscious reservation and that he must wish to succeed on the given target without question of any kind. It thus served as a piece of evidence that the attitude of the subject, conscious and unconscious, is all-important.

### DR. WILLIAM MCDOUGALL'S EXPERIMENT

Probably no one else was more concerned in the research on PK than Dr. McDougall. With his own deep concern about the question of the relation of mind and matter, with a mind quite open to persuasion, but with the caution of a scientist, he followed with strong interest JBR's accounts of the extra-chance scores he was getting in his PK tests.

When the school year ended and McDougall left the campus for his summer vacation in England, however, the only research that had been reported to him was that of JBR himself. Margaret P.'s notebooks had not yet been turned in; Hilton's work, Smith's, and Frick's were all in the future. Nevertheless, McDougall was so intrigued with the possibility that a mental effect could be demonstrated on the fall of dice that he started an experiment of his own after he arrived in England. His results were considerably different from those already reviewed.[8]

The project extended over the five months he was visiting in England, and involved eight subjects besides himself. They were mostly his relatives, with his two sons and himself being the principal ones. They threw a single die at a time, always from a narrow-necked vase, and eventually, although not equally, for each of the faces of the die. But the total result was not statistically significant, the deviation being only 49 on a total of 269 runs. This gives a CR of 1.64, a result that might occur by chance about once in 10 such series.

Of course, as McDougall could not know, since even Hilton's results were not available, the throwing of a single die is now almost unanimously considered to be a less favorable technique than throwing a larger number at a time, because it is slower and more monotonous. But he probably reasoned that to get a single face on a single die should be easier than to try as JBR's subjects had to get a combination of faces on a pair of dice.

The use of the vase, rather than throwing the die by hand, gave a control against skillful throwing, and the use of each die face as target should have been a control against dice bias. The results on that however were ambiguous, because of the uneven

___

[8] Rhine, J. B., and Humphrey, Betty M., "The PK Effect: The McDougall One Die Series." *J. Parapsychol.*, 1943, 7, pp. 252–263.

numbers of trials per face. And so the report of this work, like Margaret P.'s notebooks, was stored away and practically forgotten.

But in 1942 McDougall's report was brought out again with the rest to be analyzed for position effects. Very interesting ones were found in it, although McDougall, who died in 1938, never knew it.

The data were typical only in showing a marked chronological decline, for when the sessions were divided into the three successive periods over which the experiment extended, the hits were $+31$, $+17$, and $+1$, respectively. But the really significant result was atypical. It came in connection with the QD analysis. Although this showed a significant difference between the first and fourth quarters, it was in the reverse direction from that expected, just as was true in Margaret P.'s experiment with doubles as target. These two experiments were the odd ones in the 18 used in the 1942 analysis for position effects. All the rest had shown a decline from the beginning to the end of the pages on which their data had been recorded.

In these McDougall data, the first quarters of the pages taken all together had yielded 34 hits fewer than would be expected by chance, and the fourth, 30 *more*. The difference yielded a very significant $CR_d$ of 3.32; $p = .0009$. To make the effect all the more definitely striking, it was not caused by just one individual who might have had a personal peculiarity of some kind, but it was shown in the records of each of the three main subjects and even in those of the group of miscellaneous subjects. So universal a tendency running opposite to the one generally observed in nearly all other experiments seemed to indicate that some special condition must have caused it. Different possibilities as to what the special condition could have been were suggested. The most likely one involves peculiarities of procedure and peculiarities of subjects, too. In the first place, the conditions of throwing were unique in that although one subject at a time threw the die for a run of 24 throws, the others, or at least three to five of them, were present, watching and waiting for their turns as they all sat around the table onto which the die was thrown.

It seems likely that the results here were connected somehow with the intellectual climate that would have prevailed with the kind of subjects these were. The subjects were people on a level of sophistication such that they must surely have suffered a considerable inner conflict in taking the PK hypothesis with even sufficient seriousness to make a game of testing it. Possibly only the age and eminence of McDougall himself, as the experimenter, accounted for the fact that they complied and very well may not have prevented them from feeling a little self-conscious and foolish in even entertaining the possibility that they could influence the die by will power. Under such conditions, it is almost certain they would have begun their test runs with at least a mild mental conflict, which would only slowly have decreased as they began to get into the spirit of the game.

Whether such psychological factors were or were not responsible cannot, of course, be decided, but one fact about the series is clear. At least the effect of depressed scores at the start, whatever its nature and explanation, did gradually change, as shown by the total number of hits on all the available page quarters pooled (39 runs with a deviation of +15 had to be omitted in this analysis because they were broken up by entries on different days). These were −34, +15, +22, +31. Such an ascending trend, shown in all the four series that make it up, is strong evidence that a lawful influence is behind it. That it was shown by means of a technique as unpromising as the throwing of a single die is now considered to be, makes it seem rather remarkable that any sign of PK whatever should have been indicated.

### FRAGMENTS

By 1942, when the analysis of records for position effects was made, a number of minor experiments, hardly on the level of completed projects, had accumulated, for a policy was initiated almost from the start of the PK research not to discard data if made by or under the supervision of one of JBR's research associates—student helpers whom he had trained and authorized for the purpose. Instead, the records were filed against any future charge that PK data were selected.

In 1936 and 1937 a number of such experiments carefully recorded in bound composition books so that no data would be lost or selected were made by or under the supervision of J. S. Woodruff and Margaret Pegram, both research associates at the time.[9] They had used in all 24 subjects, and all of the fragments had involved throwing six dice for the six face. These numbers by this time had come to be generally preferred because subjects had come to feel they could "do better" with them. They probably did not analyze the reason for their preference beyond the obvious point that six dice at a time were more fun, quicker and easier than smaller numbers, while larger numbers were less convenient to handle. Also with six dice, the target face was likely to come up just by chance on practically every throw, and subjects always felt encouraged to see the face for which they were throwing, if only for a spurious reason. The preference for the six face was thought at the time to be due to the better contrast: six spots stand out more than lower numbers. Also it would be favored if the spots were hollowed out.

The accumulation included a total of 7,776 runs. The total deviation was 2,541; the average per run was 4.33, which is a good, but not an exceptionally high rate. But with the large number of runs, the CR, 15.79, with an astronomical probability against chance, is, of course, tremendous. But even if chance alone would not explain such a result, was it the result of PK? Or were the dice in all these experiments very biased for the six face?

No controls on face bias had been run; so again, the question could not be answered at the time, not until years later when the

[9] Rhine, J. B., and Humphrey, Betty M., "Position Effects in the Six-by-Six Series of PK Tests." *J. Parapsychol.*, 1945, 9, pp. 296–302.

records were analyzed for position effects. Yet, when that analysis had finally been made, the $CR_d$ between the score for the first and fourth quarters was 2.42; p. = .015. Whatever bias for the six face the dice may have had, and they probably did have some, it could not be the whole explanation of results like these.

Another fragment too must be mentioned for completeness, but it was not carried out under a qualified experimenter.[10] It was the work of a young private, Marvin Schwartz, at an Army camp in World War II. He had heard of PK and wrote for instructions for an experiment he could carry out by himself. The single peculiarity that came out of this effort was that he reported a significant *negative* deviation. It rated a CR of 2.74; p = .006.

In the middle 1940s when Schwartz's report was completed, the negative deviation, although not the first that had been reported, was still something to be puzzled about. Anyone with a bit of knowledge of statistics knows that deviations from mean chance expectation are just as significant (and would mean as much PK) if they go below as if they go above the mean. This of course was appreciated then, and that it must mean that PK had somehow been involved but it was years later before its significance was fully appreciated. At the time, since Schwartz's record had not been made under approved conditions, it was filed and only written up as a minor article some years later.

### INADVERTENT PK?

This chapter on the early explorations of students and others connected with JBR at Duke by rights should end here. But another report that came out years later shows a possible PK experiment, which, although not in the slightest way connected with those at Duke University, certainly belongs, if anywhere, with these first exploratory tests.

[10] Rhine, J. B., "The Schwartz PK Experiment." *J. Parapsychol.*, 1946, 10, pp. 208–212.

In 1947 it came to light that quite unintentionally some experiments made in England as early as 1934 were probably PK tests. These experiments were made with the intention of testing for precognition but later, after the Duke PK work was published, the experimenters realized that they may have been making PK tests instead. Their results were only marginally significant, but the attempt is of some interest if only to show how an undeveloped topic like that of PK—precognition, too—may later be shown to have involved unexpected angles.[11]

The two experimenters were Frazer Nicol and Whately Carington, two psychic researchers who had long been interested in experiments in ESP. After reading some cases that suggested precognition, Carington had become intrigued with the question of whether it actually occurs. Accordingly, he called for volunteers to do what he thought of as precognitive guessing; among other volunteers who responded was Nicol. It was his work that later seemed probably to have involved PK.

Nicol had first attempted to make precognitive guesses, but without much success. He then came upon the idea of using one die which he called a "selector" die, to throw (from a cup) the uppermost face of which he recorded. Then he threw a second die, the "working die," and the uppermost face of that one was recorded opposite the first. If they matched, it was counted a possible hit for precognition, the idea being that the face on the first die had "predicted" that on the second. However, if Nicol more or less unintentionally but quite naturally began to will the second die to match the first, the test very well might have become one of PK rather than precognition. The results were not high enough, however, to have led originally to a conclusion that precognition had been involved, and so the data were stored away and nearly forgotten.

When the report of the Duke work on PK came out, the two

[11] Nicol, J. Frazer, and Carington, W. Whately, "Some Experiments in Willed Die Throwing." *Proc. Soc. psych. Res.*, 1946–49, 48, Part 173, pp. 164–175.

men reassessed the earlier results and decided they had a bearing on that phenomenon. It was not strong or conclusive enough to stand alone, but they thought it had a degree of supporting value. Especially because Nicol one night, working until early morning hours, had made 2,640 throws of a single die (110 conventional runs) and secured 493 hits. When the expectation on this particular die was calculated from all the data accumulated on it, and its bias thus taken into account, the chance of getting so large a deviation was about one in 10,000. Even taking the expectation at one in six or 440, the deviation would be significant with a CR of nearly three, on which $p = .003$. And so it looked as if PK must have been involved.

It was true, as these two experimenters thought, that their results standing alone would have had no value in establishing as unexpected a phenomenon as PK. At the time they were made the fact that all of Nicol's work was unwitnessed would have kept it out of the highest category. But today with all the evidence now on record showing that PK is a reality, his work can be taken largely for its historical interest, for another possible instance of the way a PK effect occurs and also for an example of the kind of insight that sometimes eventually throws new light on old data. It showed too how the technique that originally was taken as adequate for exploring precognition became entirely inappropriate once the possibility of PK was recognized.

The main contribution made by the studies reported in this chapter and Chapter 2 was that they gave distinct encouragement to further experimentation. Most of the results were extra-chance. They gave evidence that here was something to explain. The various counter possibilities did not seem to account for all of the deviations, but even so, no one could be comfortably certain yet that those possibilities had been ruled out. Controls had been introduced against dice bias and "tricky throwing" and although they may not have been perfect, they had not appeared to cancel out the extra-chance scores.

Then when different physical aspects of the experiment had been tried out, no direct relationships had been shown. Instead it appeared that the results tended to follow psychological influences. Of course the tests had been made to see whether a psychological influence could be detected, and the evidence of it was suggested in experiment after experiment. It was a challenge to go on and find out for sure what these results could mean. It probably could have been but little stronger, if the CRs had been even higher than they were.

# CHAPTER 5

# The Parapsychology Laboratory and Confirmatory Experiments

WHEN the research on PK began in 1934, JBR could give it only limited attention, even though his initial results had given a very intriguing lead. He was a full-time instructor in the Psychology Department and had an obligation to teach psychology. His research, although encouraged by Professor McDougall, was still an avocational interest and had to be limited to whatever spare time he had.

However, after his book-length monograph on ESP was published in the spring of 1934, JBR's relationship to the Psychology Department was affected. Even though the book appeared obscurely, the claim that an extrasensory ability in ordinary subjects had been demonstrated in a university psychology laboratory was news. To the surprise of JBR and his co-workers—it was picked up immediately by some of the foremost science writers of the day, led by Waldemar Kaempffert of *The New York Times*.

The result was a wave of publicity, for the public was at once interested. At the time, perhaps even more than would be the case today, such publicity about a piece of research was anathema in scientific circles. Just as medical men did not advertise their methods in the daily press, scientists did not promote their discoveries in popular media. JBR's colleagues therefore were sensitive to this publicity and were not certain that JBR had not somehow had a part in stirring it up. They felt that to be thus thrust into the limelight did not reflect credit on their department. Instead it seemed like notoriety that could only excite criticism and even ridicule from their profession.

As mentioned in Chapter 3, the first reaction from the psychology profession in general was mildly tolerant, and a few psychologists tried to conduct ESP tests. But the results they got with this obscure and unstable faculty were apparently not very encouraging. Before long some psychologists published sweeping criticisms of the claim that an extrasensory way of getting information had been demonstrated. These criticisms, however, were almost entirely unfounded as careful examination and explanation later showed.[1]

However, in 1935, even before the controversy with critical psychologists had developed, a new building for the Duke Psychology Department became available on the campus. JBR then asked for separate status, name, and location in order to ease the tension all around.

His request was granted. He was given space completely independent of the Psychology Department. His research unit was given a name of its own, the Parapsychology Laboratory.[2] The "psi research," as the combination of ESP and PK projects came to be called,[3] was no longer connected with the Psychology Department. However, JBR's actual membership in the department,

---

[1] Rhine, J. B., and others, *Extrasensory Perception After Sixty Years*. 2d ed. (Boston: Bruce Humphries, 1966) pp. 183–212. (First published in New York: Henry Holt and Company, 1940.)

[2] The Parapsychology Laboratory of Duke University with JBR as Director continued until 1965, when he retired from the university. During the years of its existence it became something of a center, small though it remained, to which many researchers in parapsychology, more or less isolated as they usually were, turned for help of various kinds. This included persons in foreign countries and also students in various colleges who were given a degree of financial assistance as well as help in the planning and evaluation of experiments.

In 1965, the Foundation for Research on the Nature of Man (FRNM), founded in 1962, took over the sponsorship of the work of the Parapsychology Laboratory, now under the name, The Institute for Parapsychology, with JBR as director.

[3] Psi, a Greek letter, was proposed by Dr. R. H. Thouless, English psychologist, and Dr. B. P. Wiesner as a term to cover both the ESP and PK areas of parapsychology. It was selected because it was a neutral term that carried no implications as to the nature of the two processes.

in which in time he became a full professor, continued as before, until 1950 when his teaching duties were reduced to half-time. It was fortunate that from the start many of his students had become interested, too. In the first few years it meant that much more ground was covered, if only on an exploratory level, than he alone could have managed.

As the new laboratory came into being, a small research fund was given JBR by the university for expenses. He also began to receive small grants from private individuals outside of the university who had become interested in the research. Now, he could hire a stenographer, a student assistant and pay his other urgent research expenses.

As the PK researches continued to yield extra-chance results, thus encouraging the idea that a new phenomenon was being discovered, variations in methods and equipment were introduced. Other experimenters elsewhere were encouraged to undertake PK experiments, too.

The first assistant at the new laboratory was Charles E. Stuart, a graduate psychology student, who had been an outstanding member of one of JBR's earlier classes. He had served as subject and student experimenter in ESP tests and was also one of JBR's subjects in the initial PK research and so became interested in PK as well as ESP.

But Stuart, like JBR, could only give part time to parapsychological research. He was now a graduate student working for his Ph.D. in the Duke Psychology Department. So while further investigation of PK was high on the priority list, only a limited amount of time and attention could be given it. Consequently, the research continued to be carried on only sporadically, and although JBR was much involved, closely associated and interested in it, the projects that were undertaken were still more or less spontaneously decided upon by individuals who elected to carry out experiments rather than according to an ideal plan or chart that would have prescribed what should be tried next.

Perhaps the main distinction between the first of the projects that now followed and those of Chapter 4 is that the individual experimenters in the earlier tests were simply trying to see if evidence could be obtained that even *looked like* a PK effect. They needed first of all to convince themselves that extra-chance scores could be produced. They were pioneering in the real sense of the word, developing the very methods themselves that could determine whether PK had occurred.

Those who next came on the scene, however (in what can now be seen as a second stage), knew that extra-chance scores had repeatedly been obtained. But greater concern was growing over the possible alternatives to PK that might account for such results, and so over the next year or two the more emphasized objective was to perfect the methods and tighten the controls against possible normal causes of the results.

The more obvious alternatives to PK were, of course, the same two that had been in mind from the start of the research—dice bias and skilled throwing. Attempts at controls on each had been made, but had yet to become standardized practice.

### THE STUART–GIBSON EXPERIMENT

The first experiment after the new laboratory had been set up was in line with the idea of widening the circle of PK experimenters and of encouraging others at other places to see if they too could get evidence of PK.[4] This experiment was carried out in September 1935 by Edmond P. Gibson, a practicing engineer of Grand Rapids, Michigan under Stuart's supervision.

For some time before this, Gibson had been in correspondence with JBR in connection with some ESP tests he had made with his wife Lottie and other subjects. But he had had no personal contact with the laboratory.

Now, however, Stuart was sent to meet the Gibsons, confer

---

[4] Gibson, Edmond P., and Rhine, J. B., "The PK Effect: III. Some Introductory Series." *J. Parapsychol.*, 1943, 7, pp. 118–134.

about their ESP tests, and, naturally, to discuss the new PK work that was being reported. Spontaneously, they at once wanted to try out the PK idea themselves, and an experiment was started practically on the spot.

The conditions under which the experiment was made show that this was still a transition stage from the early freely exploratory methods to more standardized ones. A control on throwing was introduced by always using a dice cup with roughened interior (a corrugated rubber lining or something of the kind) from which to throw the dice, but no systematic control on dice bias was made. And this factor, as well as the spirit of "I wonder if I can get it too," makes this experiment as much like those of Chapter 4 as those that came in this second stage. Nevertheless, and even though spontaneous, the results were intriguing and also introduced the Gibsons to PK research, Gibson mainly as an experimenter, Lottie as a rather exceptional subject.

Stuart, of course, knew of all the PK work that had already then been reported and, therefore, because of Hilton's results, he believed that more than two dice could be used successfully. He decided to use six here. He knew, too, from Smith's results that single faces as well as, or perhaps better than, combinations could serve as targets. He decided to use single faces. But he did not build a control against dice bias into the experimental plan because the subject felt she could do better with targets she selected herself, and for her encouragement he thought he should allow her to do so. She chose the five and six faces more often than the others; fortunately, however, a control on the dice did develop incidentally.

Six medium-sized dice were selected and used throughout. Lottie Gibson was the main subject. The results were recorded in columns of six throws each, 36 die falls instead of the 24 per run that soon became standard. Then 20 of these columns were recorded across the record page as a unit that consequently was referred to as a set, and three such sets were entered one below the other on the page. However the 20 columns were not necessarily all thrown for the same target or at the same time. The set here therefore was not necessarily a unit task as had been the case with the sets recorded by other experimenters.

Two of the four series of tests made turned out to be of special interest. The first was important mainly because in it Lottie got a highly significant result. Converting her columns to conventional 24-throw run units, she threw a total of 210 runs and got hits 91 above chance. This yielded a CR of 3.44; p. = .00058. But, of course, if that series had stood alone, it could not have been said with certainty how much of the deviation was the result of biased dice.

Happily the second series, carried out with the same dice, incidentally corrected the defect. In this a comparison was attempted of the effect on PK of three different light conditions, ordinary daylight, red light, and darkness. In the dark period the record was taken by flashlight. Eighteen runs were made in each condition. But in the first two (the one in daylight and the one in the red light), the results were practically at chance, while the 18 runs in the dark gave a negative deviation, a −24, a value which if taken alone would give a highly significant CR of 3.10; p = .0019.

These results were unexpected and puzzling to say the least. The same subject who had scored positively in the main series in daylight—when light was not a specified condition—here failed to score significantly when it was used as a test condition. And in addition here the deviation in the dark was significantly *negative*. This must mean that something prevented even chance hits from occurring.

In the ESP research negative trends had been noted frequently, and they had been both puzzling and frustrating. And now here the effect was appearing in PK tests, too. (The negative deviation reported by Schwartz in Chapter 4 came many years after this one of Lottie G.'s.) It was all the more puzzling because it could not be interpreted as showing that PK cannot function in the dark, for in the first 18 of the 72 throws that made up the subject's 18 runs in the dark, the deviation was positive. It was only after that that the negative trend set in. Apparently something had changed as the test went on. But it was not the external condition and so it must have been an internal or psychological one. Apparently the negative scoring had been just as "easy" for the subject as her former positive scoring, but evidently some kind of mental twist had come in that deflected her "aim," so to speak. The only change anyone could think of was that as the series went on she probably experienced a change in internal reaction to working in darkness.

This tentative explanation was none too certain. As it turned out much later, however, this case was just the first of a series of negative ones that finally led to an understanding of one of the important aspects of psi, its characteristic of functioning under some conditions to miss the target, just as under others, it functions to hit it. It means that psi ability, either as ESP or PK, is not a fixed attribute of the individual like height or eye color, for instance. Instead it is a process that can work as consciously desired and hit the target or may be deflected by unconscious influences and miss it. Later, after the missing tendency came to be recognized as just as *real* as the tendency to hit, the effect both in ESP and PK came to be called "psi-missing," or missing the target by psi.[5] Lottie Gibson's negative deviation turned out eventually to have been an important item in the long road to the discovery of the laws that underlie some of the apparently inconsistent results of the PK experiments.

Going back now to the need for a control on dice bias in this

[5] NOTE: It was after psi-missing was recognized that the p-values assigned to CR's had to be doubled, because an experimenter could not be certain before doing his experiment whether the deviation he would get would be above or below MCE.

In standard tables, the p-values given (one-tailed) are based on the assumption that the deviation to be expected will go in one direction only, usually above MCE. But in parapsychology where it may go in either of the two directions, the conservative position is to take the p-value (two-tailed) routinely as doubled.

experiment, the negative deviations in this section in the dark provided a very good one. The same dice and the same targets were used in it that had given the positive deviation in the first series, and since one was positive, the other negative, neither one could be laid to bias.

Years later in 1942 when JBR and Betty H. were collecting material for their analysis, they could not use the data of this experiment, since because of the irregularities of runs and sets, it was not comparable to the others. Therefore the regulation analysis of decline could not be made on this material.

One record page was found, however, that was quite suitable for analysis as to vertical and horizontal declines. On this page each of the three 20-column sets was intact, and when this page was quartered a QD so marked was found that the $CR_d$ between first and fourth quarters was 2.86; p $=$ .004.

The experiment confirmed the effective use of six dice per throw and indicated that darkness does *not* inhibit PK, although here it produced a score-depressing effect. Besides, as far as could be determined the work showed decline effects in agreement with those found in other studies. It thus added its bit to the growing evidence of PK, even though it was obviously only a transition step from the earlier exploratory experiments to more highly controlled ones.

### THE LARGE GIBSON EXPERIMENT

The visit of Stuart to the Gibsons left the Gibsons very much bent on continuing PK research on their own. In close correspondence with the laboratory, they then undertook a series of tests that extended throughout all of 1936 and into 1937. They emphasized at the start that this would be a long experiment for they thought that certain effects might be found in a long series of tests that would not be evident in a short one. And so before they finished they had recorded results on well over 200,000 die falls. These included a number of individual test series, differing somewhat in one condition or another.[6]

The plan of the procedure was simple. They continued to throw the six dice from a cup as before, and recorded them in short columns of six throws each. The columns were grouped into 10-column sets, however, usually two across the page. This time, however, the Gibsons were alert to possible dice bias and therefore threw for all faces of the die equally and systematically. When they finished they had positive deviations for all but the one face; it was slightly negative but the positive deviation for its opposite, the six face, was much larger than the deficit on the one face. Dice bias did not produce the results. However, the run score averages were greater for the three higher faces than for the three lower ones. The fact that the subject preferred the higher could have accounted for it. A degree of bias, too, could have existed, but it was not great enough to account for the entire extra-chance deviation.

The deviations the Gibsons got in one long series of over 6,000 runs were not large, but they were persistently positive. In this series Lottie was still the main subject, but sometimes she substituted as record-taker for her husband. However, in general her scores were higher than his. Together, and with a few friends, the average run score when MCE was 4.0, was only 4.18. But over so large a number of runs it gave a CR of 7.46—which has a probability of one in millions.

In another total of 515 runs, the two worked separately and alone and found that the solitude affected them differently. Gibson's average was lower than when working with his wife; Lottie's was higher than when in his presence. The possible suggestion of these results was that Gibson needed the stimulus of an observer, while Lottie could reach a better state of concentration when alone. The totals were significant, and so these results, taken

[6] Gibson, Edmond P., Gibson, Lottie H., and Rhine, J. B., "A Large Series of PK Tests." *J. Parapsychol.*, 1943, 7, pp. 228–237.

at face value as suggestive, now appear to be early indications of personality differences that may affect the expressing of PK.

The subsequent analysis for position effects made on these data in 1942 showed strong evidence of patterning of hits. These patterns could not be explained by faulty dice or any of the other explanations counter to PK. One of these position effects that was significant was a strikingly high rate of success at the end positions of the column (the first and the sixth throws). The other was a very high rate of scoring in the first column of the 10 that made up the set.

With these significant position effects the QD analysis of course showed the usual results; a difference between the first and fourth quarters. In this instance it was not quite significant but a suggestive $CR_d$ of 2.38; p = .017.

This analysis, however, was not the only one made on these data. As a matter of fact, several others were made on them later, from different viewpoints, partly because of the size of the project, but also because it was well and systematically recorded. One of these analyses is reported next.

### PSYCHOLOGICAL FACTORS IN HIT PATTERNS

Several years after the analysis of the large Gibson Experiment by JBR and Betty Humphrey, Dr. J. G. Pratt, who had returned to the laboratory after his service in the Navy, made several analyses of Lottie G.'s data in that series of experiments. One of these will be discussed later on in this chapter, but the other is pertinent here. In this one Pratt studied the distribution of the hits in the records to see what evidence it might show of psychological factors.[7]

As a result of his study Pratt found considerable difference in

[7] Pratt, J. G., "Lawfulness of the Position Effects in the Gibson Cup Series." *J. Parapsychol.*, 1946, 10, pp. 243–268.

scoring patterns between Lottie G.'s witnessed and unwitnessed work. For instance, in both, her outstanding success occurred on the first trial of the first column of the set. But in the witnessed work the rest of the column was not outstanding, as the rate of hitting fell off at once with the second trial, and a gradual decline with no upturn at the end occurred thereafter.

But the general pattern in the unwitnessed work was quite different except for the first trial. Here too, that was the highest of all, but the second was almost as high and the rest only fell off slightly. Pratt's study thus confirmed the earlier finding that the first throw gave the highest level of scoring of all, but beyond that the patterns for the witnessed and for the unwitnessed work were quite different.

This difference was shown especially in the results on the sixth trial, which in the 1942 analysis had been reported as greater than the preceding ones. Now Pratt found that this was a tendency present only in the unwitnessed work. Just why these differences in scoring patterns should occur between witnessed and unwitnessed throwing was not simple to explain then, but that they represented differing psychological attitudes seemed obvious.

Pratt made still other analyses on these data (too complicated to take space for here), uncovering in each instance further signs of hidden lawfulness that apparently could only be related to psychological attitudes, however slight or obscure. He was so much impressed by the lawfulness he had found in various aspects of this data that in the concluding paragraph of his report he said:

The lawful regularity of these effects extending through the page, the series, and sets of high and low total scores reflects the presence in these data of a remarkably consistent and reliable psychological function and the exceptions to the picture of perfect uniformity are themselves psychologically meaningful. These results, occurring as they did without the knowledge of either the subject or the experimenter, and being so far outside the immediate purpose of the tests that they remained undiscovered for 10 years, cannot be ascribed to biased dice, wishful thinking, recording errors, or any other reasonable counter hypothesis. PK is left as the only adequate cause of these effects.[8]

It was probably because of the size of this experiment that the analyses made on it turned out to be as meaningful as they did. The original idea that a long series might have special merit thus turned out to be justified, although the Gibsons could not have foreseen, when they did the work, just what that merit would be.

### THE CUP-VERSUS-MACHINE TEST

At the Parapsychology Laboratory in the fall of 1936 JBR undertook an experiment that involved a more advanced method of control against skillful throwing of the dice than in any earlier experiment.[9] He knew that critics could still argue that subjects had some contact with the dice even when throwing from a cup. It was desirable therefore to eliminate even that slight contact and to mechanize the process completely.

A "machine" was then constructed by the use of which the subject would never touch the dice at all. It consisted of a long electrically-driven rectangular cage with sides of quarter-inch wire mesh (Figure 4) mounted on an axis through the middle so it could be rotated. Dice would be enclosed in this at the beginning of the experiment, and when the cage rotated they would be thrown from one end of the cage to the other, the interior being roughened with interposed baffles, so that the dice would bounce about actively as they fell. They could be read when at rest on the bottom at each half revolution, and the record made at once. Each such reading would be one "throw."

---

[8] *Ibid.*, p. 268.
[9] Rhine, J. B., "Dice Thrown by Cup and Machine in PK Tests." *J. Parapsychol.*, 1943, 7, pp. 207–217.

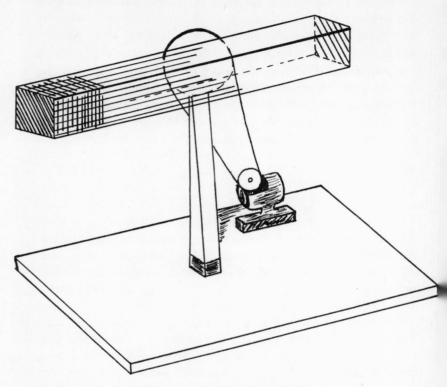

FIGURE 4.   Diagram of automatically rotated "dice machine."

In JBR's experiment using this machine, the cage was rotated at the rate preferred by the subject, usually so as to make a half revolution in from four to five seconds. JBR and his graduate assistant, J. L. Woodruff, and the former ESP subject, A. J. Linzmayer (who had become JBR's secretary) all took turns acting as subject. The target chosen was the six face, and a pair of medium-size dice was used throughout. These had the spots painted on, and no excavations, so that the danger of dice bias was reduced, but in this experiment two conditions were to be contrasted so bias could not be a counter explanation of score differences in any case.

A total of 36 runs was made throwing from a cup and 74 using the machine. In the former the average rate of scoring per run was 4.53, MCE of course being 4.0. With the machine, the rate was 4.61. Both results taken together gave a CR of 3.34; p = .0008, a highly significant figure. The reason the scoring with the machine was at a higher rate than with the cup could have been because the machine was a novelty. It also could have been because the subjects were freer to concentrate when the machine relieved them of the need even to decide when to throw. It mixed the dice and cast them too, and all they had to do was concentrate on the task of willing the target face to come up. It could be similar to the situation with some subjects in ESP tests who did better when the cards they were trying to identify by ESP were completely out of sight than when they could see the deck they were to identify and perhaps be a bit distracted by it.

With the score even better with the machine than without it, the reason for the test was fulfilled. It showed that at least in this experiment the subject's extra-chance scores were not made because they knew how to manipulate the dice. It would, therefore, be safe in the future to throw from a cup.

Later, in 1942, when the results of this experiment were analyzed for position effects, the typical QD decline was found. The difference between the first and fourth quarters yielded a significant $CR_d$ of 2.63; p = .0085.

TWO SIZES OF DICE

The availability of a dice-throwing machine was a stimulus to further tests with it. The same two students who had just taken part in the cup-versus-machine test, with the addition of Linzmayer's wife, Marion, then undertook to use it to compare two sizes of dice.[10] In earlier tests, especially the two Hilton series, different sizes of dice had been compared, and the result had not been in line with what would be expected according to mechanical principles. Now with the machine for mechanized throwing available, the group wanted to see what the effect would be.

As in the cup-versus-machine test, they threw for the six face, but used two pairs of different-sized dice thrown together. One was of medium size ($1\frac{1}{16}$ inch) and the other was smaller ($\frac{7}{16}$ inch). The various individuals took turns acting as subject and recorder.

A total of 126 runs was thrown, which yielded a significant deviation of 69, a CR of 3.37; p = .00075. Since both sizes of dice were used in each throw, each die size was thrown for the equivalent of 63 runs. The deviations on the two were practically the same, the result on each marginally significant. It was 34 on the small, CR = 2.35; p = .018, 35 on the medium, CR = 2.42; p = .015. The usual position effects were found in the data, and they were generally the same on both dice sizes; that is, the deviation of the top half of the runs was greater than that of the lower half. Then, in the horizontal direction, the first half of the pages showed more hits than the last for both dice sizes. The QD for the total, however, was not significant, the $CR_d$ being 1.55; p = .06.

From this test again it could only be supposed that the size of the dice as such did not matter. And by using the machine, so that the subjects did not handle the dice as they had done in the Hilton experiments, it looked as if even a preference for one size or the other had not been involved. In earlier work preferences seemed to be based to some extent at least on the "feel" of the dice in the hand or their ease of manipulation in a cup. But with the machine, the only difference was the visual one and apparently that did not cause perceptible preferences for either

[10] Humphrey, Betty H., and Rhine, J. B., "PK Tests with Two Sizes of Dice Mechanically Thrown." *J. Parapsychol.*, 1945, 9, pp. 124–132.

size. The decline effects so similar to those of other series again spoke for psychological, rather than physical, influences.

### THE GIBSON MACHINE STUDY

The story now goes back again to the Gibsons in Grand Rapids.[11] By the time they were finishing their large experiment reported above, the work with machines had been going on at the Parapsychology Laboratory. Hearing of it, the Gibsons set out to see what they could do with a machine. They made an electrically driven rotating cage similar to the one that had been constructed at Duke, and the experiment that resulted occupied them from February 13 to April 22, 1937. For novelty they used three dice instead of two. Target faces were chosen by the subject who kept the same target for three 24-throw runs, to make a set. The MCE for each run was, of course, 4, and for a set, 12. All faces were thrown for in systematic order.

In this experiment, Lottie G. was again the main subject, although Gibson, himself, and 13 other subjects also took part. Three of the same dice that had been used in the series with Stuart in the first Gibson work were used again here. The number of throws for each face was equalized. The control against bias thus was sufficiently tight that the results, even at the time, could be attributed to PK.

The experiment in a total of nearly 1,500 runs yielded 191 hits above MCE; a significant $CR = 2.71$; $p = .0067$. Then when the entire experiment was analyzed for position effects in 1942, a typical $QD$ pattern, both in the page totals and in the smaller unit, the set, was found. The $QD$ of the page was only marginally significant ($CR_d = 2.12$; $p = .034$) but that of the set was very much so ($CR_d = 3.15$; $p = .0016$).

---

[11] Gibson, Edmond P., Gibson, Lottie H., and Rhine, J. B., "The PK Effect: Mechanical Throwing of Three Dice." *J. Parapsychol.*, 1944, 8, pp. 95–109.

The position effects of this experiment were in fact so regular
and so typical and the control against the counter explanations
so tight, with the use of the machine and the rotation of die
faces, that the experiment was easily one of the best of its time
and the one in which with the highest degree of assurance PK
could be considered as the only reasonable explanation.

FURTHER ANALYSES BY PRATT

## 1. Target Preference

Soon after his analysis of Lottie G.'s results in the large Gibson
Experiment already mentioned, Pratt turned to the same experiment again for a different purpose. This was one suggested by
some data that he had collected much earlier, but which had been
stored away and for various reasons almost forgotten.

The data in question had been accumulated in 1940 as the
result of a series of PK tests Pratt himself had carried out in
collaboration with Joe Woodruff, when both were at the laboratory before the war.[12] At that time Woodruff, who has been
mentioned in earlier tests in this chapter, was a graduate student
at Duke, and Pratt was on the laboratory staff. This was at a time
before the analysis by JBR and Betty H. had brought out the
fact that strong position effects were occurring in most of the
PK data.

The test made by Pratt and Woodruff was a short one and
was an attempt to see what the effect would be if dice were
released to fall more quickly than they do when tumbling down
an inclined plane. A mechanically rotated cage had been constructed in which each of a pair of inlaid dice was enclosed in
a celluloid tube about 1½ inches in diameter and 18 inches long.
The tubes were connected at one end to a mechanically driven

[12] Pratt, J. G. and Woodruff, J. S., "An Exploratory Investigation of PK
Position Effects." *J. Parapsychol.*, 1946, 10, 197–207.

pulley, which raised them in a 180-degree arc then to fall free by gravity. Each tube had randomizing baffles interposed within it, through which the die would tumble rapidly and come to rest on the bottom. Here it was recorded before the next swing of the tube.

The two men took turns acting as subject and recorder. They threw 25 "rounds," a round consisting of 12 runs, one run for each face of the die by each subject. However the totals were not significant, and so no evidence was given on the question on which they had based their experiment. The method was discontinued and the data stored away.

By 1946, however, the import of position effects was being increasingly realized for the evidence they gave of psychological influences in PK experiments. After the strong evidence of such influences he had already found in Lottie G.'s data, Pratt now went back to the half-forgotten data of his old experiment with Woodruff to look for position effects and other internal evidence bearing on the matter of the psychological significance of scoring trends.

His examination did show internal patterns that were suggestive of PK. The strongest suggestion he got had to do with scoring on the lower three die faces different from that on the higher. Inlaid dice had been used, not the usual kind with depressions painted over for spots, and therefore it was unlikely that these dice were appreciably biased. Nonetheless he now found that the scores on the one, two, and three faces, were below MCE, while those on the four, five, and six faces, were above. He also found that the runs for the lower faces only, had shown a sharp decline from top to bottom. Both observations thus suggested that the psychological reaction to the lower faces was different in some degree from that on the upper faces. Parapsychologists had long been confronted with evidence of higher scores on the upper than the lower die faces. They had always had to presume that some of the difference probably was the result of bias. The present suggestion that the difference might occur without dice bias was therefore especially interesting. It seemed like a confirmation of the general assumption that both bias and preference favor the higher faces over the lower ones.[13]

The trend Pratt had observed in those data was only marginally significant, and he therefore set out to see if the preference effect would be confirmed in the Lottie G. data he had analyzed before.[14]

Because of the regular way in which the target faces had been used in this data and the fact that the numbers of throws for each face were the same, there was no difficulty in getting the totals for each of the six faces. He found, as expected, higher totals on the four, five, and six faces than on the one, two, and three faces. This difference he referred to as "target preference," although it meant only that some targets yielded higher scores than others, whether or not because of conscious preference. When he compared position effects in the three-run sets, he found them to be quite different in the sets thrown for the lower faces from those for the higher ones and much more pronounced in the latter case. In fact, the differences in hit positions in the data of the higher faces were significant in themselves, and they were significantly *dissimilar* from the patterns in the lower face sets. Evidence was found too that Lottie G. who had consciously pre-

---

[13] NOTE: Pratt also noted in his own scores in these data, a tendency toward the so-called "lag" effect, which he described as "psychological inertia" in changing targets that resulted in a carry-over of the preceding target when changing to a new one. It had been noted at various times by other experimenters but never actually measured. In these data 250 of Pratt's runs could be checked for it (initial runs of sessions could not be counted). He found the score on "lag" hits was suggestive, with a $CR = 2.03$; $p = .04$.

It seems quite likely that "psychological inertia" when it shows up as a lag effect tells something about the processes involved which may relate to the release of unconscious tendencies when conscious inhibitions are removed. However, since only occasional subjects show it, and they only at times, it is an effect that as yet has not received much attention.

[14] Pratt, J. G., "Target Preference in PK Tests with Dice." *J. Parapsychol.*, 1947, 11, pp. 26–45.

ferred the five face produced the most significant position effects when throwing for fives.

Since Lottie G. had had little or no experience with dice games before she became a subject in the PK tests Pratt wondered, too, whether her target preferences had developed after she began her PK work. He was able to get an answer on that by close inspection of her 25 pages of data secured when she had worked alone and unwitnessed. It was in these data that her personal proclivities had been most pronounced, as he had earlier found, and it was in these data that he now found that the differences in hit patterns between the low- and high-face target sets had not shown up at the beginning of the work. There was no perceptible difference between the two sets of targets in the first chronological quarter of the throws; they only developed in the latter part of the series. In fact the total data also showed that all the faces gave comparable results at first, but that later on "inhibition" came in when the lower faces were targets. The study in general confirmed even to fine points the existence of strong and consistent psychological effects in Lottie G.'s data.

## 2. Dice Bias and Manner of Throwing

In spite of all the attempts to control for dice bias in PK experiments critics had suggested one possibility of error that had not been ruled out experimentally.[15] It was the possibility that extra-chance scores like those in successful PK experiments could be secured by a combination of dice bias and the manner of throwing. The argument was that if the dice were biased for the higher faces because of the excavations, the effect would show up most of all when the dice were given a long roll. Then if the subject put more energy into his throws at the beginning of

[15] Pratt, J. G., "Dice Bias and Manner of Throwing." *J. Parapsychol.*, 1949, 11, pp. 55–63.

a run, set, or page, it might give a higher number of hits in those areas. It was a possibility that had never been taken very seriously by experimenters because they had had little reason to think it occurred. They had not observed that successful subjects threw the dice in any such peculiar fashion and knowing that bias was controlled by other safeguards this particular one had not seemed realistic. However, Pratt now decided to try to get empirical evidence for or against it.[16]

To test out the idea and to throw the dice for him Pratt secured the services of Jack Hornaday, a graduate student in psychology. Although Hornaday knew about the PK research he was not involved in it and was not told the objective of the experiment. The idea of course was that although he was to throw dice he was not to exert any PK because Pratt's objective was to see if the combination of dice bias and a special way of throwing could produce the kind of extra-chance scoring that had been secured in experiments that had been interpreted as showing PK.

In order to give the hypothesis every chance, the most biased kind of common dice, those with excavated spots, were given Hornaday and instead of a dice cup with roughened interior, an ordinary smooth drinking glass from which to throw them. He was also asked to do the task as rapidly as possible so that he worked under pressure, a circumstance not conducive to PK.

Hornaday was then instructed to throw the dice in three different sections covering three of the main variations in manner of throwing a subject might use in throwing from a cup. These were descriptively indicated as "no roll," "long roll," and "hard baffle bounce."

For the no-roll throws Hornaday was to pick up the dice as they lay on the table, place them in the glass, and then tilt it and allow them to slide out on the table with a minimum of mixing. For the long-roll throws he was to use vigor and force, drop the dice randomly into the glass and throw them so they

16 *Ibid.*

would roll as far as possible (about three feet) without hitting the back wall. In the third way of throwing he was to handle the dice even more vigorously and bounce them against the back wall. Presumably the bias would have a greater effect on the long roll or even on the baffle bounce than on the no-roll throws, if the hypothesis was born out.

In view of all the imposed "anti-PK" conditions Pratt felt that Hornaday's results should be "contaminated" only slightly, if at all, by PK.

In 15 hours of work interrupted only to eat and sleep, Hornaday threw the six white dice 1,000 times in each condition. This was the equivalent of 240 runs each, and as expected the bias showed up under each of the conditions. In so many runs the number of high faces over low ones recorded gave a significant $CR_d$ for the first two ways of throwing and a strong but not significant excess in the third. The excesses however were not correlated with the manner of throwing. The highest deviation in favor of the upper faces was secured where least expected— in the no-roll throws. The next was on the long roll and the least on the hard baffle bounce. On the first two, but not the third the difference between the high and low faces was significant, but the differences between the ways of throwing were not. Interestingly, too, in all of the cases the deficit on the lower faces was below MCE and either equal to or greater than the excess on the upper ones. This was a circumstance quite in line with expectation where bias is concerned, but quite different from that customarily obtained in the scoring when PK appears to be involved. It will be recalled that even in JBR's initial experiment (Chapter 2) and in many others in which data was secured on both the higher and the lower faces, the results did not cancel as they should have done if bias alone had been involved. Instead, in spite of any bias that may have existed, the results showed that some other factor was present too.

In this test of Hornaday's, however, the scores showed only the bias as expected, but they did not link up in a meaningful way with the different ways of throwing so that the conclusion was that this empirical control had fairly adequately laid to rest the possibility that deviations caused by bias would be accentuated by any of the special ways of throwing from a cup that a subject might use.

### 3. Areas of PK Success

In another analysis Pratt undertook to study in detail the distribution of hits on the record page.[17] Ever since the QD analysis in 1942 had shown that strong position effects are characteristic of the majority of research reports experimenters had been trying to understand the reason why the hits tended to cluster rather than to occur randomly over the experiment as a whole. Pratt undertook to find out in finer detail than previously just where the clusters occur. He hoped that the information might throw new light on the reason why.

Looking over the data of the past years for some that would be suitable Pratt chose the high-dice, low-dice series of tests that Margaret P. had recorded second in her notebooks (Chapter 4). This series was suitable because it was the work of a single subject and therefore personal characteristics if present would stand out; it was a sufficiently large group of data, well and clearly recorded; and, according to the 1942 analysis, had the marked position effects that, with only two exceptions, were characteristic of all the 18 experimental projects that had been examined in that analysis.

It will be recalled that Margaret P. had recorded the data of her throws for the high-face combinations in the upper half of the record page, for the lower ones in the lower half. In each, three sets of three columns each were recorded, each column being the record of 12 throws (one run) of a pair of dice.

[17] Pratt, J. G., "Rhythms of Success in PK Test Data." *J. Parapsychol.*, 1947, 11, pp. 90–110.

The work was significant as a whole and the high and low combination sections were each independently significant. In the 1942 analysis four kinds of position effects, or groupings of hits, had been found in this data: (1) when pooled the top halves of the runs were higher than the lower; (2) when pooled the first column of the sets was higher than the last; (3) when pooled the first of the three sets on the page was higher than the other two which were about the same; (4) when pooled the runs showed an upturn of success at the bottom as well as at the top, so that they formed a U-curve. All of these differences except the third were great enough to be significant.

With this much known about the data Pratt decided to pool that from the high- and low-dice combinations (each was independently significant), and use them both together, thus in effect doubling the amount of data for study.

He turned his attention first to the columns to see how the difference between the upper and lower halves was distributed. By dividing each half once again, thus making four segments of the runs he found that the decline from top to bottom was not a gradual one. The main part of the deviation was centered in the first segment; the second and fourth were lower, but about the same, while the third was lowest of all. This made an assymmetrical U-curve.

Next the decline within the set was analyzed and it turned out to result from an especially strong U-curve in the first column. So here it was again—the high level of hitting at the beginning of the column, and an upturn at the bottom, but mainly concentrated in the first column of the three, the second and third showing the curve only slightly. In all three columns of the set the low point was in the third segment, and it was practically the same in all three. This effect of a decline in the set thus had the same cause as the top-bottom decline in the columns.

The decline in the sets from the first to the third across the page was examined next, and here too it turned out to be the result of the higher scoring levels of the first set, which in turn was caused mainly by the high levels of hitting on the beginning and end of the first columns. The third set was practically the same as the second.

The study thus traced down the area of extra-chance scoring and found it to be mainly in the first column of the page and even in that it was clustered mainly at the top and bottom of the column. Pratt found too that the higher the score for a column the more distinctly U-shaped was the distribution of hits within it. This meant of course that the increase of hitting was more pronounced only at the ends of the run, the scores in the middle sections rising very little above chance.

The general conclusion was that most of the time spent in an experiment like Margaret P.'s was actually wasted, or, reversing the viewpoint, in most of the time of the experiment the PK ability was somehow inhibited. Although the PK force had been decisively demonstrated, it had only shown up "on the fringe of the test structure." Pratt went on to remark that "although PK thus is a real force in nature the average rate of scoring that has been achieved has been limited, and even in the most favorable trial positions it does not equal as much as twice mean chance expectation."[18] In fact no scores comparable to the highest scoring in ESP had been reported. "This all adds up," he went on to say "to the fact that the PK test . . . is a grossly inefficient instrument for measuring PK ability. By far the largest part of the test appears to be a sheer waste of time . . . It almost seems as if the test is choking off the very function which it was designed to measure.

"With such a delicate balance between the conditions in the test which permit PK to function, however imperfectly, and those which inhibit it completely, it is easy to understand why the scientific discovery of this natural phenomenon has been so long delayed."

18 *Ibid.* pp. 108–109.

On a practical level, the recommendation to experimenters from this analysis was the use of shorter columns and fewer of them in a unit of an experiment in order to "short circuit the unprofitable areas of the test structure. "At the same time, a direct experimental inquiry is needed into the causal factors which are making those areas unprofitable ones for the PK process."

## 4. *Restricted Areas of PK Success*

In a continuation of his effort to find all the meaning possible in the position effects of PK data Pratt next selected for his "microscope" another group of data that had been produced by Lottie G.[19] This was her work in the Gibson machine study. He selected it because the technique used was different from that of the large Gibson experiment he had already analyzed. It would be of interest to see whether similarities would be shown in spite of the differences. Also, he wanted to see if Lottie G., as Margaret P., had wasted a lot of her time.

In this machine experiment Lottie G. had not been the only subject, but the main one. The total deviation that had been secured was 191 hits of which 138 had been hers. She had thrown 630 runs, her CR was 3.01; p = .0026. This data of hers was thus significant in itself and so it was suitable on that score for Pratt's analysis.

The main difference in method between this experiment and the large Gibson experiment was first of all, that the dice were thrown by hand in that one, by machine in this; six at a time in that, three at a time in this; six throws to a column and 10 to a set in that, 24 to a column and three to a set in this.

[19] Pratt, J. G., "Restricted Areas of Success in PK Tests." *J. Parapsychol.*, 1947, 11, pp. 191–207.

In the earlier QD analysis of this machine experiment the typical declines had been found, and when Pratt now analyzed the Lottie G. data, he found the declines present to a significant degree there, too, in spite of the fact that the number of runs was smaller. The QD declines were shown to be present in it, so that again the data were suitable for further analysis of position effects.

Pratt first pooled all the data for the 24-throw columns of the sets to see if position effects within the columns were shown. He found them present very strikingly, and very definitely localized as well, for the greatest number of hits had been secured on the first trial of the first column, the next highest being on the last trial of the first column. Each of these positions represented 198 single die observations, or 8.25 runs of 24 dice each. The deviation on the first position yielded a CR of 4.77, p = .00016, on the last, 2.67; p = .007. These two positions (significantly higher than the intervening ones), however, were the only ones to yield significant scores. This significant scoring in the two end positions of the runs made again as in Margaret P.'s data a U-curve of performance down the run. And it was both similar and dissimilar to the curve of performance Lottie G. had shown in the large Gibson experiment. There, it will be recalled, she had had her area of outstanding scoring at the start of the first run of the set, too. But she had shown an upturn at the end of the first run only in her unwitnessed work. In the witnessed the scores had fallen off in a straight decline to the end of the column, and so Pratt had been unable to say that her work in that experiment had shown a general U-curve in the run.

However now that he found the U-curve in this 24-column data of Lottie G.'s and also in Margaret P.'s he was inclined to think that the upturn represented a reaction to the monotony of the intervening throws, but that Lottie G. had not shown it in the large Gibson experiment because there, with the columns only six throws long, the feeling of monotony had not had a chance to develop. He thought the 12-throw column that Margaret P.

had used might be a necessary length for the "end effect" to become noticeable.

However, a somewhat different interpretation is possible too, and in the quest to understand the psychological factors hidden in phenomena like position effects all angles must be considered even on relatively fine points like this.

In this instance a difference between the situation in Lottie G.'s witnessed and unwitnessed runs might have made the difference in the "end effect" of the two sections. When throwing in the witnessed condition, the other person kept the record but when she was working without a witness Lottie G. kept her own record, and naturally she would have been more aware of her stage of progress down the six-throw column then than when someone else was keeping it. It has since been shown repeatedly that position affects like these only occur when the subject is aware of the structure of the record sheet. Thus this unwitnessed section of Lottie G.'s work was actually more comparable here than her witnessed work was. It is thus quite possible to say that the U-curve in the first run of a set, characteristic of Margaret P.'s data, was also characteristic of Lottie G.'s data.

In other ways besides the U-curve, too, Pratt showed that Lottie G.'s data were similar in spite of the differences of technique. In both, the significant positions were found on the left-hand side of the page only. In both the sections of highest hitting were very much restricted to certain areas. Pratt could say consequently that location on the page affected scoring, and therefore that the psychological factor involved was related to the record structure. Such a statement, of course, was an academic way of saying that the subject's attitude in the test was affected by the stage of the task presented in a series of dice throws. And if so, it was a point worth making in order to show that PK was not an anomaly but a process following well-known psychological laws like those of novelty, monotony, and "end effects."

And, of course, these results showed, too, that probably just as much of Lottie G.'s time had been wasted as of Margaret P.'s.

## 5. Trial-by-trial Success or Failure

In his final analysis of psi data, Pratt turned his attention to the question whether success in either or both ESP and PK experiments comes in single flashes or over longer stretches.[20] He wondered if a trial-by-trial study of records when the phenomenon appeared to be functioning, would show "streaks of success," or whether each hit appeared to be independent of any others.

For his study Pratt therefore chose the data of a group of significant ESP experiments and for his PK material, he turned back once again to the Margaret P. data and to the data in the large Gibson experiment.

A method for making a comparison of the frequency of hits on a trial-by-trial basis was available.[21] It involved the counting of the number of isolated hits and groups of hits on successive trials in the data and then evaluating them in relation to the number of each that would be expected by chance.

In each of the two sets of PK data Pratt selected the highest scoring sections as more suitable for his present inquiry. In the Margaret P. data it was the first columns of the set. They gave him a total of 299 runs. In the Gibson series he found the highest scoring material in Lottie G.'s unwitnessed work and in that again in the first columns of the sets, of which there were 113.

Then for a further analysis Pratt went to some material from certain tests of sense perception to see how patterns in it would compare to those of ESP and PK. This data was from a regulation psychological test of subliminal perception. In it the subjects had been shown symbols on a screen but so quickly that they had been unable to identify correctly more than about 50 per cent of them.

[20] Pratt, J. G., "Trial-by-trial Grouping of Success and Failure in Psi Tests." *J. Parapsychol.*, 1947, 11, pp. 254–268.
[21] Stevens, W. E., "Distribution of Groups in a Sequence of Alternatives." *Ann. Eugen.*, 1939, 9, pp. 10–17.

The results of his three kinds of analyses were that the ESP and the PK material showed no "streaks of success." The hits tended to be distributed randomly. In these the subject had obviously been unable to maintain a successful stance. But in the subliminal perception data the clustering of hits was shown so strongly that a CR of 5.32; p in the millions was shown.

As a result of his studies Pratt felt that this distinction between the sensory pattern of hitting and that of the forms of psi was important as evidence of a fundamental distinction between the two processes, the latter tending to come in quick flashes, the former more sustained.

However, perhaps the question could be raised whether a 50 per cent discrimination in the sense perception data was low enough to be comparable to that of the psi data. The PK data used, at least, was far from the 50 per cent level of accuracy, which would have meant averages of 12 hits per run when MCE is four. If it had been, just possibly the successes might have tended to be less isolated, or if the rate of successful perception in the subliminal tests had been lower possibly the hits would have been more isolated.

All of the experiments presented in this chapter can be said to fall under the general topic of establishing the fact that PK occurs, by showing that significant scores were obtained that could not be explained by dice bias or by skillful throwing. It will be noted that all of the main ones were carried out in 1936 and 1937. Pratt's analyses appeared some years later. However, these are not all of the experiments that were made at the Parapsychology Laboratory during this period. Another group of tests was made in 1936, which is deferred for presentation until Chapter 7 because this work does not fall under the general topic of simply establishing PK but concerns tests made to learn something of its nature.

It well might seem that after the experiments of this chapter and the 1942 analysis of the position effects shown in their data, the occurrence of PK had been sufficiently well confirmed that no more experiments were necessary simply to get significant scores to indicate that PK had occurred, so that attention could turn to a wider range of exploration. And as a matter of fact the majority of experiments that were undertaken after the publication of the PK work began in 1943 did just that. But before the QD analysis was made little freedom was felt for wider exploration. During most of that period after 1934 when the monograph on ESP appeared, JBR and his assistants were of necessity preoccupied mainly with the controversy that developed when the revolutionary claim of ESP met the skepticism of psychologists whose dogma had always been that no such way of "knowing" can exist. Consequently much time and energy was drained off into a defense of the research that had shown ESP to be a fact. The PK research therefore could not be given first attention at the Parapsychology Laboratory. The controversy over ESP also made JBR and his assistants realize fully that they would need a very solid wall of evidence for PK if it was ever to have to stand up against a similar attack. Therefore with the time and energy available it seemed necessary to continue piling up data by the convenient and tried technique that had already yielded positive results.

But by the middle of the forties the attitude had changed. It was then that JBR said, in his 1945 editorial mentioned earlier, "merely to repeat PK tests with the simple objective of finding more evidence of the PK effect should be an unthinkable waste of time . . ." Instead experimental projects might just as well be planned to show something about the nature of the phenomenon. Even so, however, a number of projects were still ahead in which the main aim was simply to get evidence of PK. Those projects are presented next, in Chapter 6, because topically, if not chronologically, they follow those of the present chapter. They also fortify and strengthen and give a degree of variety to those already presented.

# Postscripts to Confirmation

✤

PROJECTS devoted only to showing that evidence of PK was obtained logically follow those of Chapter 5, even though chronologically they are quite out of place. After the Gibson machine experiment and then the various analyses of it, the case for PK was much stronger on statistical grounds than scientific conclusions require. However, high values are necessary to carry conviction about findings as unusual as PK, yet a point can be reached, as here, when extra ciphers in p-values seem almost superfluous. From this point on, then, further experiments with the limited objective of only showing that PK occurred would hardly seem necessary.

However the fact was that almost no one had complete information about all the evidence then (nor even now). No one then had even the benefit of a comprehensive review, so that scarcely anyone could have gotten the full impact of the evidence that had accumulated. This was partly the reason, at least, that over the following years, even up to 1965, projects were reported that had had the sole objective of proving PK, although the reasons they were undertaken varied from case to case.

Some of these experiments were undertaken before all of those already presented here were published. Several experimenters were dissatisfied with the conditions under which some of the earlier experiments had been made. But most often of all, the main reason was a familiar and natural one, that the individual wanted to see if he could get his own evidence for this rather incredible ability.

## THE HERTER EXPERIMENT

In the summer of 1942 a former psychology student of JBR's, Charles J. Herter, wanted to make a PK experiment. He had a special subject, his roommate, Charles Stoddard, with whom he had made ESP tests with interesting results. Now he wanted to see for himself if the two of them could get evidence of PK.

Charles Stuart, who by then had completed his graduate studies and received his Ph.D., was in charge of the Parapsychology Laboratory that summer. Under Stuart's guidance Herter made an almost flawless experiment.[1] By this time most of the necessary test conditions had become standard procedure. Ever since the cup-versus-machine experiment (Chapter 5) it had been considered that the use of dice cups, in which to shake and from which to cast the dice, was an adequate safeguard against skillful throwing. It was a more convenient and adaptable technique than the stationary machine and so it had become a routine method.

By this time, too, the general consensus from many tests was that six dice per throw was about the best and most generally convenient number when number of dice per throw was not the point of a study. It had been decided, too, that the safest way to choose the target was to begin with the one or else the six face and rotate targets "around-the-die."

Over a period of about a month that summer, Stoddard threw six white $\frac{7}{16}$-inch inlaid dice for eleven "rounds," each one consisting of 36 throws of the six dice for each of the six faces. The only feature of the procedure that was not quite routine was the throwing 36 times instead of 24 per run and the fact that the runs were recorded according to face, rather than in the order in which they were thrown.

The total number of runs, converted to the standard run of 24 die throws was 594. The average score per run was 4.35; $CR = 4.65$, which would not be expected by chance in a million

[1] Herter, Charles J., and Rhine, J. B., "An Exploratory Investigation of the PK Effect." *J. Parapsychol.*, 1945, 9, pp. 17–25.

of such cases. All the faces were thrown for an equal number of times; the deviation was only explainable as the result of PK.

When the record sheets were turned over to JBR for analysis that fall, they were of course at once checked for position effects. But because of the irregular way of recording, the standard QD analysis could not be made. The vertical distribution of hits in the column however showed the familiar top-bottom decline, $CR_d = 2.72$; $p = .006$.

The final sentences of the report of Herter's experiment (written by JBR) give a general indication of the appreciation that was coming to be felt at the time both of the meaning of position effects and of the circumstances under which PK is most likely to be expressed.

. . . We have to turn for an explanation of these primacy and finality effects, this terminal salience, to psychological hypotheses. . . . We therefore attach meaning to these position effects beyond the mere verification value they have for the PK process itself. The relatively uniform way the distributions appear in this study manifests an impressive degree of lawfulness at work in the process.

There is a further semi-speculative remark that may be of interest to fellow experimenters in parapsychology. Past experience indicates that the most favorable conditions for a successful experiment were present here. It was the first and only experience with PK testing for both C.J.H. and his subject. Both were deeply interested, curious about PK, and eager to see if it really would work for them. Such an attitude is highly favorable, and under those conditions, PK did work. But this does not necessarily mean that C.J.H. and C.S. could duplicate the result, for their motivation would not now be the same; and this observation, all psychologists will agree, is a datum of the greatest importance at the present stage of the inquiry.

PK IN ENGLAND: HYDE, AND PARSON'S EXPERIMENT,
AND WEST'S REVIEW

The scene now shifts across the Atlantic, where for a time the results of PK experiments were much less confirmatory than they had been in the United States. The idea of PK was still a particularly alien one there and only beginning even to be considered. The first reports of PK experiments in the 1943 *Journal of Parapsychology*, however, had not gone unnoticed. Even though these were the war years, and infinitely worse for research in England than in the United States, still in 1945 a report of several experimental attempts and one review of American work came out in the Proceedings of the British Society for Psychical Research.

One of these experimental attempts was by Dennis H. Hyde.[2] In it he gives an account of his attempt to repeat PK experiments using the "published American technique." He threw three dice from a cup against a vertical baffle, making 6,480 die falls, 270 standard runs in all. He was his own subject and recorded his results in columns according to the standard method. The total score, however, showed only a deviation of +29, which was quite insignificant. No position effects were obtained either, and the author concluded that this lack of results showed "that positive PK results are not guaranteed by repetition of the published American technique," a guarantee, it may be obseved, that none of those who had developed the "American technique" had given or implied. Some of the latter failed, too, but those struggling to make their own trails and to develop their own methods in uncharted territory have again and again shown themselves more likely to get evidence of PK than those who only repeat someone else's technique. The manner and mood are almost certain to be different.

Another experiment was by Denys Parsons, and the outcome was similar.[3] Parsons carried out a larger and more varied experiment than Hyde, but got no evidence of PK. In one section with four subjects, dice were released to roll down an inclined

---

[2] Hyde, Dennis H., "A Report on Some English PK Trials." *Proc. Soc. psych. Res.* 1942–45, 47, pp. 293–295.

[3] Parsons, Denys, "Experiments on PK with Inclined Plane and Rotating Cage." *Ibid.*, pp. 296–300.

plane, the target being either the three high or the three low faces. A small but insignificant predominance of high faces was obtained regardless of target.

Parsons then used a rotating cage, and in several different series of tests, tried out 10, 12, and 15 different subjects under carefully controlled conditions. But no significant deviations were obtained, nor were any significant declines found. The final sentence concerning them in the report is, "Failures predominate even in the first quarters and the decline effect is negligible."

Of course no one can say just why these two attempts failed. The reports are written with no reference to the attitudes of the experimenters toward the test or, in the case of Parsons, to those of his subjects. The points that are stressed however concern only the *exactness* with which the experimenters tried to duplicate the "published American technique." The impression is given that they wanted to succeed and that they proceeded with careful and studied attention to the procedure.

Perhaps it is only fair to say here that one ingredient now known to be very conducive to success in PK may have been missing in these experiments. It had not been given much emphasis in the PK publications of the times. It concerned the attitudes and spirit and spontaneity of the test "atmosphere." In spite of a few expressions in articles, like that from JBR quoted at the end of the Herter report, the significance of this psychological condition could easily have been overlooked or underrated. Even at the laboratory during the early years of research the "spirit" engendered by the excitement of discovery was taken for granted and scarcely noticed as a condition that helps "release" PK. It was ever present of course even while the need to develop sound methods was uppermost in mind.

But for these experimenters in England, the discovery of PK was already claimed in the United States. Their own preoccupation was to see if they could confirm it by the methods as reported and so meticulously carried out that no loophole would be left for criticism. It is not too difficult to suppose that consequently the intangible "spirit" of the test situation in the Duke experiments could have been crowded out. It could have been that the yeast was omitted from the loaf.

The review article in the same Proceedings was by Dr. D. J. West, even then a psychic researcher of some experience, although still a young man. His assignment was to review and survey the American PK work.[4] He covered the main lines of possible criticism with considerable minuteness. His list of criticisms are interesting here for their bearing on the weaknesses he was able to see in the American work as reported up to that date.

Beginning with the possibility that dice bias might have affected the scores, he found only four out of thirteen reported experiments that he considered free from it. The next criticism concerned the manner of casting the dice. There he considered the machine-thrown results the best, but not free from the possibility that somehow the speed of the machine might have been adjusted to favor the result. He goes still further to say, "One can also imagine human muscle action being regulated as delicately as any ordinary dice- or coin-throwing device, so that the objection could apply to hand throws as well as mechanical throws." The only way to be safe, he concluded, would be to have the machine run at constant speed. (As a matter of fact, the machine was always run at a constant speed once an experiment began, for the first hand-turned apparatus was soon converted into one electrically driven and controlled by rheostat. But no one thought of mentioning the fact, probably because none of the experimenters would have considered seriously the possibility of such a criticism being made.)

The third question raised was on the topic of repeatability. As long as some experimenters fail, as did Hyde and Parsons, West said, the implication would be that the phenomenon was still open to question. He knew they had carried out the physical requirements of the test painstakingly, and he no more than they

[4] West, Donald J., "A Critical Survey of the American PK Research." *Proc. Soc. psych. Res.* 1942–45, 47, pp. 281–290.

was impressed by the need for spontaneity and enthusiasm, to create the proper spirit, or realized that without this an essential condition for "repeatability" was lacking.

West next looked into the psychological background of the PK experiments and found it much too informal for full confidence. The research, he feared, allowed a question as to whether laxity may not have crept in "under the cloak of informality."

He then mentioned a number of criticisms that had been leveled at the early work in ESP. These were inaccurate recording, deliberate fraud, optional stopping, unreported results, "and the like." He said, however, that probably none of these could be charged against the PK work, since methods to eliminate any of them that ever was pertinent in ESP research, had now become standard.

He then discussed the use of decline effects as proof of PK and concluded that the results appear "sound and significant," although dice bias in some cases, he thought, could invalidate them, but he was not specific on the point. He concluded, however, that this possibility, although it must necessarily be mentioned so as not to be overlooked, still did not apply "to all the PK experiments, nor to the vertical declines that are included in nearly every report. Moreover, the data showed remarkable consistency in the display of decline effects giving positive quarter distributions even in experiments performed by persons oblivious to the possibilities of declines."

In his final paragraph West summed up by saying that though he did not find the PK reports perfect, he thought the faults were minor. Taking the material as reported, he thought the case was "probably even more clear-cut and conclusive than the case for ESP itself." He outlined the direction he thought should be taken to strengthen the work, but urged that further study be concentrated on finding the conditions favorable and unfavorable to PK, rather than concentrating only on further proof.

With that reasonable summation, the situation as it looked in England at the time was very well stated. As West had remarked in reference to the fact that the attempts of Hyde and Parsons had failed, "The failure of initial English repetitions to confirm the American PK results reminds one of the similar failure of the first ESP experiments in this country. In all probability history will repeat itself and English persistence will be rewarded in due course."

He might well have added that the fact that PK tests had even been attempted, considering the upset of the war, was good evidence of "English persistence." As he did say, time was necessary for attempts to get evidence of PK to be rewarded. A few years later the experiments of another Englishman, G. W. Fisk, and then one by Fisk and West in collaboration (both reported later) supplied the lack. It thus turned out that West himself was one of those "whose persistence was rewarded in due course." But before those, a successful PK experiment in England was reported from an unexpected quarter.

### "LOADED" DICE

The unexpected PK experiment reported from England, published a few years after West's review, came from Dr. E. A. G. Knowles, a young woman employed by a firm of English engineers.[5] Her report said, "To begin with I should point out that I am not engaged in psychical research, nor am I a member of any society carrying out such research. I am an engineering mathematician interested in the application of probability theory and statistics in processes of mass production."

She continued, "I had, rather incredulously, heard from my brother (Dr. Frederick Knowles) of successful experiments in the U.S.A. on the effect of concentration on the scores achieved by tossing dice." Just then preparing a lecture on "Probability, Sampling, and Significance," she decided to stage an experiment in

[5] Knowles, E. A. G., "Reports on an Experiment Concerning the Influence of Mind Over Matter." *J. Parapsychol.*, 1949, 13, pp. 186–196.

which the class could take part, for as she told her assistant, successful experiments had been conducted at an American university on the influence of concentration on the fall of dice, but, she asked, how could one believe this finding unless one tested it oneself?

Miss Knowles then decided as a preliminary to have five of her assistants each throw a dozen dice from a cup and try to get as many low numbers (faces one, two, and three) as possible. Then on a second round, each again to throw one for high numbers (faces four, five, and six). The outcome of this test was interesting for it was not as close to chance as she expected it would be. It yielded a p-value of .051, or a probability of about 20 to one against chance. Although she did not consider this result significant, in the field of engineering, she said, it would be considered encouraging and would call for further experimenting.

Pleased with the "lucky" result, the author says, "I therefore thought that as no one would believe in the possibility of influencing the fall of dice by one's mental efforts, the example might well serve as a warning against jumping to conclusions on the basis of insufficient evidence!"

But to be sure of the disbelief of the class, she asked the students before taking the test, if they believed a mental effect on dice could be demonstrated. Of course, they did not. However, over half of the students thought it was a question that should be answered by experiment rather than belief.

The experiment was tried again, but this time the deviation from chance was less than before, $p = .11$. The conclusion then was that the experiment had yielded insignificant results.

However, later it occurred to Miss Knowles to evaluate the two sets of data together, and when she did so, as she says, "I had another surprise," for she found that the outcome on so much larger a number of throws, all with an above-chance deviation, was highly significant, $p = .004$.

The numbers of high- versus low-aim throws were not equal, but in the throws for low aim, where 120 each of low and high faces

would have been expected by chance, 135 low faces were obtained
and 105 high ones. In the high aim throws where 90 of each was
expected by chance, 105 high faces had been obtained, and 75
low ones. A distribution like that could well be a surprise to a
statistician who had never before had any reason to believe what
these figures seemed to say. They seemed to say, of course, that
these dice had acted as if they were loaded for the desired faces:
for the low ones when low faces were targets and for the high
ones when high faces were targets.

Miss Knowles then thought it would be interesting to compare these results with those that might be obtained if an actually
loaded die were thrown by neutral subjects to see if results due
entirely to physical factors would be similar. She thought such
a test might permit some sort of estimate of the physical forces
that must have been involved to produce the results of the experiment. It would be a comparison of "optional" loading and
actual loading.

And so a die was loaded. On the corner where the three high
faces meet, the three spots were excavated until they met and
the grooves filled with lead, and then the spots painted over so
the loading did not show. Then this die was thrown by persons
who did not know it was loaded, and who were not instructed to
throw for any particular target. The result was as expected—the
lower faces were favored. In 905 throws the low faces came up
185 times more often than the high. This difference was roughly
comparable to the one that had been obtained in the experiment.
This, of course, did not actually prove anything about the nature
of the results obtained in the experiment, but it did give an interesting comparison.

Even though the outcome of the experiment was surprising,
and though the experimenter was one who respected statistics
fully, she voiced no conclusion at the end of her report, except
the concession that if the "observed distribution is *not* due to
chance," then the values obtained on the test with the loaded

die would give a rough idea of the magnitude "of the psychological processes in question."

### THE MANGAN EXPERIMENT

The next experimenter who came on the scene was fresh from Britain, but his experiment was carried out at the Parapsychology Laboratory. This was Dr. Gordon S. Mangan. He was a New Zealander who had just received a Ph.D. after some years of study in England, and in 1954 spent a year at the Parapsychology Laboratory before returning to New Zealand. Mangan had not faced the reality of PK until he arrived at the laboratory. Naturally the reports of all the earlier work, and of the analyses made on them, as well as the control on dice bias that now were routine methods, were readily available there. But he did not read them, electing instead to get evidence of PK if he could by his own efforts alone.

An apparatus was available (a dice box above an inclined plane, a walled-in table below, and a pushbutton to release the dice). Mangan started off quietly to make a preliminary test on his own.[6] He used 30 ordinary dice with excavated faces per throw. Although it was well understood at the laboratory long before this that such dice are biased for higher faces, and that consequently controls should be built into the experiment, Mangan simply threw them and found out for himself that the scores on the higher faces tended to be higher than on the lower faces.

However, on the basis of this outcome he planned his experiment. In it, like Miss Knowles, he threw for ones, twos, threes, an equal number of times as against fours, fives and sixes. As a result in 500 throws he had as he must have expected, a much higher deviation on the upper than on the lower face throws. On

[6] Mangan, G. L., "A PK Experiment with Thirty Dice Released for High- and Low-Face Targets." *J. Parapsychol.*, 1954, 18, pp. 209–218.

the uppers it was 242, and if the lowers had been depressed to an equal extent, he would have simply demonstrated once again that dice of this kind are biased. However, his deviation on the lowers was +45 instead of a negative to match the positive one on the uppers. His result thus told him of course that his dice were biased but that something else was involved too. If he had computed the average of the deviations he would have had the standard correction then in use in the laboatory for such situations, which in this case was $242 + 45 = 287 \div 2 = 143$.

Instead, Mangan asked a laboratory member to release 30 dice 100 times and from the results he calculated a correction of 139, only a few points different from the standard one. However, this result which he had to work out for himself probably was more satisfying to him. Probably too, this empirical control made it easier than otherwise for him to believe that he had himself demonstrated the PK effect. The fact still remained that even after correction his deviation on the high face throws was considerably higher than on the low ones. He had preferred them when throwing, however, and he supposed that his preference accounted for the differences.

### MCCONNELL'S PERFECT EXPERIMENT

A young man in the Department of Physics, University of Pittsburgh, Dr. R. A. McConnell, had been following the work in parapsychology for some time. In the early 1950s, he began to feel that the evidence for PK was strong enough that it should receive wider notice. Being a physicist, he felt that it should be of special interest to members of his own profession. But in order to impress them, he felt all aspects of the testing by which the evidence was produced would have to be completely mechanized. The chief area still not entirely mechanical was that of the record-taking. That, too, should be done by mechanical means in order to give critics no basis for their objections.

The circumstance that led to McConnell's experiment was the completion of an apparatus which was built at the Parapsychology Laboratory at Duke University. It was a dice-casting machine with a rotating cage carrying enclosed dice and an attachment to photograph and record the dice automatically, after they fell and were momentarily at rest at the bottom of the cage. When McConnell saw the possibilities of the machine, he felt it was just what he needed to to carry out his idea, and consequently he borrowed it. He arranged an experiment with it himself with the help of his assistant, R. J. Snowdon, and a graduate helper, K. E. Powell.[7]

The objectives of the ensuing experiment were clearly stated beforehand. The first was to get a statistically significant deviation; the second to get a significant decline in the number of hits. Thus it was an attempt only to get evidence of PK, and in the execution, all details of planning and control were so carried out that McConnell could say, "Among the errors of method and extraneous effects believed to have been successfully excluded in this experiment are the following: record errors, the loss or selection of data, selection of the experiment, retroactive choice of target, *ad hoc* selection of the method of analysis, 'optional stopping,' dice bias, and any hypothetical mechanical 'starting effect.' "

Nearly 170,000 die throws were made by 393 subjects over a period of 18 months. A standard procedure was used in which each subject produced three pages of data while wishing for a single target face. The first page was completed using a pair of dice, hand-thrown from a cup into a tray. After this warm-up the dice machine was turned on for the releases of the last two pages.

The total deviation of scores for the entire experiment was negative ($-91$) and not significant. But when the standard QD analysis was applied, the machine-thrown pages yielded a first-to-last-quarter decline with a significant $CR_d$ of 2.60; $p = .0093$. With

[7] McConnell, R. A., "Wishing with Dice." *J. Exp. Psychol.*, 1955, 50, No. 4, pp. 269–275.

the cup-thrown dice included, the probability against chance became still more significant. More sophisticated analyses showed that these data could not have been caused either by chance or by an apparatus defect. A check of the photos and the written records showed that no mistakes of recording had been made. Although no fault was to be found with the technique, still, when the report was submitted to a physics journal, since McConnell preferred not to submit it to the *Journal of Parapsychology* but to have it appear in a journal of more entirely skeptical readers than those who were somewhat inured to parapsychology reports, it was not accepted. McConnell recalls that an eminent physicist and member of the National Academy of Sciences wrote to him saying: "If reputable journals refuse to publish your stuff, I would, if I were you, reach the conclusion that it is not worth publishing. . . . I would strongly advise you to get back to physics." Nevertheless he persisted and eventually the *Journal of Experimental Psychology* published his report.

It would be good to say that the article produced a chorus of acclaim from psychologists. But if so, the chorus was inaudible. Nevertheless, the experiment stands for a high level of attention to the technical side of PK experimentation.

A PK EXPERIMENT IN FRANCE

In 1956–57 and again in 1957–58, a series of PK tests were made in France which really belong with those of this chapter. They came too late, of course, to be thought of as leading to the establishment of PK, or at any rate, to its establishment in the United States. Not so in France, however from which country only one experiment before these had been reported. The language barrier, as well as the Atlantic Ocean, had slowed up communication between the two countries in parapsychology as in other things.

The results of ESP tests and also of PK tests had been reported in correspondence to JBR by M. René Perot some years before any publication of them was made. In both ESP and PK tests Perot's main subject was his wife. Almost from the start of their ESP tests such high scores were reported that the question was raised whether they could be the result of some type of unrecognized slip of method or artifact undetectable at the Parapsychology Laboratory under the circumstances of distance and unfamiliar ways of reporting. Sometime later, however, it became possible to answer most of the questions. By this time Perot had written a book covering his researches and his theories about them, with, subsequently, a shorter report in the *Révue Métapsychique.*[8]

Perot's PK tests, it seemed, were begun as an attempt to repeat the American work on dice-throwing. In each of two series of PK tests, the subjects were Mme. and M. Perot, and a M. Peyrelongue. They shared the role of record-taking, sometimes Perot doing it, sometimes M. Peyrelongue. The sessions were held once a week.

Perot had the idea that results would be better if the same target was thrown for consistently. Therefore, in order not to have to rotate the target order to control for possible dice bias, he had a precision die made of plexiglass and the numbers painted on the sides in the form of Roman numerals. The target face selected for the main work was the three face, though the report said that they occasionally used others.

The die was thrown by releasing it from a box mounted at the top of a roughened incline onto a table. It was thrown 12 times per run, two of which, of course, are equal to one conventional run.

The results for both experiments were the same in that Mme. Perot's scores were very significantly high, in comparison to those that have so far been reported from other subjects. In both experiments, too, the scores of the two men were insignificant. In

[8] Perot, René, "An Experimental Study of Psychokinesis." *Révue Métapsychique*, No. 6 (June, 1967), pp. 75–83.

the first experiment, each of the three did 176 conventional runs, from which Mme. Perot had a deviation of 501, which yields a CR of 19 (millions to one would scarcely express it). The scores of the two men were both slightly, but not significantly, positive.

In the second series of experiments, each subject did 151 runs, and Mme. Perot had a deviation of 305, which yields a CR of over 12. Peyrelongue had a negative deviation of −38 and Perot himself an insignificant +13. No new aspects of PK ability except the astonishing performance of Mme. Perot were demonstrated by this test.

With this report from France, the list of experiments that add weight only to the simple fact that PK occurs is completed. Although they do not add greatly to knowledge of PK, they testify to the fact that again and again, widely separated individuals have obtained PK effects on falling dice.

In the meantime, going back now to the laboratory and to the 1930s, the trail of progress can be picked up, which shows the other experiments that were carried out that not only yielded results showing the PK effect, but also bit by bit added to an understanding of it.

# CHAPTER 7

# Physiological and Other Variables

❧

IN the PK research at the Duke Laboratory up to 1936, no special attention had been paid to the physiological state of the persons who acted as subjects. As already observed, the objective of the experimenters had been first of all just to get evidence of PK and after that to look for the most obvious physical relationships like size and number of dice per throw.

In the earlier studies on ESP, tests had been made when subjects were suffering from minor illnesses, colds, tonsilitis, and from fatigue and sleepiness. In all cases the scores were lower than when the subjects were alert and well. The conclusion was that the process of ESP was a normal one that functioned best under the same conditions that permit the higher mental processes to function. Just as the inventor, the poet, the reflective scientist needs the highest possible degree of integration for his best creation, so too evidence of ESP was shown the best under such conditions.

Earlier, in the ESP research, however, the physiological changes in the subject caused by the depressant drug, sodium amytal, had been studied. It had been found that the use of the drug (just as illness or fatigue) was accompanied by lowered ESP scores. Then when caffeine was administered after the amytal, it apparently had a counteracting effect, for scores rose again.

In the spring and summer of 1936 JBR was holding daily discussion sessions on research objectives with his graduate assistant, Richard L. Averill, and his secretary, A. J. Linzmayer, in one of which the effects of drugs on ESP were recalled, and the question arose whether these drugs would affect PK as they had

ESP; and the question and discussion led directly to an experiment.[1]

### ALCOHOL AND A PK TEST

The question was whether the effect of sodium amytal on PK would be the same as it had been on ESP. All three participants were eager to find out. The general impression had already been gained in all psi-testing (either ESP or PK) that better results were obtained when new ideas were tried out as soon as possible after they were conceived, and while interest and enthusiasm were at their highest. This time, accordingly, the experimenters did not wait for necessities, but instead they went ahead with what they had.

The main necessity of an experiment with sodium amytal was sodium amytal. It turned out that none was on hand. But someone had a bottle of gin. Rather than wait for the amytal and a test of it that could be made later, why not try the gin and test the effect of alcohol instead? Alcohol too was supposed to have a depressant effect if taken in sufficient quantity.

The experiment was started practically at once. The plan of it had to be simple and very exploratory in any case, for no medical facilities were available; so these investigators could not hope to make a finished test, fit dosage to body weight, for instance, or to give the medication "blind," for all these subjects knew the drug they would be given. They decided, therefore, simply to make a series of "prealcohol" and "postalcohol" tests to see what the difference in results would be. Since one of the three would have to be sober to take the record properly, they decided that the one whose prealcohol scores were lowest would be the record taker, the other two, the subjects.

This was the time in the laboratory when the question of

[1] Averill, Richard L., and Rhine, J. B., "The Effect of Alcohol Upon Performance in PK Tests." *J. Parapsychol.*, 1945, 9, pp. 32–41.

number of dice per throw was actively being tested. It had seemed that larger numbers "worked" as well as smaller ones. Recently as many as 96 at a time, or four regular 24-die runs in one had been tried out. Since so many dice could not conveniently be shaken and thrown from ordinary dice cups, an arrangement had been constructed to make the use of larger numbers easy. It consisted of a box to hold the dice set about a foot and a half high, over an inclined board placed at the end of a special dice table. The bottom of the dice box was movable and fastened with a catch. This could be released by a string and the bottom pulled out allowing the dice to roll down the board and spread out on the table. There they could be counted, and then returned to the box.

For the alcohol tests, then, it was decided to use the 96-dice box. Before the alcohol was taken, each of the three men made 20 throws, all for the six face. Since the postalcohol tests were also to be for the six face, the comparison between the two was what they wanted. On that account, the question of dice bias for sixes could be bypassed.

After the prealcohol tests were made, each of the subjects was given 100 cubic centimeters of gin in an equal amount of ginger ale. Twenty minutes was allowed for the alcohol to take effect before beginning the postalcohol testing. Then 20 more throws of the 96 dice, or 80 runs, were to be made.

The results of the prealcohol trials were varied and for comparison's sake can best be given here as average run scores, with 4.0 being MCE. Averill had an average score per run of 4.31. JBR's average was 4.79 and Linzmayer's was only 4.06. Linzmayer, therefore, became the observer and record taker.

When the postalcohol trials were run, all the subjects had unexpected physiological effects. Averill got sick and vomited after 14 throws and again after four more, so that for the rest of his trials, he felt very little effect of the alcohol. Still his total was somewhat lower than before and his average rate of scoring fell from the earlier one of 4.31 to 4.24. But considering that he probably had retained very little of the alcohol, it was not possible to say much about his results.

JBR "kept" his alcohol until he had completed his runs, and his results on 100 runs fell to a below chance level of 3.87. The $CR_d$ before and after was a very significant 3.36; $p = .0008$. Something certainly had lowered his PK scores. Just how much of the result, however, was caused by alcohol, it was impossible to say. Perhaps the effect before and after was the result only of expectation and suggestion. The outcome, therefore, could only be considered as evidence that the alcohol had not raised the scores.

Incidentally, the results were also further evidence that rate of scoring does not necessarily decrease with the number of dice used per throw. JBR's prealcohol average score of 4.79 was as high as any he had ever produced as a subject himself when throwing smaller numbers at a time.

### A PK TEST WITH COCA-COLA

The next day after the alcohol experiment, the two who had taken it were in no mood for further experimentation, but two days later they were again discussing drugs and PK.[2] And, as the report says, "it was generally agreed that since we did not feel as alert as usual," particularly the two who had taken the alcohol, "perhaps the time had arrived for the test of the effect of caffeine," to see if it would have a stimulating effect on PK as it had had on ESP.

Again an impromptu experiment was set up, and again one of the three would take the record, the other two acting as subjects. Only in this case, the highest scorer in preliminary or

[2] Rhine, J. B., Humphrey, Betty H., and Averill, Richard L., "An Exploratory Experiment on the Effect of Caffeine upon Performance in PK Tests." *J. Parapsychol.*, 1945, 9, pp. 80–91.

precaffeine tests would act as recorder, since presumably he would not need the stimulant as much as the others.

The test was carried out by the use of the same setup and the same 96 dice that had been used in the alcohol experiment. The same target face, the six face, was selected, too, because again the point of the experiment would be the before-and-after comparison. Also, as before, controls on the kind of drug could not be run, since the subjects knew what it was and what was expected of it. They felt that the results would be interesting if a contrast was secured, regardless of whether it could be laid to the caffeine, or to the expectation that it would raise their scores. At this stage of research, any lawful effect of the will of the experimenters on the dice which they could induce was a sufficient end in itself.

Twenty throws of the 96 dice (80 runs) were made in the precaffeine trials by each of the three subjects. Linzmayer had an average run score of 4.80; Averill's was 3.95 and JBR's, 3.85. And so Linzmayer was eliminated again, this time because his score was the highest. The other two with their below-chance scores were the ones who presumably needed the stimulant.

The caffeine was taken by each subject in the form of a bottle of Coca-Cola. After twenty minutes for the physiological effect to develop, the testing was resumed. In 120 runs, Averill raised his run score average to 4.47 and JBR in 60 runs raised his to an average of 4.64. Linzmayer who took none continued, too, but in 80 runs he averaged only 4.29. Thus he fell from the highest to the lowest, while those who took the Coca-Cola raised their scores from slightly less than chance to well above it.

Two days later, a second session was undertaken in which JBR and a subject identified only as C.D.C. took part. Each of them made 80 precaffeine runs. In these, C.D.C.'s average was 4.13, only slightly above expectation, and JBR's at 3.99, was a bit below it. Again, after the Coca-Cola, JBR's average rose markedly, being 4.64. C.D.C., however, after 40 runs, had an average of only 3.7. He said he felt no effect of the stimulant. He was a large man and they thought might well have required a larger dosage. He then was given another Coca-Cola. In his next 40 runs his average score rose to 4.88. In 40 more runs, however, his rate was lower so that his final average rate was 4.32. And so this subject's scores looked very much as if the caffeine, or at least a sufficient amount of it, rather than his expectation had acted to increase his PK ability.

The total precaffeine tests added up to an insignificant CR of .37, but the postcaffeine tests yielded a very significant CR of 5.14; p = millions to one. The $CR_d$ of the two is 2.78; p = .005. The results thus were not due to chance. Either the caffeine was a stimulant, or the subjects thought it was, for the increased scores showed that one or the other was in operation.

Scores in this caffeine experiment were kept in columns of five entries each. When these five entries for all of the subjects' precaffeine runs were pooled, the customary decline was found. The first three throws of each column had given a positive score, the last two negative, so marked that the difference was significant with a $CR_d$ of 3.68; p = .0002. The postcaffeine scores, however, though they fell off, too, did not do so significantly, or fall below the chance line. The suggestion was that the caffeine had tended to counteract the decline effect.

When these decline effects in the caffeine experiments were compared to those in the one on alcohol, an interesting difference was observed in the predrug trials. The prealcohol scores in the alcohol series showed no decline, which of course is unusual. But the precaffeine, as just discussed, dropped off significantly. Why the difference, since the general procedure, the technique, and the subjects were the same?

A main difference certainly lay in the motivation and expectations of the subjects in the two experiments. In the alcohol experiment they were trying to get the highest scores possible in the prealcohol runs; and in the caffeine experiment, they were trying for the lowest in their precaffeine tests. The results very

well corresponded to their desires. And so even the opposite decline tendencies in the predrug trials seemed to make sense and
fit the idea that the dice responded to the subjects' motivations.

## HYPNOSIS AND PK

Soon after the tests with alcohol and caffeine, the attention of
the laboratory group turned to hypnosis and the question of its
effect on PK. The subject came up partly for historical reasons. In
the early history of hypnosis, a connection between it and telepathy had been suggested by certain cases in which the hypnotized
subject seemed to experience the hypnotist's thought, even though
it had not in any way been expressed. From these occurrences, the
idea arose that if telepathy were a reality, it probably was related
to, or at least facilitated by, the hypnotic state. Therefore, in the
initial tests on telepathy (or more precisely, on perception without the senses) made at Duke University the subjects had been
first hypnotized. As it turned out, however, they did not score
significantly better when hypnotized than when unhypnotized.

Hypnosis itself then (and still today) was not a well understood
or easily standardized process. There was no way of telling if
the techniques of one hypnotist produced the same effect as
another's, or if the response of two persons to a given technique
would be the same. Even the depth of hypnotic effect from subject to subject could only be determined roughly. And so no one
could say whether lack of marked success with it in raising ESP
scores meant that no connection between the two existed or
whether the hypnosis as applied simply did not properly moti-
vate the subjects. Because of these uncertainties, because the induction of the hypnotic state is time consuming, and because
not all subjects are easily susceptible to it, its use in ESP research had soon been discontinued. For the same reasons, it had
not been introduced into the early PK research. However, after

the tests of the influence of alcohol and caffeine were made, JBR decided also to test the effect of hypnosis on the PK process.[3]

For the test, the same 96 dice and the same apparatus used in the drug tests served again, with JBR himself the hypnotist, and five of his male students as subjects. Again, too, the six face was selected as the target because subjects seemed generally to prefer it and because here again a comparison of "before" and "after" was involved so that possible dice bias did not have to be considered.

The tests were made on each individual subject separately, and began with the usual 20 pretest throws, or 80 standard runs. The subject was then hypnotized (each in as nearly as possible the same manner). The general procedure in this began by telling the subject to relax and to attend only to the words he was hearing. He was considered ready for the PK test when he reached the stage of hypersuggestibility in which he could no longer open his eyes or lift his feet from the floor when challenged to do so. He then was given positive suggestions in which he was told that he was very eager to make the dice fall with the target face up, that he would be able to concentrate on making them do so, and that he had great confidence in his ability to make them do as he willed. He was then brought to an alert state, and the PK tests were resumed. The intention was to duplicate the 80 pre-hypnosis runs, but in some cases unexpected complications arose, and the result was not the exact fulfillment of the intention. However, each of the five subjects completed one session, and one did two, making six individual sessions in the experiment.

The results of the experiment did not come out according to expectation. All of the prehypnotic runs taken together were slightly positive and averaged 4.19 per run, (MCE = 4.00) But the posthypnotic runs averaged at chance, which might seem to mean that the hypnosis had an adverse effect. However, the

[3] Rhine, J. B., "Hypnotic Suggestion in PK Tests." *J. Parapsychol.*, 1946, 10, pp. 126–140.

hypnotic process is so strictly an individual one that even the same words of the hypnotist may produce different effects on different subjects. A study of the results showed that this very thing happened here. It is necessary, therefore, to take the sessions separately, for the totals obscure the individual effects.

As it happens, the five students who took part in this experiment were identified in this report only by their initials. The first was W.R.A. His average run score before hypnosis was a slightly positive 4.19. But after hypnosis, his deviation was −30 in 80 runs, which is an average rate of 3.62 per run. It seemed to mean that the suggestions of the hypnotist had acted in reverse.

JBR was intrigued by this possibility and asked the student to remain for further testing. In this, over an hour later when no longer under hypnosis, W.R.A. did 40 more runs at the much higher rate of 4.35, compared with the earlier prehypnosis rate of 4.19. In the intervening period he had watched the performance of the next subject, C.D.C. and JBR observed that W.R.A. *acted* as if he wanted to show what *he* could do in comparison. But obviously the hypnosis had not raised the score for this subject.

The next subject, C.D.C., got a chance result before hypnosis, but a deviation of +23, an average of 4.29 per run, after. This time JBR asked the subject to continue beyond his 20 throws. He threw 40 runs more, and attained an average run score of 4.34. This showed a trend that was the opposite from that of subject W.R.A., whose score average was lower after hypnosis than before.

The scores of the third subject, C.E.W., were slightly below chance before hypnosis, and after it they went lower still, producing in the 80 runs an average score per run of 3.85. As with the earlier subject, W.R.A., this looked as if the suggestion under hypnosis was working in reverse. C.E.W. then asked for a cigarette and as he was obviously under tension, he was allowed one. His mental attitude then appeared to change and he continued until he had completed an additional 88 runs. In these he got a deviation of +34, which made his average run score for those runs 4.36.

These results with C.E.W. and W.R.A. looked as if the hypnotic suggestions had hindered them by putting them under tension. After that, JBR decided to rehypnotize any subject who, under the original hypnotic suggestions, tended to score below chance.

The following subject, D.V.H., came under the new rule, because although he achieved an average run score of 4.26 before hypnosis, the deviation was negative after it, giving a $-21$ on the 80 runs, an average run score of 3.74. He was then rehypnotized and told he should feel relaxed and free and enjoy the tests because they were like a game. The result was that he got a positive deviation and an average run score of 4.29. This was a change from his negative score under the initial hypnosis and was in line with the idea that hypnosis could have an affect, but that the way the subject reacted to the hypnotist's suggestions determined the direction, the "sign" of the scoring that would result.

The fifth hypnotic session was again with C.D.C. This time he got a prehypnotic average run score of 4.44. But his posthypnosis scores this time dropped below chance. After 60 runs he had an average run score of 3.70.

He then complained of a headache, which may have been the result of strain to get as good scores as in his first session. He was rehypnotized and given 28 more runs which gave an average run score of 4.29. Again it seemed that the kind of hypnotic suggestion given determined the direction of scoring. Although in his first session his scoring under hypnosis was positive; in this second one, his psychological attitude was different in that he expected more of himself and presumably was more tense than the first time.

The final subject, L.E.S., gave an average run score of 4.28 in his prehypnosis runs. Then, for him, apparently the hypnosis was helpful, for in the final 80 runs after hypnosis his deviation was +36, his average run score, 4.45.

It looked thus as if hypnosis did have an effect on these subjects, but an unpredictable one. In the report JBR discussed the possibility that some subjects are "negativistic," but concluded that possibility would not explain the times when their deviations were positive. Rather, he concludes, there "probably *was* conflict and strain induced in these subjects. A suggestion of strong concentration probably brings into the subject a state of general tension that is inhibitory to the process of PK. In other words, the subject tries very hard in the wrong way, inducing concentration of functions that have nothing to do with PK. At any rate, the total deviation for all runs before hypnosis was +91, after the first hypnosis ⁻3, and after the second +95. The results thus practically cancelled each other, and the total looked as if the hypnosis had had no effect.

At the time of this experiment, the results seemed to give an ambiguous answer to the question of the usefulness of hypnosis in PK. But it was shown that before an unqualified verdict could be secured, it would be necessary to know beforehand something about the personalities of the subjects, and their probable type of response to a given kind of suggestion. It was not a particularly encouraging outlook for research by persons whose first interest was in investigating PK, not hypnosis. The general opinion thus came to be that the attempt to understand the unknown of ESP or PK could not be greatly facilitated by the use of a method like hypnosis which was also, to a large extent, an unknown. Thus its use in PK was not encouraged by the results of this experiment. Nor would the encouragement have been much greater if the hypnotic sessions when the suggestions given produced positive deviations had been considered alone, for all of those scores yielded only an average run score of 4.34. While a run score of 4.34 can be impressive in so long a series, still it is no higher than many unhypnotized subjects have attained. (One of the subjects in this experiment, C.D.C., in his 80 prehypnotic trials, had an average run score of 4.44.) Thus it was understandable that no further tests of hypnosis on PK were made at the time. The experiment, however, was not felt to be a failure

then, for it not only confirmed once more the possibility of
getting evidence of PK on a large number of dice, but it also
showed that PK is a process that can be greatly influenced by
conditions and especially by the mental attitudes they produce
in the subject. It helped to encourage the search for facilitating
psychological influences in the production of PK effects. However,
this is a search that did not really get under way for some years,
although a test performed about this time was in effect a fore-
runner.

### PK AND A TUG OF WILLS

In the late 1930s an experiment started at the laboratory[4] with
something like a friendly bet between two young research assistants. The protagonists were J. S. Woodruff and Miss Margaret
(Peggy) Price, an undergraduate who then was also assisting with
psi experiments.

In his earlier experiments, Woodruff had been an outstanding
subject. In his PK score averages he had ranked among the highest
of the subjects who had so far been tested. In fact, in his results
in 32 runs of the machine tests made in the experiments of those
two sessions with either JBR or Linzmayer acting as experimenter,
he had produced an average run score of 4.84.

It is likely that the effect of this high scoring gave Woodruff
an air of self-confidence. At least he impressed Peggy P. that way.
She challenged him to a "tug of wills," in which she said she
could prevent him from scoring positively. She did not know
whether or not she could do it by willing the target *not* to come
up, or whether it would simply be by distracting him from his
objective. But at any rate, she said, she could do it if she were
free to work against him openly, to make discouraging remarks,
and so forth, while he was trying to influence the dice.

---

[4] Price, Margaret M., and Rhine, J. B., "The Subject-Experimenter Relation in the PK Test." *J. Parapsychol.*, 1944, 8, pp. 177–186.

Woodruff thought he could hold his own in spite of her. He therefore accepted the challenge, and the test that followed was carried out with an air of friendly rivalry that freed it from any element of monotony or boredom. It was the first instance in which the psychological effect on a subject of a distracting situation was incorporated into an experimental plan.

The main experiment was carried out on November 2 and 3, 1936. On November 2 Woodruff worked alone to see just how well he could do at his best and to have as it were a "control" against which results achieved in Peggy's presence could be compared. Using the machine, as in the earlier experiments in which, as already mentioned, his score had been an average of 4.84, two dice were thrown at a time for the six face for 60 new runs. In these he had a deviation of +58, an average run score of 4.97.

The next day the experiment was resumed, but with Peggy present as observer and experimenter. One could wish her actions and attitude were well described in the report of the experiment. But, characteristic of the times, the emphasis is all upon making clear that the conditions were adequate, and the statistical evaluation of results correct, and nothing is said about the actual means she took to divert Woodruff from his objective. However, since she had stipulated that she must be free to make discouraging remarks and to try to divert him from his objective, she undoubtedly interpreted her franchise liberally.

But even so, the contest started off well. For the first quarter of his runs, his results were well above chance, giving an average of 4.80 per run. But then a drop came in and the scores fell to chance. In the last half they were well below, so that his total for the entire 60 runs that day showed a deviation of $-10$. This score in contrast to those he had gotten the day before when working alone, yielded a $CR_d = 3.40$; $p = .00067$. Obviously, Peggy had won. But some days later on November 19 after consideration, they thought it might not have been Peggy after all who caused it. The two therefore made a second shorter trial, with the conditions as before. In this Woodruff threw 20 runs, but

Peggy's negative influence apparently prevailed even more quickly than before, and he finished with a total score of $^{-}3$. Although nothing further was said in this report about Woodruff's subsequent PK ability it is safe to assume that he had not lost it permanently, for he continued at the laboratory for some time and continued at times to serve as a subject in PK tests with no note made that he did not succeed as he had done earlier. It thus still looked as if it was Peggy's influence on Woodruff rather than on the dice directly that did it.

Even so, there might have been the possibility that Woodruff was simply sensitive to the presence of any observer, and that it was not the attitude that prevented scoring, had it not been for his high scoring in the earlier cup and machine experiment, in which witnesses, but neutral ones, JBR or Linzmayer, were present. Between those tests, and these with Peggy as the observer, the $CR_d$ was also significant ($2.62$; $p = .0087$). Little doubt was left then that Peggy's influence had had the effect she desired.

This little contest stands as the first reported experiment to document the fact that social conditions that influence a subject's mental state may very well affect a subject's ability to exercise PK. It was also another line of evidence besides the drug and hypnosis effects, and the position effect of hits, to show that PK is a reality and that it is a psychological one, however much it also involves the physical world.

Direct research on the effect of mental states or attitudes on PK did not follow as planned. In spite of intention to test further the effect of a wider range of drugs, no more experiments were made, primarily because of the lack of the medical sponsorship and equipment that would be necessary for the full control of such experiments. But the experimentation had gone far enough to show that PK can be affected by drugs, hypnosis, and distraction, and that was sufficient at the time.

CHAPTER 8

# New Targets and Experimenters

❦

IN the decade of the 1940s the PK research broadened on several
fronts as the objective became more and more that of exploring
the nature of the phenomenon. The added assurance the QD
analyses had given as to the basic validity of the earlier results
led to the trying out of new techniques including other types of
targets and target objects besides simply dice and dice faces.

Also, with the publication of the first reports of PK experiments in 1943, a wider circle of experimenters came upon the
scene. Earlier, all of the persons who undertook experiments were
connected with the Parapsychology Laboratory either directly or
indirectly, for no others knew about the research. But with publication of their findings, in time attempts at confirmation were
made at other places.

At first, however, only a few experimental attempts were reported from anyone not connected with the laboratory. These
were war years. It is easy now to overlook the fact that until the
middle forties the war was critical. It cast a dark shadow over
everything and was a constant preoccupation and worry to every
responsible adult, interfering with every interest and activity not
directly war-centered.

In England, as already mentioned the situation was, of course,
much worse. The "blitz" had threatened even survival itself. Even
in the best of times, the total number of research-minded persons
there, as in the United States, was small; and under war conditions it would seem as if they would have been eliminated entirely, and yet one of the first reports from abroad came from that

country. It was also the first one reported in which a kind of target object other than a cube was used.

COIN SPINNING

The first PK experiment reported from England that yielded positive results (McDougall, though British, was a Duke professor) was carried out by Dr. Robert H. Thouless, a psychologist, of Cambridge University. Thouless, who was in England throughout the war, was immediately interested in reports of PK research in the *Journal of Parapsychology* as they came out in 1943 and at once began a test of his own to see if he himself could get evidence of PK.

Casting about for a simple and workable technique, he elected to try to influence spinning coins and to see if he could cause a specified face, head or tail, to fall uppermost.[1] In order not to bias the fall by normal manipulation, even if he could have done so, which seemed unlikely, he arranged randomly in regard to heads and tails as many coins as he intended to spin in one round or run, and did not look to see which side was which when he picked each one up to spin. Then, as still another precaution, he made a preexperiment in which he deliberately inclined the coin to a given side when he began to spin it to see if that face would be favored. He found no evidence that it was.

He then conducted his experiment for 10 evenings spread over a period of two months. Each evening, 400 spins were made, making a total of 4,000 in the experiment. Each session began with a run of 10 spins for heads, then the same coins were spun for tails for a 10-spin run, and so on for the rest of the 400 trials.

At the end of the 10 series, the record showed that the target face had appeared 42 more times than the opposite one. This was not a significant value. But dividing the chronological period in

[1] Thouless, Robert H., "Some Experiments on PK Effects in Coin Spinning." *J. Parapsychol.*, 1945, 9, 169–175.

half, the excess of successes for the spins of the first five evenings were $+13 + 15 + 12 + 20 + 0 = 60$. Of the last five, $^-4 + 4 - 13 + 13 - 18 = {}^-18$. The $CR_d = 2.47$; $p = .0135$, a marginally significant difference.[2]

However, from a strict statistical standpoint, it is not proper to make this calculation, since it was not foreseen that the results would fall off in the last half. Yet, knowing that PK does occur, and that scores over a period of time do tend to decline, the significant difference given here between the two sections permitted the strong supposition that spun coins, as well as thrown dice, can be influenced by PK.

### DISC THROWING AT CHILDREN'S PARTIES

After Thouless' experiment, but before it was published in 1945, Elizabeth McMahan (Betty Mc.) at the Parapsychology Laboratory had also started a series of experiments to see if the PK effect could be demonstrated on "two-sided objects."[3] She first tried to do so by making her own objects. She cut out small squares of cardboard, colored differently on the two sides. But these proved awkward to handle, and after an extensive trial with Duke students taken individually, that did not yield significant results, she changed both the kinds of object and the age of the subjects.

Instead of the cardboard squares, she then used plastic discs (poker chips) and painted the two sides different colors. It had been found earlier in testing for ESP that children tend to make good subjects; she therefore decided to try them for her PK test.

---

[2] NOTE: The record showed that the coins were biased for tails. But with equal frequency of faces as targets the effect of this bias is fully corrected, of course just as in the case of dice bias. The $CR_d$, however, compares two blocks of data of equal size and therefore needs no correction because the bias would have been the same on each.

[3] McMahan, Elizabeth, "PK Experiments with Two-Sided Objects." *J. Parapsychol.*, 1945, 9, pp. 249–263.

Also because they had been found to score well in groups, not being so easily inhibited by the presence of others as adults usually are, she decided to stage little parties and use the PK test as a party game in which a free and easy atmosphere could be created. To help do so, prizes would be offered and refreshments served.

For these parties a cardboard tube to mix and cast the discs was devised. (Figure 5.) This was closed at one end, and a num-

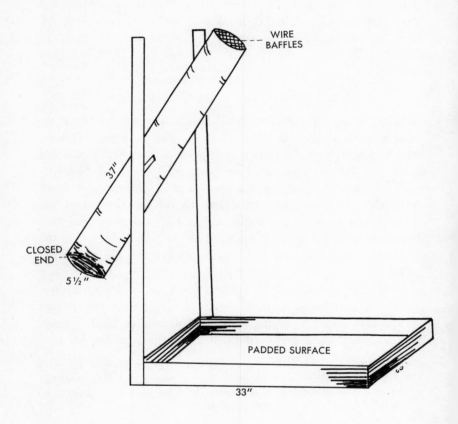

FIGURE 5.   Betty Mc.'s hand-turned apparatus for throwing discs.

ber of internal baffles to mix the discs inserted, the tube then being mounted in the middle so it could be rotated, as in the earlier "dice machine." The discs were put in the open end where they fell over the baffles to the bottom. Then the tube was rotated so that the discs tumbled out again and onto a flat surface. In this position, the faces could be counted and the record taken.

When the game or test began, all of the children gathered around to help the one who was the subject as she tried to cause the target face, designated by the experimenter, to come up. (In this experiment, however, the point was not to test the possible joint effect of extra subjects. Instead, it was thought of more as a situation that would help sustain interest.) Each subject was given 25 trials for one turn, and 10 discs were used in each, making 250 disc-falls per turn. The results of these throws were recorded in five columns of five trials each. Each subject was given a second turn when all had completed their first ones.

Immediately after the first party, it was noticed that the subjects tended to get positive deviations on their first turns, but much lower ones on the second. At the end of the four parties, the scores on the first turns showed a positive deviation; on the second, a negative, but the two opposite trends cancelled each other sufficiently to make the total insignificant. The CR of the difference however, was a very significant 3.45; $p = .00056$. This, of course, was evidence of PK.

The way of looking at a difference like the above then and today is slightly different, or at least the emphasis of interpretation has changed. Today the difference in scores between the first and second turns would seem to mean that the novelty of the first turn had worn off and by the second turn psi-missing had set in. But at the time, the results were taken to mean that primacy, the quality of "firstness," had in it something important. The suggestion then was to find a different way to duplicate the primacy effect.

One possible way to do this, Betty Mc. thought, might be by introducing for a third turn a really novel procedure, while keeping the age of subject and the party atmosphere the same. The novel procedure she introduced in her next experiment was a new "PK machine."[4]

This machine was an apparatus that operated on the same principle as the former one, only this was larger and more glamorous in appearance. Instead of the opaque cardboard sides, this was a box-like cage of wood in which white discs with red circles painted on one side and blue crosses on the other were enclosed. The revolving cage was 5½ feet long, and one side of it was covered with wire mesh so the discs could be seen as they fell over a series of baffles within when the cage revolved. A wire basketlike structure with a flat bottom was fastened to each end of the tube onto which the discs fell and were counted. The subject turned the tube for each throw, thus making one throw for each half-revolution.

In each session, two turns were given as before on the old apparatus, and then the new one was introduced, making three turns for each subject. Five parties were held in all. In three of these, the subjects were adolescents; in the other two, younger children. But in spite of the novelty of the new apparatus, after two parties the results were disappointing. The scores of all the subjects on the three turns, a total of 80 runs per subject, gave deviations of only +10 for the first, −8 for the second and then instead of an increase, a disappointing −15 for the third. The question then seemed to be whether the novelty had had any effect at all, or whether it had prevented the results of the third turn from going even lower. As a matter of fact, it seems likely that with children varying in ages from five to 11, as did some of these, up to adolescence, the "party atmosphere," after the initial turns, began to have too strong an effect, and the game, even with the new apparatus, was probably less an interesting novelty to the subjects than it was to the experimenter. By the third turn the fun of a directed game almost certainly was wearing off and

[4] McMahan, Elizabeth, "A PK Experiment with Discs." *J. Parapsychol.*, 1946, 10, pp. 169–180.

the urge for undirected activity and refreshments, was in the ascendency.

However, an attempt was then made to see if the scores on a third run without the novelty, but made just the same as the first two, would go lower than those on the second. Three more parties were then held in which all three turns were the same, all made using the new apparatus. The results were erratic. In 130 runs for each turn, the first gave a deviation of +22, the second a +32, and the third a −4. This, of course, was not an exact answer to the question. Neither did the scores add up to a significant over-all deviation.

With results like these, the question was whether or not PK had been involved at all. But again the answer was suggested when the total scores from all the parties were evaluated for decline effects. The averages for the four quarters of the record pages were found to follow the familiar pattern of distribution of hits in dice experiments. The $CR_d$ between the deviation of the first and fourth quarters was a significant 2.44; p = .0147. The results of these analyses were sufficiently in line with those found in dice experiments in which significant over-all deviations had been secured, that they seemed to show that PK can influence two-sided objects. They did not say anything, however, as to whether it operates on them as effectively as on dice. That question, however, was later made the subject of at least a minor test.

### BAILEY'S DICE VERSUS COIN TESTS

In 1945 Wilbur E. Bailey, a municipal judge of Palo Alto, California, reported an informal PK test he had made.[5] It was hardly a full-blown experiment and is reported only as a note in the *Journal of Parapsychology.*

[5] "Bailey's Comparison of a Coin and a Die in PK Tests." *J. Parapsychol.,* 1946, 10, pp. 213–215.

Bailey's tests again were the result of an individual's own curiosity. He wanted to test for PK "for his own satisfaction," rather than as a scientific project. However, the hint that his test gave had a certain suggestive value.

Bailey shook a penny in a glass and tossed it on the rug, trying to make it land with preselected target face up. He threw 10 times a session for 10 different night sessions, beginning the first night with heads as target, and alternating heads and tails each session thereafter. Like Thouless, he threw more tails than heads, but he had an over-all excess of successes of 35, a CR of 2.21; $p = .027$, not significant, but suggestive. His hits were distributed rather regularly over his 10 sessions.

Then, in the fall of 1945, Bailey threw a single die 216 times (nine runs), shaking it in the same glass used for the penny. He began with the one face and used each one in turn, and secured a positive deviation of 11 which, though not significant, was a high average per run. Insofar as the two sets of data could be compared, it looked as if the rate of scoring for penny and die had been sufficiently comparable to be interesting, especially because it was the only direct comparison that was made.

COIN THROWING IN GERMANY

Evidence of PK on discs much more conclusive than any of the above, and from what might seem a very unexpected quarter, appeared later, however. In 1950–51, a graduate student, S. R. Binski at the University of Bonn, Germany, finished a PK research project for his Ph.D. degree, which he had undertaken partly for a reason like that of Thouless, who had wanted to see if PK evidence could be obtained in his own country. Binski wanted to see if it could be obtained in Germany. But although he finished his research then, it was not reported for a number of years for a reason connected closely with World War II. In 1950 Binski, on a visit behind the Iron Curtain, was seized by the Russians and deported to the far north of the Soviet Union. Five years later he got back to Germany and completed the analysis of his experimental work at Bonn.[6]

The research had involved two projects. One was a test of PK on coins (the German 10-pfennig piece) and the other on a roulette wheel. In the coin test, 100 coins were thrown at a time, with one or the other face specified as target. One hundred and seventeen subjects were used. They were mostly high school and college students. The well-mixed coins were taken by the subject in his cupped hands, held about a yard above a low table, and dropped on it while he willed them to fall with the specified face turned up.

A total of 153,000 coin throws was made. The result was slightly positive, but not significantly so. It would have occurred by chance about six times in a hunded. But among the subjects was one young man, Kastor Seibel, a 17-year-old high school boy, whose first 1,000-pfennig set gave a deviation of 96 in the expected direction. This was a result so much higher than any other subject had achieved that special tests with him were undertaken.[7]

However, before Seibel had been in the experiment for many days, his mother, the widow of a high school director and herself a teacher, called on Binski, and the substance of a message she brought as reported in the *Journal* article was:

> My son told me about the experiments you are doing with him. I am alarmed about this and do not like to allow further experiments with my son.

[6] Binski, S. R., "Report on Two Exploratory PK Series." *J. Parapsychol.,* 1957, 21, pp. 284–295.

[7] However, targets were not alternated systematically. The experimenter preferred to permit the subjects to choose their target faces. Although the total throws of all the subjects excepting Kastor Seibel approximated a 50–50 division of heads and tails, the assumption cannot be made that the coins were unbiased. For this reason the customary method of evaluation could not be applied but a suitable one was worked out (*cf.* reference, footnote 5, p. 289) by which the value of Kastor Seibel's results could be determined without the assumption that the coins were unbiased.

For generations there has been in my family a hereditary capacity called "second sight." This capacity to foresee accidents and deaths was a heavy psychical burden for some members of my family. When the last male scion of the family, a Catholic priest, died on the foreseen day, my husband and I made an agreement that our children never should know anything about that unhappy capacity. Up to now I was able to conceal all this from my sons, and thank God, until now in none of them has there been any indication of a "dark" gift. I hope you will understand how much I am alarmed about this unexpected outbreak of the buried mystery.

The result was that Binski held a sober discussion with Mrs. Seibel about her son's capacity in the light of the contemplated investigation. He persuaded her to withdraw her objection and to allow further experiments to be made with her son. His high level of success continued and in the five final sets, he had an excess of 584 hits in the 10,000 coin throws. This is a number whose anti-chance probability can best be expressed as less than $10^{-10}$.

The tests with the roulette wheel in the second part of the study involved a departure in the test object from either coins or discs. The roulette wheel consists of a platelike shell in the center of which is a metal disc on a needlepoint bearing that may be rotated. Compartments in the disc of equal size are numbered from zero to 36 in irregular order, and all but the zero (of which there are two) colored alternately red or black. When the rotating disc is set in motion, a small sphere (marble) is spun around in the shell, and as the rotation slows down it falls into one of the compartments of the disc; whether it be a red or a black one is nominally a matter of chance.

In Binski's test, the subjects were assigned targets, red or black, into which to will the marble to fall. The group in general secured a small, but not significant, positive deviation, which would occur by chance about three times in a hundred.

Again in this, Kastor Seibel's scores were evaluated separately, and again his rate of success was exceptionally high. In 500 trials, he had an excess of 62 hits; $p = .006$. It was a rate of success comparable to that he had had with the coins and one that makes him one of the very few high-scoring subjects on record.

The fact that even one or two persons have stood out significantly from others as able to score higher than average indicates that in experiments, the use of unselected subjects for PK tests, which is a common and necessary practice, should not raise too high expectations for high PK deviations. The PK ability can no doubt be expressed to a different degree by different persons just as is that of ESP. On that account and because the same person may show PK ability more distinctly at different times, it means that statistical evaluation of the results of many subjects taken together can probably be expected to produce totals representing the lowest common average of PK achievement, not the highest possible level. In this context Pratt's remark after one of his analyses can be recalled, that "the test is a grossly inefficient instrument for measuring PK ability."

The fact, of course, that coins rather than dice (discs rather than cubes), were used in Binski's tests and that, therefore, this especially gifted subject used them, shows that the shape of the object used as such need not determine or limit the PK ability. Also, Kastor Seibel's success with the roulette shows that his ability was not limited to a particular shape of target object.

### SIMULTANEOUS HIGH AND LOW TARGETS

Back at the laboratory, about the same time that Betty Mc-Mahan was staging the first of her children's parties, Betty Humphrey (Betty H.) of the Parapsychology Laboratory undertook an experiment to try to answer a question that had long been asked around the laboratory: Can a limit be found to the mind's ability to accomplish complicated PK operations?[8]

[8] Humphrey, Betty M., "Simultaneous High and Low Aim in PK Tests." *J. Parapsychol.*, 1947, 11, pp. 160–174.

To the uninitiated, it is incredible enough that a PK effect can be registered even on a single die. How can the mind recognize the desired face as it falls out of a dice cup, much less manage to manipulate it according to desire? Even in the early days of PK testing, this question, of course, was in the minds of those making the tests, but the main objective then had to be simply to establish the fact that it somehow does so. Betty H., experimenting with herself as subject, tried to see if she could succeed on a PK task more complicated than throwing dice for one specified face.

The suggestion for the experiment came from the early tests in which the target had been either high or low face *combinations*. These were testimony, it seemed, to considerable "mental dexterity" as it might be called, for it would appear that with this more complicated target, two die faces would have to be recognized simultaneously (at some unconscious level where both ESP and PK operate) before those that add up to a combination greater, or less than seven, as the case might be, could be selected and influenced. Since such tests had succeeded to a statistically significant degree, it appeared to mean that somehow two faces had been "known" simultaneously and influenced. And so for her tests, Betty H. wanted to try something that seemed even more complicated. She decided to use two sets of dice and to make the objective on one set as high a number of target faces as possible, and on the other, as low a number of the target faces as possible. She wanted to see if results could be gotten both ways simultaneously.

With herself as subject, she used six white and six red dice, throwing all 12 at once from a dice cup onto a padded and walled-in surface. In order to guard against miscounting after each throw, she picked up the dice that were hits and set them aside for a recount before picking them up to throw again.

The target throughout was the one face. She attempted in throws she designated as high-aim to get as many ones as possible on the faces of the dice of one color, and at the same time, in low-aim throws to get as few ones as possible on the faces of the dice of the other color. The plan was reminiscent of Harvey Frick's attempt at a control on sixes by trying to get ones. But there was a difference here, as now results were equally interesting on either face since the experimenter had no previously fixed expectation.

The color to be used for both high- and low-aim throws was specified and then alternated. Since six dice of a color were used, one hit on each was expected by chance on each throw, and since they were thrown for both high and low numbers, the experiment was controlled against dice bias.

In all, 1,242 runs were made for high aim, the same for low. The total deviation for high aim was only +45, and not significant. But for low aim, the total deviation was −179, which yielded a significant $CR = 2.78$; $p = .005$. The difference between the low aim and the high was a marginally significant $CR_d = 2.46$; $p = .014$.

These figures indicated that the results of high- and low-aim tests did differ in direction according to the subject's wishes. But even so, they did not show if the differing results occurred on the same throw. It was possible that on some throws the PK effect operated to produce a positive deviation, and on others, a negative one. All the throws were counted in which at the same time the score on the six dice thrown for high aim was in excess of one (which would be MCE), and those in which the score on the low-aim dice was zero. There were 32 more successes on the high-aim dice and 32 fewer failures on the low-aim than would be expected. This gave a suggestive CR of 2.18; $p = .029$. This simultaneity thus suggested that PK was sometimes operating to produce positive results on one kind of dice and negative results on the other in the same throw.

In addition, some testimony was given to suggest a possible relation between the unconscious mental process that must have been involved and the conscious ones exerted by the subject. The author reported difficulty in keeping her mind on both objectives at once. She said she only felt that she was succeeding in the task after repeated trying, which meant toward the end of the set. Then after the interruption of beginning again on the next one, she felt the same difficulty.

The result of the experiment thus was one to encourage the idea that the mind in its unconscious reaches has the ability to cope with situations at least as complex as this one. It meant that even in this test of PK on two opposite targets simultaneously the limit of "mental dexterity" had not been exceeded.

A "BLIND TARGET" EXPERIMENT IN ENGLAND

Dr. Robert H. Thouless, who made the coin-spinning experiment described previously, later reported a series of PK experiments that he had carried out using himself as subject and dice for target objects in an attempt to study the psychological conditions that affect PK.[9] One of the experiments of this series involved a target innovation that makes it of interest in this chapter, although the rest of the work will be reported in Chapter 9.

The innovation Thouless introduced consisted of keeping himself in ignorance of the target face for which he threw the dice, so that it was in effect a "blind target." The question behind the procedure was whether in this way results could be secured that would be comparable to those secured when the subject had conscious knowledge of the target. Back of that question was a familiar one, that of the relationship of PK and ESP.

The idea that the two psi processes are intimately related had long been held by JBR, who in 1947 had devoted an entire chapter to the topic of the relationship of ESP and PK in his book, *The Reach of the Mind*.[10] In that chapter he had said, "ESP and

---

[9] Thouless, Robert H., "A Report on an Experiment on Psychokinesis with Dice and a Discussion of Psychological Factors Favoring Success." *Proc. Soc. Psy. Res.*, 1949–52, 49, pp. 116–117.

[10] Rhine, J. B., *The Reach of the Mind*. William Sloane Associates, New York (Apollo Edition, 1961).

PK are so closely related and so unified logically and experimentally that we can now think of both mind-matter interactions as one single fundamental two-way process."

Thouless too had recognized this close relationship when he with a colleague, Dr. B. P. Wiesner, had proposed the term *psi*, a Greek letter, to cover them both.[11] As already mentioned, the term has been in general use ever since to indicate the two processes when referred to together. Taking into account the similarities between the two processes, and that PK may be the motor or dynamic aspect of a unitary process, with ESP the cognitive one, he continued, "Further evidence that they are related phenomena would be found if it were discovered that there was a correlation between success in card-guessing experiments and in the correspondence between intention and result in dice-throwing experiments." In the experiment with blind targets, Thouless was obviously carrying out the procedure he had suggested in his article.

For the experiment, targets were selected by randomizing six cards marked to represent the die faces one to six, and laying them face down in a heap. He then made one throw of four dice for each of the hidden faces, willing the face to come up which was indicated on the card—the first throw for the first card, the second for the second, and so on—and recording all four uppermost faces after each throw. After thus throwing the four dice six times "blind," the record was then checked with the targets.

The result of the test was that in 2,592 trials, a deviation of +33 was secured. The CR of this was an insignificant 1.80; p = .07, but Thouless considered the suggestive results encouraging and that the method might even have an advantage over tests in which the subject knows the target because there would be less tendency for the subject to use conscious volition. He had found from his own experience that conscious trying did not necessarily help results.

[11] Thouless, R. H., and Weisner, B. P., "On the Nature of Psi Phenomena." *J. Parapsychol.*, 1946, 10, pp. 107–119.

This was the first PK test made with blind targets and, although suggestive, was not definitive. But a definitive test of the same idea was made a few years later.

## A "BLIND TARGET" EXPERIMENT AT THE
## PARAPSYCHOLOGY LABORATORY

After Thouless' blind target experiment, Dr. Karlis Osis at the Parapsychology Laboratory in 1953 went to work on the same question: are ESP and PK two aspects of the same basic process? He attempted to answer his question by a technique similar to the one Thouless had used.[12]

Osis knew that earlier in ESP studies evidence had been found to indicate that the process of extrasensory perception goes on in a single step; that it is a unitary one. Even when the target to be recognized is a complex one, as when the task is to match one ESP symbol with another, it does not appear that the symbols must first be recognized and then judged to be similar or dissimilar to each other. Instead it appears that only one mental step is involved and that the result is simply a judgment that these two are alike, or unlike, as the case may be. If ESP and PK are one, then, the subject should be able to "know" the target (unconsciously, of course) by ESP and direct the PK process accordingly just as well as if he had conscious knowledge of it.

A test was then performed involving three subjects, Mrs. Klara Osis and Miss Mable Sones, a laboratory visitor, and Osis himself. For the test, each subject was given an opaque envelope that he was not permitted to open. It contained the target sheet which had two eight-item columns, each of which had spaces for the targets and results of each throw. The targets for each throw had been determined by a random process and filled in in the ap-

---

[12] Osis, Karlis, "A Test of the Relationship Between ESP and PK." *J. Parapsychol.*, 1953, 17, pp. 298–309.

propriate spaces. Each face was thus the target an approximately equal number of times, and the dice were inlaid. On the outside of the envelope a target sheet like the one inside, but unfilled out, was clipped.

In the test then, the subject, with one of these envelopes before him, threw a die willing it to match the unknown face indicated on the hidden sheet, then the next, and so forth. He recorded the result of each throw on the other sheet. The Osis couple recorded for each other, but since this was frankly an exploratory attempt, Miss Sones worked alone and recorded her own results. However, later the envelopes were always opened and checked by Osis or his assistant.

Because of other pressures, Osis planned only two short sessions of 20 runs each. In one the two women were to be subjects who tried to see how many hits they could make. In the other, Osis planned to be the subject himself, and since he thought he usually scored below chance in tests, he intended in this one to try to miss the targets, or in other words, his objective was to get as low a score as possible. He knew the number of trials he was projecting was so small that results would have to be high if the experiment was to have a chance to achieve statistically significant results. On that account, he tried especially to interest his subjects deeply and to make the tests when all were in fresh and happy moods.

The results (converted to standard 24-item runs) for the 20 runs of the high-aim test for the two women together gave a significant deviation of +23; CR = 2.82; p = .005. On the low aim, Osis himself on the 20 runs had an insignificant deviation of −15; CR = 1.84; p = .065, or about six in a hundred by chance. Thus, his deviation, though in the intended direction, was not significant. The difference between the high and low aim tests was, however, a very significant $CR_d$ = 3.29; p = .001.

It looked as if the fact that the targets were hidden had not appreciably reduced the scores of these subjects, for the results were as good as any they had ever got in PK tests when ESP was not involved. The suggestion, therefore, if not the conclusion, was like Thouless', that ESP and PK are essentially one process.

## 1. *Hard vs Soft Surfaces*

Three more research projects belong in this chapter because of innovations in the targets. Chronologically, however, these experiments were carried out considerably later than all of those already reviewed. These were made by Haakon Forwald, an experimenter who had made a long series of experiments in PK with a different technique before beginning those that classify as belonging in this chapter. His more complete introduction is reserved for Chapter 12.

The first of these experiments of Forwald's was divided into two sections.[13] One section was carried out in 1956–57, the other in 1960. Each section involved four series in which two different dice sizes were used; one five millimeters per side, the other 13 millimeters per side. Comparisons of dice sizes, of course, had been made before. The innovation here was the introduction of two different throwing surfaces for comparison. One was soft, made by putting a thick piece of soft cardboard, much like blotting paper, on the table; the other hard, the bare table top.

In the 1956–57 section of the experiment the targets began with the one face and took the rest in order around the die. The dice sizes and the different surfaces were permuted so that each combination was used in a separate series of tests. A series included 36 sessions, each of which included six sets, and each set included a total of 36 die falls for each face of the die. Four series were made, in one two 13-millimeter dice were thrown on the soft

13 Forwald, H. "A PK Experiment with Die Faces as Targets." *J. Parapsychol.*, 1961, 25, pp. 1–12.

surface; in the next three of the five-millimeter, on the hard surface. Then in the final two series the surfaces were the opposites.

In the entire section, 31,104 dice were thrown; the deviation was +264. This gave a very significant CR of 4.02; p = .00007. However, the results of the four different conditions varied widely. The small dice on the hard surface yielded the largest deviation, +123 in 216 sets; also a highly significant CR = 3.75; p = .0002. None of the other combinations were independently significant.

However, when the results were tabulated according to the target faces, a complication was found that confused the interpretation of the result. All but nineteen hits of the entire deviation of +264 had been on the one face, with much smaller numbers on the rest, the threes and the fives even being slightly negative. This might have looked like a bias for ones, even though the controls were adequate. But it also could have meant that ones were very much preferred by this subject. However, another possibility existed, too, based on the course of Forwald's earlier work and explained later in Chapter 12. Although the technique was different there than here, a comparable situation existed in that, in both experiments, his throwing was done in sets, and in the other he had tended to do his main scoring on the *first throws* of the sets. Here in this experiment, the one face had always come first. There was no way, therefore, to tell if the large number of hits was due to bias or the position of the throw, or to a preference for the one face.

However, to help decide this point, when Forwald undertook his second section of the experiment in 1960, he reversed the target order and began with the six face to see if he could clarify the situation.

In this second section, he made the same number of trials as before. The total deviation he secured was even greater than the first one. This time it was +345, a CR of 5.26, and yielded an anti-chance probability in the millions. However, on the four series this time, the results on the first throws of the sets did not stand out particularly strongly. The highest score of all was again on the one face, which this time came last. By itself, it gave a deviation of +108 and was again significant with a CR of 4.02; p = .00007. It thus still looked as if this subject had a preference for the one face. However, in his earlier work, Forwald, usually his own subject, had shown a tendency to fail to get a trend in results once he became conscious of it. He may have done that here, but the question whether he did or did not could not be answered, because in his other work the single trend that did not get lost when he noticed it was that toward high scoring on the first throw of the set.

However, the high deviation on the one face may be explained; the effect that did not change the second time around was that of the high deviations with the small dice on the hard surface. This time it was even greater than before, being +135 as against the earlier +123. These dice on the hard table top bounced much more than any of the others, including the large ones on the same surface. It looked, therefore, as if the bouncing and longer time for random motion of these dice was conducive to PK. Forwald's own suggestion was that much greater opportunity was given in the longer journey of the small dice on the hard surface for PK to act than in any of the other situations. He thought the result suggested that the PK effect worked during the whole time of movement, gradually controlling the die so as ultimately to bring it to position. This impression of his was one that had long been held as one of two possible ways in which the "mechanics" of the PK process might work. For many years the question had been discussed among those who made experiments, whether the falling die was affected by a general steady force acting on it all the way as if, some said, the center of gravity had been shifted, or whether instead a determining force was applied when a die happened to reach an instant of near equilibrium. At such a time, presumably a slight "push" in the proper direction could cause the target face to come up, even though without it, it might not have. The question, of course, was not settled.

## 2. Controlling "Sameness"

Forwald next began to inquire whether he could increase the number of doubles he could get beyond that that would be expected by chance, not a double on a specific face, but any double. Therefore, he undertook an experiment in one part of which he tried to get doubles with as few throws as possible; and in the other, to see if he could avoid them, or in other words to see how many throws he could make without getting a double.[14]

Although Margaret Pegram had made a test involving doubles in one of the earliest PK experiments on record, no one since had reported an experimental attempt in which the target was not either a single face or combination of faces. And even so, Forwald's experiment was somewhat different from Margaret Pegram's. She had thrown for specified doubles, the expectation of which was one in 36. But Forwald's innovation was to aim at the concept of sameness, rather than to produce two specified dice faces simultaneously. He wanted to see if he could control sameness by getting it to occur more frequently than it would by chance when he so wished, and less frequently when he wished to avoid it. Of course, in throwing for unspecified doubles, his theoretical chance of getting a double was one in six throws.

With the same pair of 13-millimeter dice used in the previous experiment, Forwald simply shook the dice in cupped hands and dropped them from a height of a couple of feet onto the hard surface of a table that was ringed with books to keep the dice from falling off. As they fell, he reported he looked aside or shut his eyes, because he felt that he could succeed better this way. Other subjects have found other ways or attitudes which they have thought contributed to success. Usually all such variations in attitude sooner or later "wear out" and prove themselves to

[14] Forwald, H., "A PK Dice Experiment with Doubles as Targets." *J. Parapsychol.*, 1962, 26, pp. 112–122.

be only devices of passing—probably of novelty—value. At any rate, none of those reported so far have proven to help generally, or very long.

In a test of this type the basis for evaluation is different from throwing for single faces. In this, the number of throws that will be required to attain the objective is the unknown quantity while in the ordinary singles test, the unknown is the number of faces that will appear in a given number of throws. Consequently, the formula for evaluation is different in throwing as Forwald did and, to the nonmathematical, more complicated. However, evaluation can be made by the appropriate formula,[15] and using it, Forwald found that the 150 doubles he had obtained in 788 throws gave an encouraging CR of 1.67; p = .09; high enough that he then started on a confirmatory series.

In part 1 of this series, trying for doubles with as few throws as possible, he succeeded in getting 960 doubles with 554 fewer throws than expected. This was the equivalent of a quite significant CR of 3.26; p = .001. In part 2 then, he tried to reverse the process and avoid doubles for as many throws as possible. Again he was successful in his attempt, but not to as great an extent as before. This time he got the same number of doubles as before, 960, in 414 throws more than would be expected by chance. The CR on this, 2.44; p = .015, is still significant, however. The $CR_d$ between the two numbers is 4.03; p = .00006.

As far as one man's test and testimony can go then, this result seemed to say that so "blind" a process as *sameness* on concealed dice faces can be influenced by PK. These tests were made, it must be remembered, some years after the "blind target" tests of Osis and others had been published. In a way they too, had given testimony to the subjects' ability to respond to sameness, although in these other cases the sameness was between the hidden target face and the face secured in the test.

In attempting to account for the fact that his results were lower

[15] *Op. cit.*, p. 115.

when he tried to avoid doubles, Forwald proposed the idea that the emotional concomitant of success in the two opposite tasks was different. He says in wishing for doubles, the attitude was a calm, expectant one, but when trying to avoid them, he found himself likely to develop a state of anxiety lest a double appear, and the latter attitude he thought was less conducive to success than the former, which very well may have been an insightful observation corresponding to the fairly frequent observations of others, too.

### 3. Another "Blind" Test

Still with curiosity unsatisfied, Forwald extended the idea to a "blind" situation of another kind. If "sameness" could be obtained with dice faces, perhaps a die face and a card symbol could be matched also. He thus seemed to have approached the "blind target" idea of Thouless and Osis by his own experimental route. The task seemed essentially similar to that in the doubles test, though at first it appeared more complicated.[16]

As a sort of a code by which to connect the die faces with the symbols Forwald assigned each die face (except the six face, which he disregarded) one of the five card symbols: one, star; two, circle; three, square; four, cross; five, waves. He then shuffled a pack of ESP cards and without looking at any of the faces placed the pack face down on a table beside him. This was the target deck, the order of which he wanted to determine by throwing a die 25 times.

It will be observed that his method was practically like that of Thouless. When Thouless threw his dice, he was trying to secure the die face that was specified on the hidden target. Forwald was trying by his die throw to match the ESP symbol on the hidden card, which was also the case in the Osis test.

---

[16] Forwald, H., "An Experiment in Guessing ESP Cards by Throwing a Die." *J. Parapsychol.*, 1963, 27, pp. 16–22.

The tasks themselves thus were basically the same. In each, a combination of ESP and PK would be called for.

Taking a single die, Forwald dropped it on a table from several feet above so that it bounced and rolled considerably, while he willed that the face that would come uppermost would be the one that would match the first card in the deck; then he threw it again for the second card and so on, consecutively. He recorded the uppermost die face for 25 throws and only then checked this list against the actual order of the cards. However, as he threw, he paused perceptibly after each five throws, so that the 25-throw run was structured into five segments. In 2,500 trials, he had a deviation of +73 with a very significant CR of 3.64; p = .0003.

Forwald then repeated the test with the opposite intention of seeing how many card symbols he could miss. In other words, he now wished to avoid making hits. His scores this time on 2,500 trials yielded a negative deviation of −38. This number by itself, though in the desired direction, was not significant, but the difference between the two series was very much so, giving a CR of 3.93; p = .00008.

A check was made on these data to see if the usual decline effect had occurred, but it had not. Neither did the record show Forwald's usual high score at the beginning of the subsets of five trials in the runs, which might have been expected from the regularity with which it had occurred in his other dice work.

His results this time were only similar to those of his earlier experiments in that the score was higher when he was trying to make hits than when he attempted to miss the target. Nevertheless, with scores as significant as these, it looked as if this "blind" experiment, like those of other experimenters, had succeeded in showing either that PK and ESP can work simultaneously or that they are but aspects of a single process.

The list of innovations involving simple variations of faces as targets ends here, but because PK research was mainly an extracurricular activity pursued by individuals whose major preoccupations lay elsewhere, a lot of work was done that did not take the form of formally planned projects and that was never reported. For example, no formal study comparing the most favorable number of dice to be used per throw was ever published, though the general experience of many researchers seems to show that the number *per se* is unimportant so long as it promotes a quick and interesting experiment in contrast to an uninspired, long drawn out, and boring one.

Another unmentioned kind of test involved a comparison of the shapes of objects. Spheres (marbles) were tried, usually with unsatisfactory and inconclusive results, and cubes made with rounded corners were compared with square-cornered ones. But no significant difference was found except that some subjects preferred one kind rather than the other. The same result came from a comparison between very lightweight cubes (balsa wood) and very heavy ones (lead). Results followed preference, not weight, and with experimenters preoccupied with other matters no reports were published. Discussions about the mechanics of PK action too, were among the items that might have been but never were made into published reports.

However a type of target material quite different from dice must be included here even though research on it is recent and preliminary, and conclusions far from being established. This target material is that of radioactive substances; the objective: to hasten or slow down the disintegration rate of the elementary particles involved.

FIRST REPORT OF A TEST OF PK ON RADIOACTIVITY

In the 1950s a number of persons privately reported success in attempts to influence the rate of disintegration of radioactive substances by will power. But the claims were difficult to establish objectively. However, the first published report of such an attempt was made by John Beloff and Leonard Evans in 1961.[17] Although no significant results were secured it was an interesting attempt, both for the logic that produced it, and for the effort involved.

Dr. John Beloff, the senior author, a psychologist, then of Queen's University, Belfast, had long been interested in psychical research for somewhat the same reasons that led Dr. William McDougall many years before to become involved in it. In fact, Dr. Beloff's position in the field of psychology was much like that of McDougall in character.

As the report states, the investigation was undertaken because it seemed possible that if PK is a reality, subatomic particles might be more easily influenced than macroscopic bodies. Being statistically random in behavior they may be "nature's own dice," he reasoned. Further, a PK influence on the subatomic level would not be running counter to Newtonian dynamics as PK apparently does with larger bodies. Instead, the influencing of elementary particles would involve the principle of quantum indeterminacy, which, he suggested, might "allow a certain loophole."

In trying to set up an experiment as a result of this reasoning two types of apparatus were tried out. The first was a "spintharoscope." This in principle consisted of a radioactive source and a phosphorescent screen on which scintillations were produced by the particles emitted from the source, the number of which could then be recorded.

In the experiment the subject was to try to increase the number emitted. The substance used was an isotope of plutonium. But the scintillations were too feeble to be counted reliably. The attempt to work with this apparatus consequently had to be given up.

The second device tried was similar to a Geiger counter. The

---

[17] Beloff, John, and Evans, Leonard, "A Radioactivity Test of Psycho-Kinesis." *J. Soc. psy. Res.*, 1961, 41, pp. 41–46.

source of alpha particles used with it was uranyl nitrate in crystal-line form. Thirty student volunteers were used as subjects.

Each subject served for one session which consisted of three runs of 10 one-minute trials each. The trials were run in pairs, one of which, the positive, was an attempt to increase the count, the other, the negative, to decrease it.

Each subject initially was informed about his task, which was to exert a "psychic influence" on the number of radiations re-corded on the dial. He was offered an incentive of half a crown if he could produce an excess of 20 in his positive over his nega-tive trials.

The total results were slightly negative. Some of the usual tests for possible hidden PK effects were then made. The results, for example, were examined to see if there might have been a com-bination of significantly high and significantly low scorers whose results would have canceled in the totaling. That situation, how-ever was not found—no subject had had a deviation above 5 per-cent in size, and in a population of 30 subjects the range was well within chance distribution. Two of the high-scoring subjects were tested again in a second session but their rate did not hold up. Six subjects won the half crown, but could not repeat their first preformance. A slight over-all decline was also found, but it was not significant. However, to those familiar with the elusive aspects of PK, slight indications like these might well be taken as encouragement to further testing, rather than as simple null results.

The author in discussing the outcome of the experiment com-ments on the fact that an unsatisfactory condition for PK may be inherent in a test of this kind in that it gives the subject nothing on which to fasten his attention. It is not possible to visualize a single emission comparable to that in which successful PK subjects may visualize a die face target for instance, and apropos of that thought, the question arises whether a dice test would have succeeded under the conditions of this test, had one been included for the sake of comparison. And unless it had been included and had succeeded when the one on plutonium failed, other conditions besides the target substance might be the reason for failure.

One reason for instance could be that the subjects were not sufficiently indoctrinated on the topic of PK to accept a task like this as a reasonable one. It may have seemed quite impossible to them to be able to influence subatomic particles "psychically," and therefore the challenge of discovery may not have been induced. At any rate, in an experiment like this it would be necessary to know whether these subjects under the psychological circumstances of the test would have given evidence of PK on "macroscopic" material.

It may be observed, too, that the general results of all of the PK experiments would scarcely lead to the supposition that the smaller the object to be affected the greater would be the likelihood of success. If so, smaller dice should have succeeded better than larger ones. But they did not. At the other side of the equation, however, it might seem that research would be justified. If the mind has real force, how much force has it? As far as tests so far have gone, none of the systems in which the PK force has been tested could be considered very large.

However, even though Beloff considered his test a failure, he expressed the hope that a different way of assessing the "quantal phenomenon" may be found which will give information about PK.

### SECOND REPORT OF PK TESTS ON RADIOACTIVITY

Another attempt to influence subatomic particles by PK, also unsuccessful, is that of two investigators from Churchill College, Cambridge.[18] In this case again the method was considered to be

18 Wadhams, P., and Farrelly, B. A., "The Investigation of Psychokinesis using beta particles." *Jour. Soc. Psych. Res.*, 1968, 44, No. 736, pp. 281–288.

especially sensitive because the force needed to change the course of a subatomic particle would be infinitely small.

The instrument used in this experiment was a Geiger–Müller tube; the material, or source of the beta particles, strontium-90 of millicurie strength. Profiting from the earlier report of Beloff and Evans these experimenters provided a definite "physical" task for the subject. It was to deflect the particles, or stop them, so that they would not enter the tube. If successful the number recorded should be reduced below the ordinary average.

The measurement with this setup was between periods of concentration and nonconcentration, rather than between the positive and negative attempts. In the test the subject looked at the gap between the source and the tube and willed the particles away from the tube.

The periods of concentration and nonconcentration were randomly distributed. Counts were made in sets of 10, of one minute each, with half a minute in between for recording.

The two experimenters themselves were the main subjects. They explained that their idea was to test whether any trace of PK could be found in normal people, without any "emotional excitation." By using a technique like this with an apparatus which would register a very small effect they thought they could test their hypothesis. It was apparently based on the assumption that if PK is an inherent ability and shows up in what might be called a gross form in experiments as with dice when subjects are emotionally involved, or at least interested and enthusiastic, then a slight residue should be detectable at any time by a sufficiently sensitive mechanism. The assumption, however, may well be gratuitous since it is not suggested by successful experiments.

Seventy-five readings were made by the two experimenters plus a few by others. No significant differences were found. One of the subjects had initial success at the 5 per cent level, but it faded out. His results at the beginning of the trials (early in the day) also showed a suggestive 5 per cent level of significance, but they declined as the test proceeded. Here, too, these slight irregularities just possibly might be signs that could be read as encouraging; but with these data as they stood, no conclusions could be drawn. Nevertheless, the results could be taken to indicate that the hypothesis had not been confirmed. No slight residue of PK was observed in normal people without "emotional excitation."

However, it cannot be said that the requirements now known to be necessary for successful PK experiments were fulfilled either in this experiment or the preceding one, so that failure to obtain evidence of PK cannot be interpreted as bearing either positively or negatively on the question of whether radioactive substances can be influenced by PK.

### THIRD REPORT OF PK TESTS ON RADIOACTIVITY

The third recorded attempt to affect the disintegration of a radioactive substance by PK was reported as successful. This does not mean, however, that "three is a charm," for this one was actually carried out second. However, because of various circumstances, including language differences, Wadhams and Farrelly of the experiment reported just above were probably unaware of it when they made their own.

The experimenters in the present case were two French scientists, Dr. Rémy Chauvin and Jean-Pierre Genthon, the former a biologist, the latter a physicist.[19] Although the experimenters were French the first report of their work appeared in a German journal of parapsychology.

In this experiment a Geiger counter was used, uranium nitrate the radioactive substance. The task was to influence the rate of occurrence of the blips on the counter. One minute was set as the time for a trial, either to accelerate or to slow down the blips.

---

[19] Chauvin, Rémy, and Genthon, Jean-Pierre, "Eine Untersuchung über die Moglichkeit Psychokinetscher Experiemente mit Uranium und Geigerzähler." Zeitschrift für Parapsychologie und Grenzgebiete der Psychologie, 1965, 8, pp. 140–147.

After the trial, a minute of "uninfluenced time" was inserted. This was followed by another minute of trial, the objective of which was the opposite of the first. The comparison thus was between the accelerated and the slowed down periods, similar to Beloff and Evan's positive and negative trials. The unit periods of testing both for an accelerated and a slowed down effect thus were relatively short, lasting only three minutes in all.

The subjects used in this test were children, seven in all, between the ages of 8 and 17. They were relatives and friends of the experimenters and had taken part in ESP tests earlier and also in PK tests with dice. Thus they were already somewhat "indoctrinated"; and as children, the seeming "impossibility" of PK doubtless would have been less likely to have inhibited them than if they had been adults.

The subject of general atomic theory was discussed briefly, but the subjects did not appear to be much interested in it. They were interested in the Geiger counter, however; and, as can readily be imagined, watching it and trying to influence it gave them the proper incentive.

Two of the subjects, 13-year-old boys, achieved highly significant results in the direction intended. A simple basis of judgement was used. When the result was better than 50–50 in the intended direction the trial was considered a hit, the reverse, a miss. The magnitude of either hits or misses was not taken into account. The actual scores are not reported, but only that on this basis, the results of one subject reached $p = 3 \times 10^{-12}$, the other $3 \times 10^{-11}$, very highly extra-chance values of course. The authors felt that the principle involved was the same as that in dice tests. The senior author, Chauvin, was reported as continuing the research, but at the stage of this first report the authors considered their work as only exploratory.

In the first of the projects of this chapter, target changes were only cautious ventures with a new shape of object, discs instead of cubes. The results eventually seemed to indicate that shape of target object as such did not make any very pronounced difference in results.

Then the later projects, those of Betty H. and the several experimenters who used "blind targets," took the inquiry into greater and more fundamental differences of target objectives. They showed quite clearly that mental processes much more complex than might have been expected could go on below the conscious level. While even in the simplest dice test it was logical to suppose that ESP must play a part, in these it was much more obviously so, and also the process that produced the results appeared to have been a surprisingly complicated one. However, it is at least interesting to suppose that its complexity is mostly a figment of rationality. Actually at the unconscious level, it very well may be that the addition of a bind target, to be identified by ESP, was not really adding a new dimension to the test but only more of the same. At least the results appeared to say so, since they were achieved apparently at about the same rate of speed and similar level of effectiveness as any other test.

But, whatever the unconscious process may be, the introduction of the tests on microphysical substances at least adds considerably to the range of targets tried. One initially successful project, out of three so far, can well be considered only par for the course. Further experiments on the topic now can be awaited with some expectation that the success will be confirmed. Here too, as a kind of standard, the psychological conditions must be good enough for dice tests to succeed before the PK effect on microparticles can be considered to have been tested. The least that can be said for the range of targets and target objects used in these experiments is that they seem not to have come to any final limit beyond which the PK effect cannot go. The results with the new ventures at least were not discouraging but rather can be taken as invitations for further diversification.

CHAPTER 9

# Mental Influences on PK

ALMOST as soon as PK research began signs appeared that the phenomena, to a large extent, followed mental rather than physical rules. If they had not and if instead the results had seemed to be directly related to the mass of the objects, the course of PK research would no doubt have been quite different than it has turned out to be. Instead of being complicated and baffling and revolutionary in its implications it might have been quick and easy and fitted in with scarcely a ripple. A relatively simple stretch of physical research would have lain ahead in which the size and reach of the effect would soon have been measured. The main problem would have been to find out how the force that initially affected the objects was transferred from the mind—i.e., the brain—to the object. Presumably then it would have been discovered that only an obscure and until then overlooked kind of energy transformation was involved. But soon all the pieces of the puzzle would have fitted together nicely, no established principles would have been violated and only a small repair job in physics would have been called for.

But it did not turn out that way. The puzzle was much more complicated. The PK effect was not tied up neatly to any of the obvious physical realities. Instead, the vagaries of mental processes were involved, and these are far more uncharted and difficult to understand and forecast even in this twentieth century than the physical ones (which, it might be remarked, as well as being less complex have also been studied over a much longer period).

The results as they accumulated not only showed that mental influences sometimes obscured the physical ones, as in Hilton's inquiry on the effect of size of dice, but also they sometimes

showed up in entirely unexpected ways. Frick was not expecting
the result he got when he tried to control for sixes by throwing
for the one face. Betty Mc. was not expecting her first sessions
with the children to be invariably better than the second. Even
JBR with his hypnotized subjects was inquiring whether (expecting that?) they would perform according to suggestion. In
short, none of the experimenters who got results like these were
expecting them. But these unexpected results had causes too. These
were indications that more was involved than simply the conscious
attitudes and expectations of the people in the tests. Unconscious
mental processes too were affecting the results.

However just when or where or how strong such influences
might be was difficult to foresee or measure. Psychological effects,
unconscious as well as conscious, vary with the time and place
and personality. It is easy to record a subject's hits or misses but
not so the thoughts he had as he made them, the shades of feeling or emotion he may have felt, or the degree of concentration
he achieved. These factors, it would seem, once past are gone
forever and even the grossest kind of measurement could scarcely
do them justice. And yet these unrecorded attitudes and influences do leave traces that can be recognized and interpreted.

While every experiment has its psychological overtones, in the
present chapter experiments are presented in which psychological
effects seem to be particularly conspicuous. Some of these experiments were designed to illustrate a given psychological effect
but most of them had other primary objectives. The first one
presented below had a different objective but it illustrates a
psychological attitude or lack of attitude of the subjects toward
the tests that had not existed in the earlier experiments.

### NASH AND HIS CAPTIVE SUBJECTS

In 1940 Dr. Carroll Nash, then a biology professor at the
University of Arizona, used his 113 subjects in a PK test[1] and

[1] Nash, Carroll Blue, "PK Tests of a Large Population." *J. Parapsychol.*,
1944, 8, pp. 304–310.

thereby set a record for numbers. No one before had used so many. In another way, too, the test was unique. These students did not know about PK, and the experimenter did not discuss it with them. As he says, they were selected "through no volition of their own." The test was given as if it were part of their academic requirement. He simply told them that they were to roll the dice with the specified face uppermost. They were thus, in effect, captive subjects, quite the opposite from the early PK subjects who had a strong investment of personal interest in the outcome of the test.

This experiment, however, was an original one, for Nash quite independently of any suggestion from Duke had thought of using dice to test for PK. He had been following the reports of research in ESP since the first issue of the *Journal of Parapsychology* in 1937, but nothing had yet been published about PK. He then wrote to JBR suggesting the use of dice as a method of testing for "telekinesis" (the old term that had been applied to the alleged movement of objects without contact in mediumistic séances). He was thereupon encouraged to make such a test himself, but the fact that the method was already in use at the laboratory and had been since 1934 was not mentioned to him. It was thought better to leave him uninformed so that he could develop his idea independently. The use of a dice cup was recommended, however, and also equal numbers of throws for each die face and, if possible, a large number of subjects. Nash took the suggestions.

The objective of the experiment he carried out was to test the effect of throwing one die at a time versus throwing all six at once. Each subject made two sets of experiments, a set consisting of six "runs" of six die falls each, so that the MCE per set was six. The targets for the six runs were rotated so that throws for all six faces were balanced.

Forty-nine subjects threw one set with one die at a time, the other set with six. The rest threw both sets with six dice per throw. The average per die (MCE was 6) secured on all of the one die per throw sets was 5.69, while the average of all of the six dice per throw sets was 6.31. The $CR_d = 1.67$; p = .09, an insignificant value, even though the trend was in line with that of all the other experiments in which one die thrown at a time was contrasted with a larger number. The experiment was the first one to document the fact that subjects are unlikely to succeed without having an incentive or any personal involvement in the test.

The next test is in contrast because in it the subjects were highly motivated. The purpose however was quite other than an attempt to show the effect of high motivation.

### PREACHERS VERSUS GAMBLERS

A PK contest was staged by one who could be called an "inspired" experimenter, even though he was still at the student stage. It was in the spring of 1943, and a young man from the Duke Divinity School, William Gatling, was among those who had been in JBR's psychology class. By the end of the term, he had absorbed the idea not only that PK, as well as ESP, really occurred, but that it, too, had implications for religion that a young divinity student should take seriously.

Gatling believed in the efficacy of prayer, and was convinced that sometimes it is answered in ways that seem miraculous. If the answers meant that circumstances including sometimes physical ones were changed according to the objectives of the prayer, the question was the means by which that change was brought about. Once Gatling recognized that PK might be a reality he saw it as the possible means. Possibly then, with prayer the method of formulating the wish, PK produced the result. Even if a higher personal agency intermediated, PK would still be required.

Gatling then came to JBR, who as an experimentalist said, "Why not try it out?" Such an experiment might not show if an external agency was involved but at least it could show if prayer was a good method by which to secure strong motivation in a test. But it would be necessary of course to contrast that form with some other way of strongly motivating the subject to get high results in order to show whether it was prayer per se or simply strong motivation that had led to the success. It was then decided that the motivating objective of professional "pride" that gamblers may have might well offer such a control.

Gatling accepted the idea and as a result found four young men on the campus who were noted for their good luck at crap shooting. And then he recruited three of his fellow divinity students to join him and set the two groups to throwing dice to see which one would be the better.[2]

The technique they followed in this contest was simple and well controlled. The dice were always thrown from a cup with roughened interior, six at a time, and in equal numbers for all the die faces, the ministerial students presumably prefacing their tests by prayer, although it is not mentioned in the report, and neither is any mention made as to any preparation the crap shooters may have made beforehand.

The results of the contest no doubt surprised both groups of contestants for neither side was able to get much ahead of the other. After a total of 1,242 runs, they were still practically tied. The crap shooters had thrown 540 runs with an average run score of 4.52 (MCE = 4). The divinity students had thrown 702 runs with practically the same average run score, 4.51.

When the results of both groups were added, the totals with the run score average of 4.52 gave a CR of 9.97, which would not occur by chance in billions of tests. The result was the *highest* that had ever been reported over as large a number of runs as this. The deviations for each face were positive. Beginning with the one face, and in order around the die, they were +50, +113, +136, +73, +133, and +136. The scoring rate of the individuals varied widely, the highest being that of one of the crap shooters, who averaged 4.80 per run against that of Gatling

[2] Gatling, William, and Rhine, J. B., "Two Groups of PK Subjects Compared." *J. Parapsychol.*, 1946, 10, pp. 120–125.

himself, the highest of the ministerial students, which was 4.69.

The decline effects in the data proved to be in general in line with expectation. Although the score for the pooled third quarters was a little higher than for the first, the difference between the first and fourth gave a marginally significant $CR_d$ of 2.22; $p = .026$.

Since the rate of scoring in this contest was unprecedentedly high, it might have been said, if only successful gamblers had been involved, that these were selected subjects. But the divinity students were not selected for dice-throwing ability, but because of their convictions. The suggestion, therefore, is that whatever the prayer may have done, certainly the strong motivation which the competition induced, was effective. Beyond doubt, these subjects had a higher stake in the outcome than do ordinary ones.

The experiment then made an especially clear example of the effect of strong interest in the outcome on the part of the subjects. While many of the early tests had suggested that such interest was effective, this one showed it neatly in one package, so to speak.

However, it should be noted even here, that not all of the subjects did so well. One of the divinity students finished with a very small total deviation ($-2$), and the lowest crapshooter had only $+9$ to show—not a score that would be likely to win a crap game. The results thus suggest, too, that personal variation (presumably here in response to stress) is a factor to be taken into consideration in producing PK. It is the same observation made in the experiment with hypnotized subjects in Chapter 7.

### A HELP-HINDER CONTEST

Another experiment that took the form of a contest, though not on so high a level of motivation, was performed by Betty Humphrey a few years later.[3] In this she attempted to produce

[3] Humphrey, Betty M., "Help-Hinder Comparison in PK Tests." *J. Parapsychol.*, 1947, 11, pp. 4–13.

differing psychological attitudes in the subjects by the plan of procedure.

The question Betty H. wanted to answer was whether the psychological influence that induces PK is additive, or in other words, whether two subjects would be more effective than one. She set up her experiment so that in one part of it, two subjects would be concentrating on a single target to see if helping helped, as in effect the two subjects would be doing. In contrast, in certain of the tests, the second subject would be trying for a different target from that of the first. This was to see if hindering hindered, but it should be observed that the word hinder in this context is a misnomer. The two subjects in these tests simply had different targets, and since six dice were thrown each time, presumably each subject could have affected an individual die which the other was not affecting. In a true "hinder" situation, the conditions would have to be such that both subjects were necessarily trying to get different faces to come up on a given die at the same time.

As the experiment was set up, two subjects were present at a time, besides the experimenter who kept the record. On a given turn, one of the subjects was designated as the "thrower." He released the dice and was, in effect, the subject. The other, who tried to help or hinder, as the case might be, was the "observer." The two roles were alternated at the end of each turn, so that each person served at times in each capacity. A turn usually consisted of 12 throws of six dice for a given target. The dice were thrown from a cup onto a padded table.

In order to minimize the conscious effect that might be made on the thrower by knowing whether he was being helped or not, he was kept in ignorance of the observer's target. To do this the thrower first chose his target face for the turn and showed his choice to both the experimenter and the observer. Then, to determine whether the observer was to help or not, the observer got his own target by throwing two dice, shielding them from the sight of the thrower. If the sum of the upturned faces was an even number, he was to help; if odd, not. If he was to help, he would try for the same target the thrower had chosen. If not, he would take for his target the higher of the two faces shown on his dice, unless it was the same as the one chosen by the thrower. In that event, he would take the lower one. Then, so that his hits could be recorded, he would show his target to the experimenter without letting the thrower know what it was. Thus, those two knew what the target was, but the thrower did not. They tried to give the thrower no cue as to whether he was being helped or hindered during his turn.

The result was that on the 177 "help" runs, an average run score of 4.54 was obtained which gives a highly significant CR of 3.91; $p = .0001$. The CR of the entire "hinder" section was not significant, and the $CR_d$ between the help and hinder section was 2.07; $p = .038$—a difference not significant, but suggestive.

The experiment as a whole seemed to show that the two subjects working together were more effective than when each was trying for a separate target. However, neither subject was tested alone, and so it could not be said whether helping really helped, although that was suggested by the fact that the average run score, 4.54, was fairly high. However, it certainly was not twice as high as a good subject working alone might expect to get. And so the additive factor, if such there was, must have been a relatively slight one.

The results of the hinder section were not completely interpretable either. If the observer had scored well or better than the thrower, it could have been said that he succeeded, or at least that an effect had been demonstrated. But since neither one alone secured a significant deviation, it could not be definitely concluded that PK was involved here and even though the CR of the total scores of both series if taken together yielded a significant value, this did not prove that the hinder section involved any PK effect.

It is possible too that the observer may have been unfavorably affected by knowing constantly in the hinder section whether he had failed or succeeded in getting his target. To offset this possibility, it would be necessary that both individuals be kept in ignorance of the other's target.[4] Such an experiment was promised here, but no further report on the point was ever published.

## THE ROSES TEST THEMSELVES

In 1948–49, Ronald Rose, an Australian student of anthropology, and his wife began to prepare themselves for studies of various aboriginal tribes.[5] Among other objectives, they intended to include tests for ESP and PK. In preliminary preparation, they tested their own ability to get evidence of the phenomena from subjects. In these tests, Rose, with an unspecified number of subjects, including his wife and himself, made as many as a hundred PK runs, but none of the subjects except Mrs. Rose got significant scores. Rose's own deviations were positive but much lower than his wife's. On that account, the interest of the report centers on the contrast between his own results and those of his wife.

Six dice were released at a throw, mechanically, by the withdrawal of a ruler, so that the subjects had no physical contact with them. The experimenter did the recording, Mrs. Rose substituting in this for her husband when he was the subject. A point was made in the entire experiment of keeping a record of all the uppermost faces of each throw.

The dice were thrown in groups of 25 throws or the equivalent of 6¼ standard runs for a given target. The subjects were permitted to select their own targets and, therefore, the number of

[4] A recent still unpublished experiment carried out in mutual ignorance of the other person's target has given quite different results and suggests that the interaction between the two is very subtle and complex. Different personalities and circumstances also may yield different trends impossible to predict. Much, more experimental data on the topic are needed.

[5] Rose, Ronald, "Some Notes on a Preliminary PK Experiment with Six Dice." *J. Parapsychol.*, 1950, 14, pp. 116–126.

faces used was not equalized. This target selection also permitted to a degree the then recently raised criticism of some of the earlier PK experiments, which was that the results could have been caused by precognition rather than an effect of mind on matter.

The idea behind this criticism was that the subject, if given the freedom to select the target, might arrive at it because by precognition he could divine the die face that was going to come up by chance on the next throw or series of throws. If so, the hits that would result would not have been produced by PK, but rather because the proper target had been selected. Of course the subject would have been equally unconscious of just how he did it in either case.

It seemed at least a theoretical, although remote, possibility and one that had not been taken seriously in the early years of PK research. In the early dice work, subjects had sometimes been allowed to choose their own targets if they cared to. Many of them thought they succeeded better when they did so than with a target imposed on them by the experimenter. However, sometimes the plan of the experiment had precluded their choosing of the target. Later it was found that if the experimenter gave the subject no choice, the imposed target apparently served as well as the one he chose himself. This had been shown by "around-the-die" tests, for instance, often made in order to control dice bias.

In her test Mrs. Rose's score was a +83 in 331¼ runs, which is an average run score of 4.25 (MCE = 4) and gives a significant CR of 2.51; p = .012, while Rose on 331¼ runs had a deviation of +41, an average run score of 4.12 and an insignificant CR of 1.14; p = .25.

Mrs. Rose had elected to throw mainly for sixes, so that her result could not be interpreted as free from the possibility of dice bias. However, the fact that the faces of all the dice were recorded for each throw made it possible to count the number of sixes that came up when some other face was target. It was found to be so low that little bias for sixes seemed to be indicated, and the number of sixes she obtained in 125 runs when the six face was target (+85), and the number she obtained when it was not (−14), was significantly different, CR = 3.59; p = .0006.

Rose's scores however were not significant, and even the trends that were suggested were opposite to those of Mrs. Rose. They thought their results reflected their differing personalities and the different attitudes with which they approached the tests, as well. Rose described Mrs. Rose as having been especially interested in PK and keenly interested in getting significant results. When she threw the dice, she exercised a perceptible effort of will, often calling the target face aloud with determination.

On the other hand, Rose said that although he was interested, he did not enter into the experiment with so strong a determination to produce significant results as his wife did. He was trying mainly to introspect and see if he could find a key to the conscious control of PK. The attitudes of each, he thought, were indicative of personality traits he could recognize. One of these was that his wife was quick in adapting to new situations, while he was slow, which showed that the two personalities were quite different. One of the unsolved questions of PK tests, and of ESP tests, too, is which effect is stronger—basic personality characteristics or the more temporary mental states like the mood of the moment or the degree of interest in the test.

The second experiment the Roses carried out involved a special kind of test subject. This must have meant a special kind of attitude toward the tests.

### THE ROSES TEST AUSTRALIAN ABORIGINES

Soon after their preliminary tests, the Roses began to make psi tests on some detribalized natives at the Woodenbong Aboriginal Settlement in New South Wales.[6] They knew that the tribal beliefs and practices of these natives were rapidly changing

---

[6] Rose, Lyndon, and Rose, Ronald, "Psi Experiments with Australian Aborigines." *J. Parapsychol.*, 1951, 15, pp. 122–131.

to those of the white community even on the subject covered by
the term ESP. According to general accounts, a high level of
extrasensory "knowing" had existed in the group in its tribal
state. Some of the older members still believed that they once
had had almost constant telepathic experiences and that certain
"clever men" still had such ability. But many of the younger
persons considered all this superstition, although even they were
certain they would "know" of the death or serious illness of a
relative at a distance.

The Roses felt that formal tests to see if these people had
great psi ability should be made at once before the change had
gone further. Accordingly, in August 1949, at the aboriginal settlement, Rose and his wife tested 23 subjects for ESP. One person especially, Lizzie Williams, an elderly half-caste, gave an especially high deviation. In addition, the CR for the group was
significant.

The Roses wanted to introduce PK tests although the topic was
strange to these subjects, for they did not consider it a capacity
they themselves might possess. They believed that powers of that
kind belonged only to the "clever men" who could call up or
disperse storms and kill or cure by magic. Consequently none of
them had any belief that he himself had an ability to affect matter
directly. The Roses had $\frac{5}{16}$-inch plastic cubes made, which,
instead of having spots, were painted contrasting colors on anti-
podal sides, black and white, red and yellow, blue and green.
With these cubes, they felt that considerable interest in throwing
for a specific color was aroused. Twenty subjects in all took part
in the tests. Each color was the target an equal number of times.
The record sheet used provided for 24 runs, four of each color.
Each subject did a minimum of 24 runs, but one subject, Nellie
Charles, did many more than the rest, and scored much higher.
She was the granddaughter of Lizzie Williams, whose deviations
on the ESP tests had been high.

The entire group of subjects completed a total of 1,896 runs,
with a deviation of only +128. This gives an insignificant CR of

1.61; p = .11. But Nellie Charles, on 600 runs, had a deviation of + 108, a CR of 2.41; p = .016, which could have been considered significant if it had stood alone. But statistically it had to be averaged in with the rest, and theoretically the question left undecided whether this subject had given evidence of PK, but of course the indications were fairly strong that she had done so. It well could have been that the group was not properly motivated, whatever that may have implied, and that only Lizzie Williams had the necessary characteristics to produce results in this situation. After all, in the Roses' tests at home, the miscellaneous subjects, even Rose himself, had not given significant evidence of PK.

The Roses felt strongly that their tests were encouraging and that they should be repeated soon, before the cultural change had gone farther and blotted out the aboriginal attitude toward psi ability and its possible high level of expression. No one else however took up the challenge, but the Roses in a short report a year after the first one,[7] told of conducting a series of ESP and PK tests with a group of natives at Tabulam, New South Wales. However, they gave no details unfortunately, only reporting that the results were "quite insignificant." This is probably an example of an experimenter's lack of interest when he has no significant result to report. Besides, Rose was an anthropologist, not a parapsychologist and may have had no interest in the reasons for failure.

In December 1950 and February 1951 the Roses visited and tested two groups of natives in Central Australia. One of these consisted of detribalized Aranda people, the other of almost fully tribal members of the Pitjendadjara tribe. Again with these subjects, details are not given and it is reported only that insignificant scores were obtained, both in ESP and PK. In the latter, however, it is said that 1,128 runs were made with 12 regulation dice per throw instead of the colored ones used before. Whether for this

[7] Rose, Ronald, "Experiments in ESP and PK with Aboriginal Subjects." *J. Parapsychol.*, 1952, 16, pp. 219–220.

reason or not, it is of course impossible to say, but the deviation was only a +7. Only one subject produced results that at any time looked interesting. This one, in his first session of 24 runs, had a deviation of +26, a significant CR of 2.91. But his final deviation in 144 runs was only +30, CR = 1.37; p = .17. So he, like Nellie Charles, remained only in the suggestive category. Rose further stated that tests on aboriginal "clever men" showed no special ability, but again no details were given in his paper.

In a follow-up study a few years later, the Roses went back to the aborigines at the Woodenbong settlement in New South Wales.[8] They spoke of the natives now as semicivilized and "absorbed in the white community." In the few intervening years, too, because of deaths and illnesses, less than half of their previous subjects were available. However, out of the 12 subjects they used only one had not been tested before.

A number of well-controlled ESP tests were given and the results were highly significant, and higher than they had been on the earlier occasion. But PK tests again were failures. Using inlaid dice, the subjects threw 12 at a time from a container onto a blanketed table or floor, with each face the target an equal number of times. But none of the subjects secured a positive deviation of more than 10 (CR 1.12), and Nellie Charles, the highest scorer before, here scored a −11, the lowest score of all.

Naturally the Roses were disappointed in their failure to get evidence of PK as well as of ESP. The main reason for it they could offer, since they felt that all conditions had been optimum, was the "relative physical indolence" of the subjects, as shown by their lack of initiative and drive in their everyday affairs. However, if this was a fair estimate of the situation, it is possible that such an attitude on the part of the subjects meant that the objectives given them were not sufficiently compelling. They probably were more nearly like Nash's subjects as far as their interest and involvement was concerned, than like, say, the preachers and

[8] Rose, Ronald, "A Second Report on Psi Experiments with Australian Aborigines." *J. Parapsychol.*, 1955, 19, pp. 92–98.

the gamblers. Whether or not any means could ever be found to rouse these natives from their "indolence," unless that goal were accomplished probably nothing but failure could be expected no matter what the culture of the subjects.

In tests for PK, just as in intelligence tests for instance, techniques designed for individuals of one kind of cultural background cannot necessarily successfully or fairly be transferred directly to persons of a different background.

### THE VASSES AND THE ROSES

Another husband and wife team, Dr. and Mrs. Paul Vasse, reported a PK experiment about the same time as the Roses.[9] It is of interest in its own right and also in the comparison of the attitudes of each of this couple with those of the Rose couple.

Dr. Vasse was a practicing M.D. in Amiens, France; his wife Christiane, a teacher in a primary school there. Both thus were busy professional people. Their interest in PK originated with Mrs. Vasse (so that she, like Mrs. Rose, presumably had a stronger personal interest in the outcome of the PK experiment than her husband had).

Christiane Vasse's attention was turned directly to the field of parapsychology when she came upon a suggestion in her reading that the germination and growth of seeds could be affected by human thought. That led her to make a simple test. She planted a plate of seeds on her window sill and attempted to influence those in one half of it to grow faster than those in the other.

In a few days, the growth in one half was obviously better than in the other. The difference was sufficiently striking to show in a photograph taken when the seedlings were a few inches

[9] Vasse, Paul, and Vasse, Christiane, "A Comparison of Two Subjects in PK." *J. Parapsychol.*, 1951, 15, pp. 263–270.

high. She then wrote to the Parapsychology Laboratory and sent copies of the pictures of her plants. JBR realized that in spite of these encouraging results, many controls would be necessary before the point could be made that human thought had caused the difference. Such controls would be difficult to carry out in an impromptu setting like hers, for all the variables, heat, light, water, and soil chemicals were involved. He suggested that a simpler plant experiment be tried, that of phototropism, the tendency of plants to turn to the light. Consequently, a trial was made using young corn seedlings. She tried to prevent their bending toward the light.

In this experiment Dr. Vasse, as well as his wife, had an experimental plate of seedlings, but while the results on hers were encouraging on his they were not, and in neither case were they entirely definitive. The Vasses felt they were on the trail of something that needed further study, but the plant experiment was too difficult to control under the home situation. They needed an easier technique. By the route of this reasoning, they were persuaded to try a PK test of the more standard dice-throwing type. They decided to use the technique that Margaret Pegram had used and to throw a pair of dice for high dice and then for low dice. As will be recalled, high dice include all combinations of faces over seven; low, all under seven, and the expectation for high or low in a run of 12 throws of the pair is five.

The Vasses threw their dice from a cup onto a padded surface, with 12 throws of the pair per run. The records were kept in a notebook, odd pages for Mrs. Vasse, even for Dr. Vasse. They took turns recording for each other, and each page of the record book contained two columns of three runs each, one was a record of the throws for high, one for low dice.

The results were that Mrs. Vasse threw 135 runs for high dice, with a highly significant deviation of +69; CR = 3.48; p = .0005. For low dice, she threw 111 runs, with a deviation of +45, a still significant CR of 2.50; p = .012. Her husband, on the other hand, threw 96 runs for high, with a deviation of +11, and 138 runs for low with a deviation of +10, neither one significant.

When Christiane's sets on the page were compared, the one on the left, which of course had been thrown first, was higher than the one on the right. The columns, too, showed the pattern already familiar from the work of Margaret P. and Lottie G. That was that the first columns were highest, the middle ones lowest, and the end ones somewhat higher again. But her husband's average scores were practically the same on his two sets on the page, the patterns of the two thus being quite individual.

The general patterns of the results of the Vasses was inescapably similar to that shown by the Roses. In both cases the women's scores were significantly high; in both the men's were not. The women's results but not the men's showed characteristic declines. The over-all personality patterns, as they might be involved in the matter of PK results, appeared to be similar, too.

Although no personality sketch was included in the Vasse report as it had been in the one by the Roses, a gross comparison is possible because Christiane later visited the laboratory and its members became acquainted with her. Then later still, some of the laboratory members met her husband, too, in France.

The similarities between the two couples that could be noted were not atypical of many married couples. In both of these it appears the women were more spontaneous and extroverted than their husbands. In both, the men apparently were more of the reserved scientist type. In both, the wives were the more personally interested in getting results in the experiment. It was suggested, too, that the wives were more adaptable to the test situation and probably felt fewer reservations when taking part in it. The Vasse conclusion in regard to their own differing results was that one can expect differences in PK scoring trends to follow the differing individual attitudes toward the test, and the differing psychological developments in the course of the tests.

Of course it was just by chance that two couples like the Roses and the Vasses should have reported tests that showed the similarities they did, about the same time, and in spite of the distances that separated them, one in Australia the other in France. No more such "object-lesson" cases have shown up since, although to a degree one can see a similarity in the record of the Gibson couple. Lottie G. consistently scored higher than her husband and personality characteristics were somewhat like those of the Rose versus Vasse couples. However, in this case, Gibson's initial interest was probably greater than Lottie's.

Of course when one tries to make a psychological distinction between the men and women in cases like this of the two couples, only the results they got in their tests are objective facts. Their attitudes are much less tangible. It would be desirable in such cases to go a little farther experimentally and administer psychological tests, as Rose suggested, but at least, the differences here seem obvious enough to be noticed, even if they were not measured. It should be observed, however, that the higher scoring of the women is not necessarily based on sex, for many of the best PK subjects have been men.

In the next two experiments to be presented a quite different psychological effect appears, and it is all the more striking because as the experiments were made it was entirely unintentional.

CONTRASTING ATTITUDES IN TWO EXPERIMENTS

## The First Experiment

Mrs. Laura A. Dale, research associate of the American Society for Psychical Research in New York, undertook two PK experiments. The first one was started after she read a review of the work at Duke in the *Journal of the American Society for Psychical Research* by JBR on the results of the PK tests to that date, 1943.[10] The review stressed the findings of the QD analyses that had then been so recently discovered and also the fact that as far as the experimental results indicated, PK appeared to be affected by psychological influences rather than physical realities like size and number of dice thrown.

On the basis of the results as reported, then, Mrs. Dale planned her experiment with two main objectives in mind—first to see if evidence of PK could be obtained, and second, if it could, whether the subjects' attitude concerning the possibility of PK would affect the results, as it had been found to affect those of ESP. In ESP it seemed that those who believe in the phenomenon (the sheep) tend to get positive deviations, while those who do not (the goats) tend to deviate in the negative direction. No one had yet attempted to see if PK would show a similar effect. In addition, Mrs. Dale had in mind the testing of a large number of subjects, rather than the somewhat limited numbers that had been used in all but one (Nash's) of the cases that had then been reported. As a still further addition, she intended to see what differences in scoring men and women might show.

Mrs. Dale then secured the services of 54 college students from several New York colleges, 29 women and 25 men. They came as paid volunteers, and so were not captive subjects like Nash's, nor yet quite the same as the free-will subjects of most other experiments to date. However, at each session (of which each subject had only one) the nature of the test was explained so that each one knew what the test was about when he took it. After this explanation, each one was asked to indicate whether or not he believed that such a phenomenon as PK could occur. After that came the PK test.

For the test, four dice were thrown at a time, and four runs were thrown for each die face in succession. The results for each die face were recorded on separate sheets, so that for each sub-

[10] Dale, L. A., "The Psychokinetic Effect: The First A.S.P.R. Experiment." *J. Amer. Soc. psych. Res.*, 1946, 40, pp. 123–151.

ject a six-page record resulted. The number of the first face thrown for by the subjects was staggered among the students to avoid a primacy effect, for if all had begun with the one face and if high scores had been obtained on it, it would not be clear whether the results were due to the first position in the series of throws or to a preference for ones.

The dice were first shaken in a dice cup, then dropped into a receptacle placed at the top of an inclined chute. From the receptacle, they fell down the chute over many interposed baffles so that they bounced around freely, and came to rest on the bottom of a 12 × 18-inch dice box.

A total of 1,296 standard runs was made, and an over-all deviation secured which gave an average run score of 4.13, a significant $CR = 2.60$; $p = .009$. This, of course, was strong indication that PK had been involved.

The sheep-versus-goat division did not show the results expected. The 41 students who were sheep had an average run score of 4.117 (4.0 of course, was MCE). The 13 who were goats, had an average of 4.176, practically the same as the sheep.

When the hit distribution of the four runs recorded on each record page was obtained, a marked decline across the page was found. The first runs pooled had yielded a deviation of 100 hits, the last only 4. The $CR_d = 2.07$; $p = .03$—a result that was suggestive and in the typical direction.

When the hits that occurred in the top half of the runs were compared with those of the lower half, the value of the top halves was significant ($p = .0008$) but the lower was almost at chance. The $CR_d = 2.11$; $p = .034$. This decline, too, was in line with the findings of most other workers in comparable situations.

Since each subject served in one session only, no chronological decline in the ordinary sense could occur, but the records of each test had filled a page, one for each die face, and therefore had made a chronological record of their individual tasks. Mrs. Dale had noticed that as the sessions progressed and she and the subjects got better acquainted, they all felt more relaxed and began to enjoy the procedure. She added that even the "no" subjects (the goats) began to talk to the dice, by the third or fourth sheet. The deviations on all of the record sheets *inclined*, too, instead of the decline the experimenter had expected if the novelty wore off and the subjects began to get bored. The first three pages gave a total deviation of +54, but the last three, one over twice as great, +117. The difference was not statistically significant, but great enough that Mrs. Dale felt that the trend had followed the social situation.

The remaining analysis, that of the rate of scoring of women versus men turned out to be of special interest. The deviation for the women was +139. The CR was a significant 2.89; p = .004. For men the deviation was only +32, with an insignificant CR = 1.63; p = .10. However, both showed very similar declines across the record pages. The women had deviations for the two halves of the record sheets (the first two of the four runs per page) of +101, and for the second half (the last two runs) of +38; the men, +54 and −22 for the respective parts of their pages. Thus, for both over half of the hits were on the first half of their record sheets, so that the men's results even though so little different from chance in totals, showed typical PK fluctuations in scoring rates. This suggested that the men's scoring was simply depressed for some reason, but essentially similar otherwise, to that of the women.

Mrs. Dale made a probably meaningful commentary in regard to her own attitude when testing the two sexes. She felt on the whole, she said, "rather tense and on the defensive with the male subjects, and wondered if they did not find the whole thing a ridiculous performance. But with the women subjects she felt more at ease and enjoyed their sessions thoroughly." It seemed not unlikely then that the male subjects had worked in a different social climate than the female and that this factor, too, like the incline during the session, was the result of a general condition. Here it looked as if it was directly related to Mrs. Dale's differing attitude toward the women and the men.

In view of the way the results came out and of the fact that Mrs. Dale herself was the only "constant" human factor in the situation, since the subjects came for one session only, she raised an interesting question, which, although not touched on in any of the previous PK reports, is one that can be raised in any experiment in which an experimenter and at least one subject are involved. That is the question: Who does it—the subject or the experimenter? Since the effect occurs without the introspective awareness of the person who causes it, it is impossible to be sure which one is the effective personality. The primary objective of most of the PK tests has been simply to produce results. The question of which person is responsible for them only comes up later. However, in most of the experiments in which more than one individual subject was tested, each one showed what seemed to be individual levels or patterns of scoring, and so the general assumption (a working one only) has been that the one who actually manipulates the dice or other objects is the one who exerts the influence.

In the present case the question was raised by Mrs. Dale and discussed at some length because she felt that in several ways the pattern the results took fitted her own attitudes more than one could assume they fitted those of the stream of subjects.

She reported that the PK experiment had special interest for her because of some of her own experiences that she thought were psychokinetic. On account of this she had a very strong interest in the outcome. But the stream of subjects could hardly have had as strong an interest in the results as she had. She felt, in fact, that the subjects may have served more to stimulate her own PK ability than to demonstrate their own. Even the lower scores secured by the men, she felt could have been the result that their presence made on her, and her ability to score, instead of the result of their own PK. Because of this difficulty of telling whether the subject or the experimenter actually exercises the PK that may be demonstrated in an experiment in which both are present, it well may be as Mrs. Dale suggests that the inherent ability of any given individual can never be known unless he tests himself alone.

Soon after finishing her first experiment Mrs. Dale planned the second one, to confirm and improve on the results of the first.[11] This second experiment was also carried out at the headquarters of the American Society for Psychical Research. It was conducted from May to December 1946 and was made up of three sections—(a), (b), and (c), which followed each other. Each had a different specific objective. A short outline of each section will be sufficient to give a general idea of the plan and scope of each.

(a) The objective here was to test the effect of distance on PK. (The only test on the topic that had been reported was Nash's first distance test, which is presented in the next chapter. In it the observer remained near the dice during the trials when the subject was 30 feet away from them.) For Mrs. Dale's experiment an arrangement was set up by which a subject 100 feet from the dice could release them from a container to fall down an incline and come to rest below. A camera and lighting equipment was so arranged that a picture of the dice at rest was taken automatically. Besides that, the two experimenters and the subject also took records of the results.

Since women had scored higher than men in the first experiment, Mrs. Dale selected all females as subjects this time. Forty-eight dice were released on each throw. Die faces were rotated as targets. Subjects alternated in throwing first at a distance, and then close up. In the distance experiments, all three individuals walked the 100 feet, each time coming back after each throw to record the dice and replace them in the container.

[11] Dale, L. A., and Woodruff, J. L., "The Psychokinetic Effect: Further A.S.P.R. Experiments." *J. Amer. Soc. psych. Res.*, 1947, 41, pp. 65–82.

Everything was controlled and in order for a perfect experiment. But the deviations turned out to be quite negligible.

(b) This was an attempt to repeat the original successful experiment. Since section (a) had failed to produce results, it seemed reasonable to think that perhaps too many departures from the earlier situation had been embodied in it and that some of these changes had prevented the operation of PK. The distance test was eliminated accordingly, and the equipment for throwing that had been used initially was reintroduced instead of the more complicated machinery of section (a). This time only six dice were used at a throw. Fifty-four subjects took part, again all women, and 1,296 runs were made. The result, however, was still a negligible and slightly negative one.

(c) The objective this time was to find whether a relation existed between ESP and PK. Fifty-four subjects, both men and women, were employed. Four dice were used and the same throwing equipment as in section (b). Instead of beginning with PK tests, an ESP test was introduced first. In this the subjects began with six runs of "DT clairvoyance," which means they guessed the order of six decks of ESP cards concealed in boxes on the table before them. Then each subject, as in the successful experiment, performed four runs of PK for each of the six die faces. Everything was controlled and rotated, of course. Finally, the ESP scores and the PK scores were correlated to see if they showed a relationship. A total of 1,296 PK runs were thus made and 648 decks of cards guessed. The PK runs yielded a deviation of −22. The ESP runs yielded an insignificant total of +70. They did show a touch of significance, however, in having a steep chronological decline to which it was again suspected that the experimenter herself may have inadvertently contributed. This was suggested by the fact that she added up the ESP scores when half way through the experiment and found that a deviation of 100 existed, which at this stage was significantly high. But the subjects of the last half showed a negative tendency and with a deviation of −30 reduced the total to insignificance. The author speaks of the "bad magic" which had been thought by some investigators to accompany the practice of evaluating results before the end of a project. That "bad magic" was in evidence here, and today it would be considered as the result of an attitude change in the investigator, since her degree of anxiety would increase as she realized the deteriorating situation and hoped and feared for the outcome. On the other hand, the PK scores were not tallied up in the middle of the experiment and they did not show a chronological decline. But neither did they show a significant correlation with the ESP scores.

This second attempt, thus, in spite of its magnitude and faultless design, or because of it, was a failure. Practically all the results were within the limits of chance fluctuation. The experiment nevertheless attests to the effect of a change in attitude, for as Mrs. Dale realized, her approach the second time was much different from the first, and with mental processes as subtle as the conscious and unconscious ones involved in situations like these (as revealed in her own analysis given below) changes are surely created, too, in the attitudes of the subjects.

Mrs. Dale's idea in her earlier experiment that she herself had probably been the effective "subject" was strengthened by the results of the present one and especially by these of section (c), in which she herself, by her midway checking of the ESP scores, could have been the effective influence. Her own idea of the probable reason for failure here is revealing. She says:

Despite the fact that *objective* experimental conditions . . . were similar in Series I and Series IIc, the results of the latter series did not confirm those of the former. The principal *psychological* variable may have been the attitude of the experimenter. The first series was undertaken in a spirit of adventure; there was intense curiosity to see whether or not the Duke results would be repeated under the conditions specified. Series IIc, on the other hand, was undertaken, as it were, from a sense of duty, and the experimenter's morale was low after the failure of Series IIa. She felt "morally obligated," however, to attempt to repeat the earlier experiment from which positive results had derived. Major interest from her point of view focused upon the ESP task, which provided something new in the test situation. One other factor may also be mentioned—even at the risk of sounding as if an alibi were being put forward! In a three weeks' period, the experimenter worked with over seventy individual subjects, each session lasting from an hour to an hour and a half. . . . It is believed by the experimenter that such intensive work, resulting quite naturally in fatigue and strain, is not conducive to the best results.

Rather than an alibi for null results, the great amount of hard work the tests of the second experiment involved can well be taken as a fairly reasonable explanation of the disappointingly low results. It was becoming clearer even then that PK does not necessarily function because of conscious trying to cause it to do so. The necessary conditions for the release of an unconsciously based ability are more subtle than simple direct conscious effort. The difference between the psychological situations in Mrs. Dale's first and second experiment was of course primarily a difference in herself as experimenter and indicates that the experimenter's attitude can affect the subjects in tests. In this instance the change was unintentional, but inherent. No amount of will power could bring back the first fresh enthusiasm of the initial experiment. One of the challenges of present-day research still is to find indirect ways to offset such inadvertent results of changes in the mental attitudes of experimenters as well as subjects that tend to follow when an initially successful test is repeated.

### DR. THOULESS' STUDY OF PSYCHOLOGICAL FACTORS IN PK TESTS

The first person who took as a stated objective the study of the psychological factors that affect the success or failure of PK tests was Dr. Robert H. Thouless, whose experiment with coin spinning has already been reported.

Later, in the fall of 1948, he paid a visit to the Parapsychology Laboratory at Duke University and became acquainted at first hand with the PK research going on there. When he returned home he used his Christmas holiday period to push through a further series of PK tests, because it was a time when he could give such a project his almost undivided attention.[12]

His objectives in this project, as stated were: "First to see whether I could increase the relatively scanty record of PK success reported from Great Britain. Second, to try to devise a method of experimenting which would eliminate the possibility of success being due to an unconscious skill in throwing or third, to precognition of the way the dice would fall."

In the entire experiment, Thouless worked alone. He threw four dice at a time, either by hand or by the device mentioned below. He constantly watched his results for suggestions that might have a bearing on the nature of the PK process. The experiment consequently was divided into parts, some of which were developments from observations made in the preceding one or questions that arose because of it.

While the contribution of the experiment as a whole comes mainly from the individual sections, their strength is increased by the fact that the total scores were significant. The experiment included 23,144 die throws, and yielded a deviation of +169⅔. This gives a significant CR of 2.99; $p = .003$. In addition, in those sections that permit the analysis, a significant chronological decline occurred, and a drop in scoring rate within individual sessions.

Since the total scores were significant, the separate sections of the experiment, of which there were three, can be taken the more seriously for the suggestions they make, whether or not they were statistically significant when taken alone.

Section 1. The point in this experiment was to remove en-

---

[12] Thouless, Robert H., "A Report on an Experiment on Psychokinesis with Dice, and a Discussion of Psychological Factors Favoring Success." *Proc. Soc. psych. Res.*, 1951, 49, pp. 107–130.

tirely the possibility of unconscious skills influencing the way the dice fell. A mechanical device for releasing the dice by a hinged bottom in the container was constructed, and the dice for each new throw were replaced in the same order and position. To avoid the possibility that the results could have been due to precognition, which, as explained in the foregoing section, was a recently raised counter explanation for PK results, Thouless devised a special method of target selection, which would make the precognition explanation impossible. Other experimenters had attempted to obviate the precognition possibility by selecting the target face by various randomizing means, including having subjects throw for targets "around-the-die," which was a method that controlled against dice bias and precognition. Thouless however decided to use a target order determined by a Latin square. This device, he felt, not only ruled out precognition, but had the advantage that the various sections of the experiment as well as the whole would be made up of individual tests having each face of the die represented as target an equal number of times.

A six-by-six Latin square was used for the determination of the targets for all sections except section 3. A six-by-six Latin square is an arrangement of the numbers one to six in six rows so that each digit occurs but once in each row and column. By following such a prescribed order, the subject would have no freedom to select targets by precognition.

A total of the 16,232 die throws was made, which yielded a deviation of 103⅔ hits, a nearly significant CR of 2.18; $p = .03$. Some of these throws were by hand from a cup, some by the machine. As other experimenters had found before him, the scores on the machine throws were somewhat higher than on the hand throws, but in them especially a strong chronological decline came in. The difference between the scores of the first 24 runs and the last 24 was 34. This gave a significant $CR_d = 2.7$; $p = .005$.

Section 2. Thouless then undertook a second experiment to see what caused the decline and if the reason was what he thought it was. He felt it could have been the result of the intense and concentrated effort he had made to crowd the experiment into the brief time of his vacation period. It seemed to him that the more he tried to hasten results, the less he succeeded. (Compare with Mrs. Dale's second experiment.) Therefore, he decided now to avoid the intense strain and concentration of the first experiment, and begin another which would be taken rather leisurely, and in shall sessions, at convenient intervals.

He used the machine for all of the official tests of this experiment. At each occasion he limited the throws to three for each digit of one column of the Latin square and set the limit of the whole project at 36 sessions, which would complete the square.

This experiment started off with positive scores, but after the first five sessions they began to decline. To see if the reason was the repetition of the task, a novelty was introduced in which he began reciting poetry as he threw, while still hoping the proper faces would come up. The method also tended to reduce conscious tension, which appeared to be a factor that inhibited PK. With this procedure, the scores continued to be positive until almost the end, the device thus appearing to be one that counteracted the tendency for the scores to decline. At the close of the experiment, the 2,592 die falls gave a marginally significant deviation of +42, a CR of 2.22 for which p = .026.

Section 3. This series of tests was the one involving "blind targets," already reported in Chapter 8.

As a result of his observations in these three series of experiments, Thouless discussed a number of points that could have a bearing on the success of a PK experiment, including the motivation of the subject. He thought that a balance between two strong and too weak a desire to succeed is necessary. Anxiety about succeeding militates against success, but a degree of desire is necessary. A gamelike atmosphere, he felt, is usually advisable because it can help reduce the tension that is likely to build up and that tends to defeat itself. He thought, too, it was advisable to set a limit to an experiment and not check results until then, in order to avoid the anxiety that might result (Mrs. Dale's "bad magic").

The chronological decline, Thouless thought, seemed to be a result of the repetition of the specific task and not a general falling off that would apply to any PK task that might be interposed at that time, for the decline seemed to be averted by introducing a novelty or distraction into the procedure. This tendency for scores to rise when a new condition was introduced did not necessarily mean that the new situation was intrinsically better than the previous one, only that it had the aura of novelty.

The question of optimum length of session was more or less uncertain, but Thouless' general impression was that comparatively short periods give the best results, for he had had better results when only three runs were made on each occasion than when a greater number was made. When the scores for each run of the three were pooled, the extra-chance scoring was found to have occurred on the first run, a result similar to that found by other experimenters, too. But later when a test was made using only a single run per session, the scores were at chance. Of course, the failure to score on the single runs could have had some other cause, especially since the experimenter was also the subject. Possibly an "innocent" subject would have performed differently.

By the time this research was done, Thouless' suggestion was that all kinds of emotionally stimulating conditions could well be introduced in the course of testing sessions, but they would need to be varied according to the results secured, some persons responding best to one kind of stimulus, others to a different kind. Thouless felt that he was still far from having solved the problem of successful PK scoring, but it is clear, too, that he had touched upon some important "do's" and "don'ts." Considering the great variation in the personalities of experimenters as well as subjects, he was probably correct in concluding that a foolproof formula for success is not possible even for ESP experimentation, and, he felt, even less so for PK since on the whole he thought it was the more "dirigible" of the two, in the sense of being the more quickly affected by the psychological attitudes of the subject.

## A PK BASEBALL GAME

Incidentally, Thouless' suggestion that a gamelike attitude would be likely to promote the occurrence of PK was tested later, but by a person who had probably not read the Thouless report. This was Douglas Steen, a businessman-physicist in Los Angeles, California.[13]

Mr. Steen had been following reports on PK experiments with interest and noted that they almost characteristically showed a chronological decline in success. This seemed to imply a drop in morale which he thought could be offset if a technique were devised that would automatically keep up the subject's interest to the end. For this purpose he, like others in the realm of ESP, thought that a test imbedded in a gamelike procedure might do it. The spirit of play, of fun, would create the proper attitude while the objective of winning would prevent a decline of interest as time went on.

Mr. Steen probably was a baseball fan. At any rate, the game he proposed to simulate was baseball. From the PK angle, it would mean that the objective would be to influence several targets simultaneously in a more complicated manner than had yet been tried in any test.

Steen worked out a method of procedure involving throwing one red and two white dice for each play. The red one would indicate the nature of the play, specific plays being assigned each face (for instance, the one or two face indicated a hit). The white dice would show the player's response (for instance, the combination four–four indicated a home run, with specific plays assigned each of the other combinations).

The object as in the real game was to score runs by registering hits, and consequently, the combinations that could bring this about could only be secured to an extra-chance degree by the

[13] Steen, Douglas, "Success with Complex Targets in a PK Baseball Game." *J. Parapsychol.*, 1957, 21, pp. 133–146.

proper manipulation of all three dice, a task certainly more involved than had been attempted in any preceding PK research. In this case, while a hit would be recorded if the white dice showed a combination in line with the play indicated by the red one, if the white dice turned up a favorable combination not called for by the face shown on the red, a "latent" hit only could be registered. This, of course, was less to be desired than an actual hit.

The game proceeded by innings as in regular baseball. The players were seated at opposite sides of a large rectangular playing surface with a small pool of red and white dice handy, but the same dice were always used throughout a given game. The dice were shaken in a glass before throwing. All three were recorded on each cast, the red one first. All plays thus could be checked and evaluated later.

Steen then tried out his baseball game with two subjects, whom he identified only as A and B. Between November 1949 and December 1950, he played 100 games with A and 14 with B.

The question of how to score the records was difficult, but the objective of course was to get actual hits, which meant the three dice in winning combinations. Latent hits meant that only two of the three dice were in accord with intentions. Thus it turned out that one measure of the amount of PK in the data was the proportion of actual hits and misses to latent ones. In the entire data, this comparison showed that the ratio of actual hits and outs to latent hits and outs was marginally significant; $p = .016$.

It was found, however, that a chronological decline over the period during which games were played had occurred. When the number of real and latent hits and misses in the first 40 games was contrasted with the number in the last 40, the difference was quite significant; $p = .003$.

Then when the record of "success" on the red die alone was analyzed, it gave still another indication of chronological decline. The successful scores, of course, were those when faces one or two came up. In the first 40 games, 32.9 per cent of the casts were successful, but in the last 40 (in both of which Steen and subject A were the players) the percentage of success was only 29.7. The p value of such a drop was .00002.

The results thus showed in several different ways that the complex target had been successfully hit well beyond the number of times that would be expected by chance. The PK force apparently acted in a way that took account of the relation between the red die and the white ones. The experiment thus added its bit on the question that had concerned Betty H. in her high-versus-low experiment (Chapter 8) and suggested again that PK can be shown even when the mental processes involved are quite complex.

The idea behind the game was that it would be a technique that would prevent a decline by bolstering the psychological attitudes of the players, but the fact that one did occur chronologically gave the best basis for statistical measurement. However, the game very well may have prevented a decline "in-the-run" so to speak. The desire to win may have kept results from falling off within an individual game. Or possibly the strength of desire to win decreased; if so, that could have been the cause of the decline.

The baseball game did offer a suggestive technique that might have been further exploited, although no further reports of its use have been recorded. As a technique for stabilizing the attitude of the subject, it apparently was successful only to a limited degree. After all, the problem of stabilizing the subject's attitude is hardly one for which a permanent, hard-and-fast technique can be expected. So far no technique has been shown to have a permanent effect on PK. But the successes achieved in this game experiment as a whole fairly well validated Thouless' idea that a gamelike attitude is likely to favor the expression of PK.

## PK AND PERSONALITY TESTS

About the time of Thouless' study on the effect of psychological attitudes on PK, a graduate psychology student then at the Parapsychology Laboratory, R. L. Van de Castle, attempted to correlate PK test results with certain standard personality measures.[14] Personality measures are based on the assumption of a degree of stability in the personality characteristics they measure, and thus are different from tests depending on temporary influences of specific situations.

The first of the psychological tests Van de Castle used was the Expansion-Compression Test. This is based on the manner in which a subject makes a freehand drawing. It had been found that certain personalities tended to draw boldly and clearly, and make good use of the drawing space, while others tended to make small cramped drawings, with faint lines, often using only a small amount of the available space. In these differences, personality differences, too, were indicated.

Van de Castle's results, after careful separation of the two types of drawings from a total of 31 subjects in which the two tendencies had been rated for their degree of strength, suggested a relationship between the personality types and the PK scores. A five-point scale was used to judge the expansive-versus-the-compressive type of drawing, and the level of PK scoring was found to vary according to the subject's rating on the drawings. The most expansive subjects (of which there were only three) had the highest scores, with an average per run of 4.22, where MCE is 4, while the lowest and most compressive group (again only three subjects) scored below chance, an average of 3.70. Although not statistically significant, the scores followed a smooth pattern of decline with decrease in expansive tendencies.

Another test that Van de Castle used was the sheep-goat difference, which Dale and Nash, too (Chapter 10), had used before him. Mrs. Dale had asked her subjects to say whether or not they thought PK was possible, thus dividing them into two groups, one of sheep, the other of goats. Van de Castle had asked his subjects if they thought PK was theoretically possible

[14] Van de Castle, R. L., "An Exploratory Study of Some Personality Correlates Associated with PK Performance." *J. Amer. Soc. psych. Res.*, 1958, 52, pp. 134–150.

and divided them into three groups, sheep, goats, and undecided.

The results of Van de Castle's test was that 13 subjects (sheep) said yes, and they had an average run score of 4.12. Nine (goats) said no and scored 4.03, and nine indecisives averaged 3.99. These averages too were not significant but suggested a tendency of sheep to score more positively than goats.

Van de Castle's subjects were also given the Rosenzweig Picture Frustration Test. It is a projective technique that attempts to measure the person's reaction to frustration by recording his response to a pictured frustrating situation. What would you do if: someone spattered mud on you? if you missed the train? But in this test, too, the result was not significant.

Among the battery of psychological tests to which this group of subjects was subjected was also the Rorschach mentioned by Rose above. This test involves 10 cards, each with a distinctive ink blot, which the subject interprets according to the idea it suggests to him. One of the features that can be judged from this test is that of spontaneity. From the differences on this point made in connection with the subject's responses to the ink blots, those rated as the most spontaneous seven out of eight, scored above chance with a +52; the least also seven out of eight, below, with a −23, a very suggestive difference. As the author said, "Further research may indicate that some other yet untried personality measure will turn out to be more powerful in separating high- and low-scoring PK subjects. Or perhaps no personality measure will be found that is actually related to PK performance. Regardless of the outcome, the question of what, if any, possible relationships exist between personality and PK definitely needs to be answered. . . ." No one however has attempted to answer this particular question. The situation still stands today much as the experiments reported in this chapter leave it.

As already indicated some of the projects of this chapter were specifically designed to test a psychological influence on PK, and some had other objectives. Those of Humphrey, Thouless to some extent, Steen, and Van de Castle each had a psychological point in perspective.

Humphrey's test suggested that two subjects in a test apparently do interact on some level, although the manner and extent of the interaction was not settled. Thouless showed the delicate balance between effort and boredom necessary for success with emphasis on method, the introduction of novelty. Steen too showed the precariousness of the proper balance of motivation, and Van de Castle, the difficulty of relating PK performance to specific personality traits.

In the projects in which the experimenters had individual objectives, the same theme came through, although of course inadvertently. The experiments of Nash and Gatling showed the contrast between subjects with slight as opposed to strong desire to succeed. Rose's test with aboriginal subjects, too, seemed to raise the issue of the proper level of motivation of subjects. Then his experiments with himself and Mrs. Rose, in conjunction with those of the Vasse couple, still seemed to illustrate the same point, or at least that of the effect on results made by the attitude toward the test taken by the subject-experimenters. Mrs. Dale's experiments were somewhat different in that the changes in attitude shown were apparently on the part of the experimenter primarily. However, her own differences of attitude both between her men and her women subjects and between the experiment as a whole the first and the second time, no doubt meant a change too in the subjects, however subtle and unintentional it may have been.

The general impression can scarcely help but be that the mental influences that seemed to operate here were very determinative of the level of results achieved. Within the range of average run scores shown by some of Gatling's subjects on the one hand and the general level of Nash's on the other, with the rest of the experimenters and subjects in between, the higher scores are found where the higher motivation appears to be.

Naturally the strength of motive or kind of attitude of different people cannot be expressed in CRs or p-values. Difficulties of measurement are too great. But even so these experiments tell something that cannot be overlooked about the circumstances under which PK is manifested most strongly.

However, even at the highest, PK results still are far from perfect. The degree of control of his ability that even the best subject ever shows is relatively small. But the hints given in experiments like these indicate the direction that methodological advances should take. They also show something of the kind of psychological factors that inhibit or enhance its operation.

# CHAPTER 10

# Variations in External Conditions

❧

I N the early exploratory and confirmatory periods of PK research, during which the first necessity an investigator felt was simply to get evidence of PK, the main variations that were introduced concerned the size and number of dice and various controls against skilled throwing and dice bias.

By the middle 1940s, however, when the trend of experimentation was toward a broadening of the conditions of research, variations in external conditions began to be tried out. Most of the experimenters who were involved in the innovations of this kind, as it happened, were not directly, or even indirectly connected with the Parapsychology Laboratory. One exception to this, however, was an experiment made by Betty McMahan of the laboratory, the Betty Mc. of the children's parties (Chapter 8); and for the effect of mental influences it showed the experiment could well have been included in Chapter 9.

## CHILDREN'S PARTIES IN THE DARK

Between April and September 1945, after finishing the initial experiments with discs already reported, Betty Mc. began a new series of tests still using discs, still the same apparatus and also the same subjects with the same social setup—children's parties. This time, however, the objective was a new one, that of trying out the effect of throwing in the dark.[1]

[1] McMahan, Elizabeth A., "A PK Experiment Under Light and Dark Conditions." *J. Parapsychol.* 1947, 11, pp. 46–54.

The effect of darkness on PK had already been touched on, as it will be recalled, in Chapter 5. Lottie Gibson threw dice in one series of tests in darkness and secured a significantly negative deviation. It seemed that the situation had somehow affected her ability to score positively. It had changed the *sign* of her deviation, to speak mathematically, but today the result can be taken to mean that the change in sign resulted from her reaction to working in the dark. But at the time Betty Mc. undertook to make PK tests in darkness, the question whether PK would occur in the dark was still considered to be sufficiently unsettled to deserve a further experiment.

In the tests that ensued, the subjects were all either adolescents or younger children, and all girls. Five parties were held, all at night, because the lighting was more easily controlled then. An equal number of tests, still using discs, were made when the lights were on and when they were off. In the latter condition, the record was taken by flashlight.

The disc-throwing apparatus, it will be recalled, consisted of a long cage mounted in the middle so it could be rotated. At each end, a wire basket was fastened and when one end of the cage was lowered, the discs gathered in the high end would tumble over baffles to the lower, where they could be counted before the next semirotation of the cage. In the light-versus-darkness tests, as before, 10 discs were used for each throw. A blue cross was painted on one side, a blue circle on the other. Two throws, or 20 disc falls, were counted as a run.

Each subject threw two runs at a turn under a given light condition and for a given face of the disc. When all subjects had had a turn, each one had a second turn in the reverse light condition, and for the opposite face of the disc. A die throw determined whether the first turn for each subject would be taken in the light or dark, and which side of the disc would be the target with which each subject began. This routine was followed except when it was necessary to use the conditions or disc faces still needed to equalize the numbers of each.

With conditions thus balanced, a total of 220 runs (of 20 discs) were thrown in the dark, the experimental condition. The deviation, while not significant, was +54. The deviation of the same number of throws in the light (−61) was not significant either. The difference between the two, however, was marginally significant (CR = 2.45; p = .014). It seemed thus that PK was probably involved, even if neither deviation alone was high enough to be significant.

An added reason for thinking that PK had occurred was because of the differences in deviation between the first and second turns. While not significant, the first turns gave a positive deviation of 21, the second a negative one of 28, just as had been true of the total deviations of the two turns of the earlier disc experiments. In fact this tendency for first and second turns to yield such different results is the outstanding one shown in the entire set of projects of this particular experimenter and, of course, is not an effect that would be apt to occur by chance alone, or by any other likely alternative to PK. Instead it shows that the contrasting conditions the experimenter meant to test in each set of experiments did not produce effects for either alternative that were nearly as pronounced as the simple one of preference for a first over a second turn. Although this result was not the one the experimenter was looking for, it was an unmistakable sign of lawfulness.

However, the result of the darkness tests here, needless to say, was a surprising one at the time. It had not been expected that these subjects would score below chance in the light, because on previous occasions when darkness was not involved, they had tended to score above chance in light.

Besides that, the positive deviation they now secured in the dark ran counter to Lottie Gibson's negative one. Results like these were difficult to account for before the psi-missing concept had developed. However, it seemed to be indicated that the subjects' attitude toward working in the dark was the factor that caused the difference, just as it had seemed to be with Lottie, for subjects in these tests were children and they had given evidence that they liked working in the dark. They thought the tests made when the light was turned off, when they all tried to get the target face to come up in the dark, were more fun, more interesting and exciting than the ordinary ones in the light. But Lottie G. was an adult working alone. After the first novelty wore off, the darkness must have been more of a bother to her than a stimulus, and so her attitude and the attitude of these groups of children can readily be supposed to have been quite opposite. As a result each group scored positively in the condition they liked the best. But why did they score below chance in the other?

Results like this have occurred so often in parapsychology tests that the effect has even been given a name. It is called the differential effect. It apparently means that when comparisons are made that are at least partly unconscious the mental process involved on the less-favored item is different from that of ordinary judgement. In ordinary conscious judgement in a case like this, the person presumably would continue to score the same as before in the light but simply do a little better still in the dark if he enjoyed that condition more. But it appears that when this choice is made unconsciously, the less-preferred condition becomes automatically "blocked," and therefore a negative score results. Apparently a situation is created on the unconscious level that is a little like the blockage that sometimes occurs, say when an individual must suddenly introduce a friend but cannot recall his name. Only in the test, however, he is unaware of the blockage until his negative score shows it.

The reasons for the blockage in such negative scoring are still being studied, but in the meantime experimenters now know that a comparison like this is almost certain to call out the differential effect. Thus it no longer seems in such cases that the unconscious process is operating illogically. Once the laws governing mental action at a level below that of consciousness are known, they too can be seen to have a real sequence or logic. If on an unconscious level the effect of novelty is as strong as many experimenters think, and as Thouless, for one, showed it was for him, it is logical that Betty Mc.'s subjects should have responded best to the novel condition. To these children it did not matter half so much that the condition was darkness per se, as that throwing in the dark was something different, more interesting and exciting than in the light. The result therefore was logical, once the experimenter learned to interpret it.

Even at the time of the experiment, however, the results in the dark were considered to have been caused at least partly by the novelty of the situation and not as the direct result of darkness as such. Instead, the kind of result seemed then and still seems to be a function of the psychological atmosphere.

At the time also, the central logic back of the idea of holding children's parties to make PK tests (like that later expressed by Thouless and worked into Steen's baseball game) was that best results would be secured in happy carefree situations such as those involved in parties and games. In such circumstances psi would be more easily shown than in more rigid laboratory circumstances. The general level of results secured in these parties was not high enough, however, to bear out this expectation fully, in spite of the fact that the parties as such seemed to be successful social occasions enjoyed by all. It may well have been, however, that the parties were in themselves so much fun that the experimenters' objective of getting evidence of PK was overshadowed in the minds of the subjects by their own objective of having a good time. If so, the tests themselves actually became of rather secondary interest to the subjects, and they certainly were such by the time the second turn came and refreshment time approached.

### NASH'S FIRST DISTANCE TEST

About the same time Betty Mc. was testing the effect of darkness on PK, an experiment to test the effect of distance on it was started by Dr. Carroll Nash (Chapter 9). Now at the American University in Washington, D.C., Nash tried to find the effect that would be produced if the subject in a PK test were so far away from the dice that he could not see them fall.[2] In this case, he did not himself conduct the experiment, but a senior student assistant, Mary Lou Courtney, acted as observer-experimenter.

In all of the tests that had been reported thus far, the subjects had been within a few feet of the falling dice. (Mrs. Dale's distance test came later.) This was the first reported attempt to see whether scores would be affected if the subject was farther away from them. Nash, again like Mrs. Dale, also took up the suggestion from Schmeidler's work on ESP, that scores can be affected by the subject's belief or unbelief in ESP. He, too, wanted to see if PK scores would be similarly affected and the sheep tend to score higher than goats, as in general, they have tended to do, the former usually in the positive, the latter, in the negative direction. The supposition is that the goat attitude is more likely than the sheep attitude to produce conflict, consciously or unconsciously, and hence to lead to psi-missing, while the sheep attitude is less complicated and the subject more likely to respond spontaneously and without the reservations of the doubter, his deviation, therefore, tending to be positive.

Nine subjects were available to Nash, ranging in age from 15 to 44. To separate the sheep and goats they were asked if they believed that PK was a scientific fact and that they could demonstrate it. Six answered yes, and the others, no.

In order to permit a subject to throw the dice at a distance, a device was constructed with which the cubes could be released from a container by a long cord, and permitted to roll down an inclined board covered with corrugated cardboard to come to rest on the surface of a dice table below.

With this arrangement, half of the runs were made with the subject at a distance of 30 feet from the dice. But in alternation with the distance throws, an equal number of throws, for com-

[2] Nash, Carroll Blue, "Position Effects in PK Tests with Twenty-four Dice." *J. Parapsychol.*, 1946, 10, pp. 51–57.

parison's sake, were made with the subject only three feet from the dice.

The recorder, Miss Courtney, took the record from a fixed position near the dice table. She recorded the results on horizontal lines, each with 16 entries, but instead of regular chronological order, she put the three-foot results on the left half of the record sheet and the long-distance results on the right, dividing the two blocks of data down the page by a median line.

Twenty-four dice were thrown at a time, each throw thus constituting one run, and 16 throws, or one line of entries across the record page, was considered a set. The throws of a set were all made for a single target which the subject himself picked at the start, but subsequently he threw for all faces of the die in turn. As it turned out, the various faces were used nearly, but not quite, the same number of times.

In the beginning, distances were alternated with every throw for the first 8 throws, which made a half-set. But then for the first throw of the new half-set the subject kept the same distance as at the preceding trial, but after that, alternated again as before. In this way, the half-set was emphasized to the subject and his first throws for the two half-sets of a session were at opposite distances.

The subjects threw 47 sets in all. The total deviation achieved was +312, which was an average run score of 4.42 where 4.0 was expected. The result yielded a highly significant CR of 6.23, which would not occur by chance in millions of such cases.

The deviation at three feet was +179; at 30, +133. The deviation at both positions was independently significant but not the difference between them, and this fact seemed to mean that the greater distance had had no significant effect.

However, the fact that Miss Courtney had been in the same position near the dice throughout the series raised the now familiar question of "Who did it?" Was she, rather than the person who pulled the string, the effective subject? Although she was not consciously trying to influence the dice, she had strong reason to wish the experiment to succeed; thus the possibility of unconscious influence could not be eliminated, and the interpretation of results as far as distance was concerned had to be left undecided.

On the sheep-versus-goat test, there was no significant difference between the run score averages of the sheep and goats, although the average run score for sheep was a bit higher than for goats. This was similar to Mrs. Dale's result, and also to Van de Castle's, and seemed to show that this particular kind of difference in the attitude of the subjects toward the test, while showing a slight tendency in line with that generally found in ESP results, did not affect PK as much as it did ESP. If so, there can be some logic in it for PK has an objective side that ESP does not. The actual throwing of the objects has an appeal of its own to sheep and goats alike that could very well tend to make the latter forget their reservations, as they get caught up in the "game."

As the scores were kept, with the two distances recorded on separate sides of the page, they were not actually in chronological order. But the chronological order of the throws regardless of distance could be reconstructed, and when this was done, in order to see if the usual QD decline was present, the $CR_d$ between the first and fourth quarters was 2.83; p = .0046. Thus this measure, as well as the total deviations, bore testimony to the presence of PK. But the objective of the test, to find the effect of distance, if any, was left unanswered, for the experiment had not clearly tested it even though the suggestion was given that it had no appreciable effect.

### NASH'S SECOND DISTANCE TEST

Two years later Nash again supervised a test at American University on the unsettled question of the effect of distance on PK.[3] This time the plan was to remove the ambiguity of the first

[3] Nash, Carroll Blue, and Richards, Alice, "Comparison of Two Distances in PK Tests." *J. Parapsychol.*, 1947, 11, pp. 269–282.

experiment by having the observer move with the subject each time the subject threw from the longer distance. (The same improvement in conditions Mrs. Dale included in her second experiment, which was also reported in 1947 but which unfortunately did not yield significant results.) However, even though in this test the intention was to repeat the earlier one with the necessary modification, some other changes too were introduced in the procedure.

One of the changes was unavoidable. Mary Lou Courtney was no longer in school, and another senior student assistant, Alice Richards, conducted this experiment. The other changes were made because it seemed as if they would be improvements. One was a reduction of the number of runs in a set from 16 to eight. Before, the half-set of eight runs had seemed to be taken as a unit by the subjects, and so this time the decision was simply to call the 16 runs of a session two sets. And because the constant shifting from three feet to 30 feet on every throw had seemed to be a nuisance and interruption, this time the subjects were asked to throw eight times at one distance and then eight times at the other.

Instead of the sheep or goat distinction, several other secondary objectives based on personality ratings were introduced. But the results showed nothing of interest in connection with them, so they need not be discussed here. Also, a test of the effect of giving or not giving rewards for high scores (two movie tickets) was included.

Forty-eight subjects participated. Again 24 dice were thrown at a time with the target faces systematically varied. A total of 1,536 runs were made. The deviation was +158, the CR was 2.21; $p = .027$—a value of only suggestive significance. The lowered level of scoring in this experiment compared to that of the earlier one is reflected throughout the various sections of results. Nevertheless, the trends shown have interest, especially those of the main objective, the comparison of the two distances.

At three feet, the 768 runs yielded a deviation of only +39, while the same number at 30 feet yielded a much higher deviation of +119, with a marginally significant (if taken by itself) CR of 2.35; p = .02. Since at the 30-foot distance no one remained near the dice, this time the point was strongly indicated that the interposed distance had not inhibited the operation of PK. The lower score at the shorter distance could be taken to mean that somehow the subjects had been more challenged and motivated by the tests at 30 feet than by those at short range.

The results on the comparison of rewards with no rewards were the opposite of that that had been anticipated. They yielded a CR of 2.04 for the no-reward trials, 1.09 for those with reward. Although neither was significant, it was reasonably clear that the offer of rewards had not raised the scores. But the idea of winning a small reward may have been slightly embarrassing to subjects the age and stage of these, or it could have been that the idea was merely a distraction and tended therefore to depress scores.

The outcome with regard to decline effects was even more contrary to expectation. In only one aspect was the expected decline found. That was between sessions when the first was a marginally significant CR = 2.18; the second only an insignificant CR of .95. In all other aspects, the expected declines were inclines instead. Chronologically, the last half of the experiment was significantly higher than the first, and also an incline was found in the sets on the page with a significant $CR_d$ of 2.73; p = .006, most of which occurred in the sessions of the last half of the set.

Since these subjects, like Mrs. Dale's, were mostly different in the second part of the experiment from those of the first part, the incline in results is comparable to the one she found. It therefore raises the same question: Were the subjects of the second part so much "better" than the first, or was it the experimenter who changed? Alice Richards, like Mrs. Dale, was present throughout, and at the end of the first half, she knew the deviation (−39) was slight. Although she was acquiring greater familiarity with the test and probably deeper interest in it, she probably too was feeling an increasing urgency to get results. If so, she could have transferred a higher level of motivation to the subjects who came later than she did to the first ones. Thus, in effect, indirectly or directly she could have been the one who exercised the PK, at least in this latter half of the experiment when she knew scores would have to improve if the project was not to be a failure. Also, presumably, she would have known the significance of PK at a distance better than her stream of subjects could have, and thus been particularly interested to see if PK would be shown at 30 feet. The situation, was really very like that of Mrs. Dale's and the question of who did it, again looked more as if the answer might be that it was the experimenter rather than that the subjects, whether she did it directly by her own PK ability, or indirectly by her effect on the subjects.

The experiment, however, again seemed to say that distance, at least up to 30 feet, does not inhibit PK. The question of longer distances still remained to be tested.

MCCONNELL'S DISTANCE TESTS

Some years after Nash's tests of PK at a distance, another experiment that bore on the question was made by Dr. R. A. McConnell at the University of Pittsburgh, who conducted a PK experiment presented in Chapter 6.[4] His new experiment was not aimed primarily at testing the effect of distance on PK, although he was interested in that aspect, too. He knew that earlier tests had given reason to think that the distances that had been thus far tried had not been prohibitive, and it suited his purpose very well now to separate his subjects from the dice and thus incidentally to make another test of the effect of distance on PK.

McConnell's major interest in this experiment was to see if
---
[4] McConnell, R. A., "Remote Night Tests for PK." *J. Amer. Soc. psych. Res.*, 1955, 49, pp. 99–108.

subjects could demonstrate PK when sleeping. He knew that ESP and PK both involve unconscious mental processes, and he thought it possible that they could operate during sleep as well as, or possibly better than, when the subject was awake. He thought, too, that PK might be a more favorable phenomenon than ESP to test during sleep. For one thing, it would not involve the uncertainties of recall and other difficulties of technique that beset ESP tests when the subject is sleeping. PK instead would leave objective evidence. The same dice-casting machine was available that he had used in his earlier test, the one that photographed the dice as they lay at the completion of each half-revolution of the revolving cage in which they were enclosed. In addition, the machine could be connected with a timer and set for a specified period to run for a given number of revolutions. The record then could later be taken from the photographs.

In the experiment that resulted, nine subjects, including McConnell himself, were tested. Each of them was at his own home, the nearest at least a mile from the machine, which was at the university. The subjects were first made familiar with the machine. Most of them participated in a preliminary daytime test with it. They were instructed to select their target for the specified night, preferably during the afternoon before the test, tell it to no one, but have it in mind and to think of it especially for 15 minutes before going to bed. During that time and before going to sleep, they were to try to avoid emotion-rousing thought on other topics, and to will their target number to come up during the test.

The testing periods with the machine were 15 minutes long, beginning at some agreed-upon quarter hour between midnight and 5 A.M. A quarter-hour chime clock was lent to the subject, to be placed in a nearby room several nights in advance of the first test. In this way, without necessarily being wakened, the subject could know at least subconsciously that the experiment was about to begin.

The results of the experiment as a whole were not significant.

Nearly 18,000 trials were made and the over-all deviation was +73.5, which yields an insignificant CR of 1.47; p = .14. But McConnell's own scores, taken alone, were significant. In 5,537 trials, his deviation was +66.5; CR = 2.40; p = .016.

Of course, from a statistical standpoint, it is not proper to take only one subject's scores from a group. But when trying to learn about an unknown like the effect of distance—and sleep—on PK, one is entitled to pick up every suggestion possible and remember it for future reference. This is particularly true when what seems like "mitigating circumstances" accompany it. In this case, it was McConnell himself who scored the major part of the total deviation of the entire experiment. No one would argue against the idea that the experimenter's interest and motivation in a test like this is likely to be higher than that of any of his subjects. And so the fact that his scores were the highest of all is meaningful. It gives a strong suggestion that such an experiment as this can succeed, and that the distance was not a barrier. Just how much it tells about the effect of sleep on the PK process can be left a question because it is not known whether or not McConnell was fully asleep when the machine was in operation. In any event, the experiment was encouraging and suggestive, even though not actually definitive.

A "BLIND" DISTANCE TEST IN ENGLAND

One of the most significant distance tests to date was reported from England in 1952 by G. W. Fisk, a member of the English Society for Psychical Research, and his colleague, A. M. J. Mitchell.[5] Fisk had earlier devised a special technique by which "near-misses" in ESP responses, a phenomenon commonly referred to as "displacement," could be evaluated. By using a target arrangement like a clock face, not only actual ESP hits could be counted

[5] Fisk, G W., and Mitchell, A. M. J., "The Application of Differential Scoring Methods to PK Tests." *J. Soc. psych. Res.*, 1953, 37, pp. 45–60.

but the misses could be evaluated as to their actual distance from the target position. Now he wanted to find a way to show whether displacement occurred in PK, too. It was in the course of making an experiment to test this possibility and of finding a way to evaluate it that Fisk made his distance experiment.

The procedure on which Fisk's major interest was centered in the light of other features in his test is of only incidental interest here. The method was based on the fact that in throwing dice for a specific target face, three possibilities can result. The desired face can fall uppermost and that, of course, would be a hit; or one of the four sides adjacent to the target face might be on top. That would be a near-miss, or a displacement of one; finally the face to come up might be the one opposite the target, a complete miss, or a displacement of two. By assigning a hit a zero value, a near-miss a value of one, and a complete miss, a two, Fisk had the basic data from which he could compute the amount of displacement present in PK results. He called this the "dice orientation" or DO method. He could also, of course, evaluate the same data by the old "face value" method (FV) and compare the two. He found evidence of displacement in his experiment. Evaluation of results obtained by the DO method showed that the amount of PK was greater than when he used the FV method, thus showing not only that displacement occurs in PK as well as in ESP, but also that his DO method was more sensitive than the other. The only difference in the method of experimenting was that if the DO method was to be used, the upper faces of all the dice of each throw must be recorded and not only the number of hits.

The experiment on which Fisk made the DO measurement may have been suggested by the "blind target" tests that had been reported by Thouless shortly before (Chapter 8). Thouless, it will be recalled, had thrown for concealed targets; only after throwing an entire run had he permitted himself to learn what the targets were.

Whether or not Fisk was aware of Thouless' test (Osis' similar one had not yet been published), he planned his own to cover the same points, by having subjects in their homes, at whatever distance, orient their PK tests to targets displayed in his home in Devon, England. The plan thus was one of testing with blind targets that were also at a distance.

Fisk initially selected the targets by throwing a die and taking the uppermost face as the target for the day. Later, to insure randomness, he selected the target by the use of a random number table. He displayed each target for 24 hours and changed them each morning at 8 A.M.

Fisk provided his subjects with a pair of dice (⅝ inch) which he had first tested for appreciable bias. Each subject in his own home made 100 throws of the pair from a cup every day and then mailed the results to Fisk.

Ten subjects took part in the test. The distances involved ranged from three to 300 miles. The total score secured was high enough to give an anti-chance value of 4,000 to 1. (A slight correction should be made for unequal number of targets.) Most of the deviation was contributed by four of the subjects and by one in particular, a woman, Dr. J. Blundun. She was an M.D. and lived 170 miles from Fisk. In 10,000 trials, her deviation was +117.3; p = .0015—a highly significant score secured with both the blind target condition and a longer distance than had been tried before.

A SECOND "BLIND" DISTANCE TEST IN ENGLAND

Work with Dr. Blundun did not stop with the 10,000 trials that were listed in Fisk's first report. Four years later, he, in collaboration with Dr. D. J. West, the English psychic researcher mentioned earlier as writing a critical review of American work on PK, reported further work with Dr. Blundun.[6] Altogether,

[6] Fisk, G. W., and West, D. J., "Psychokinetic Experiments with a Single Subject." *Newsletter of the Parapsychology Foundation, Inc.*, Nov.–Dec., 1957.

four more series were attempted with her under somewhat varying conditions. In the first and last of these series, the targets were enclosed and sent to Dr. Blundun so the feature of distance was not involved, although the targets remained concealed and the results were sent to Fisk to check. Results in these were marginal, slightly higher when assessed by the DO method. In the second experiment the subject became ill and the experiment was not finished. The third was of the most interest here because in this the targets were again at a distance, and also because of a variation in procedure involving their location. Formerly, all targets had been dispayed in Fisk's home in Devon, but now every other day the target was displayed instead in West's home in London.

At this time Dr. Blundun had never met either of the two men, but both had corresponded with her—Fisk, of course, in connection with the test made four years before. Whether West's correspondence had concerned the test, or whether she had any reason to think of him in connection with this test, is not stated. At any rate, she was not told of this change in procedure and because the targets had been in Fisk's home before, she must have thought they were there this time.

Targets were displayed on 60 consecutive weekdays, thirty days by each experimenter. The subject made 48 trials each day (16 throws of three dice apiece). The target faces were balanced and random. The result was a marginally significant score on Fisk's targets and only a chance total on West's. While the highly significant scoring of this subject's initial trials four years earlier was not duplicated in these later tests, the fact that she did not score on West's targets is a point of some interest here, and not too surprising, for even though PK apparently can operate "blind," it still needs to be *directed*. The directing, of course, is a function of the subject's, and may not be only a conscious orientation. As parapsychologists are coming to recognize, it may also be an unconscious and unintentional process. But in Dr. Blundun's case here, apparently neither a conscious or unconscious reason existed for her to orient any of her PK tests to targets not displayed in Fisk's home.[7]

The special contribution of the work with Dr. Blundun was the evidence it gave on PK at a distance and PK with blind targets. While it might have seemed an impossible task to expect PK subjects to succeed in hitting targets they did not know, these results look as if the task was made no more difficult thereby, for the levels of scoring reported by the four investigators who have tried the "blind" target condition, Thouless, Osis, Fisk, and Forwald were comparable to those generally reported when targets are known.

The studies of differing external conditions presented in this chapter seem to unite in suggesting (as in Chapter 9) that the outstanding feature shown by the results is that of *psychological changes resulting from them*, more than from the actual objective circumstances. In the dark, the subjects scored according to the situation they preferred; at a distance, they succeeded as if it were not there, as far as the tests permitted a comparison. In Nash's second test, the best suggestion was that the experimenter

[7] Another possible interpretation comes in, too. In earlier tests of ESP, Fisk and West had collaborated by having each prepare part of the test material in a test that Fisk administered. The result was that the subjects, who did not know of West's part in the test, gave significant deviations only on the material that Fisk had prepared. This has sometimes been taken to mean that some sort of preference for one experimenter over the other was being shown by the subjects. But as with so many first impressions in psi tests, later work is throwing a different light on the point. In this case, recent and still unpublished results show that subjects seem to discriminate (in precognition tests) between the persons who later check their records. But it is not a matter of preference of one person over the other, but of preference for the person who gives the test, and who, therefore, the subjects take for granted will check their responses, over the other person who will do so, and toward whom the subjects' attention has not been directed. This work is still in the pioneer stage, and may seem tenuous, even in psi research, but it begins to look firm enough to give fairly strong support to the idea that West's negative results are not necessarily against him personally, but only against him as a second and unknown person in the tests.

affected the results. But if so, the effect was a psychological one, whether she was actually the subject herself, or whether her influence operated through the student subjects. In the first of Nash's distance experiments, too, the question was whether the experimenter was the subject and produced the higher scores when the student subjects were 30 feet away. However, in light of McConnell's and Fisk's tests, the question whether a distance of 30 feet would be prohibitive is well bypassed, for both of them produced significant scores at a much greater distance than thirty feet.

The general impression given by all these tests then is that the physical conditions as such were not limiting factors. It was the internal conditions created within the people involved that really mattered, and this finding is well in line with the results shown in Chapter 9, in which it was the mental influences of the people involved, whether subjects or experimenters, that really affected the results.

CHAPTER 11

# A New Order of Target: Placement PK

ABOUT 1950 a new *order* of PK target objective was introduced into the research. It meant a basic change of technique. It also permitted new consideration of the old question of the nature, specifically of the "mechanics," of the PK process. Although in the new tests, dice (cubes) were still the target objects, the objective now was to divert their fall to a specified *place* (the right or left side of the dice table) instead of with specified face uppermost. Tests with this objective came to be called placement tests.

The question of just what the mechanics of the PK process could be was one that had often engaged the speculations of experimenters, but had seldom, if ever, been mentioned in their reports. JBR, in his book, *The Reach of the Mind*, had shown that PK is evidently dependent on the ESP ability.[1] He says, "When the subject influences the dice, he has to follow them in some intelligent way to exert whatever causitive action is responsible for the results. Naturally he has to do this exerting at the right point of space and the right instant of time. The essential mental action on the rolling cube takes place somewhere in its course before it comes to rest. . . ." Thouless, Osis, and Fisk, in their tests with blind targets, had then established the close relationship of PK and ESP, experimentally. But still the finer pointed question, *how*, remained.

Around the Parapsychology Laboratory at least, considerable off-the-record speculation on the question had gone on for years, even though it is probably true also that many of those engaged

[1] Rhine, J. B., *The Reach of the Mind*. (William Sloane Associates: New York, 1947), p. 128.

[ 218 ]

in research never thought much about it. Like the young gambler who brought his idea to JBR, and apparently never asked himself how he could make the dice come up according to his wish, so too, many of those who took up and followed his technique, spent little if any time asking how they were able to get PK results. They were too deeply engaged in finding out *whether* they could do so. But once the idea that PK does occur began to be taken seriously, the question of what principle must be involved began to be discussed more and more, although still very little, if any, reflection of it seeped into the reports. The general feeling then was that time spent in untestable theorizing would mostly be wasted time, and particularly so, early in the research when actual data that could be interpreted as giving information on the point were so few.

However, two different opinions began to be favored and advanced by different experimenters. One was something like a "loading" hypothesis, exemplified, in a way, by Miss Knowles' experiment in which she compared "psychic" loading with actual loading (Chapter 6). This idea was that a comparatively stable influence could be affecting the objects during a run, or set, just as if loaded dice were involved. The advocates of this idea felt that the force must be an internal one and probably not actually in conflict with physical theory.

The other idea was more in line with the one expressed above by JBR. It was that an external force was applied and that it was a temporary one, exerted at a critical instant to deflect the falling object from its course. It came to be called a *kinetic* theory in contrast to the *loading* theory. This idea seemed especially appropriate in the tests for dice *faces*. The new kind of test, the placement test, brought new considerations into the situation.

COX'S CHECKERBOARD TEST

In 1946 W. E. Cox, of Southern Pines, North Carolina, a businessman with an avocation of mechanical engineering and one who was actively interested in the problems of parapsychology, began to make PK tests with dice. He had been a frequent visitor at the Parapsychology Laboratory and over the years since has kept up an "honorary" association with it. The line of testing he initiated, however, was the result of a reflection of his that if rolling dice could be controlled as to face, it should also be possible to make them fall in a designated area, and *place* them according to will.

The change from face to place, however, called for radical changes in technique, including even changes in the numbers of hits to be expected by chance per die per throw. After trying out a number of preliminary arrangements to test his idea, Cox finally settled on one by means of which he made three series of tests.[2] As it turned out, the technique he introduced was in itself only an introductory and transient one and not very typical of the placement technique that was worked out later. But it was a first step, and a comparatively complicated one.

In these first experiments, Cox used the top of a portable typewriter case as a relatively deep open-topped receptacle into which to drop dice, as he willed them to fall in specific areas. The areas were indicated by lines marking off the bottom of the case like a checkerboard. There were 16 each way, making a total of 252 squares, eliminating the four corners, which were rounded. The squares were then numbered consecutively one to six beginning at the "top" row and continuing in such a way that no two adjoining squares had the same number. The objective was to make the dice when dropped in the box come to rest on certain squares designated by a given number, as, for instance, on the four spaces or the two spaces.

Using different subjects, Cox instructed each to take a cup containing 24 dice, and hold it about a foot above the center of the box and then invert it and spill out the dice while willing them to fall on the squares that had been designated beforehand.

[2] Cox, W. E., "The Effect of PK on the Placement of Falling Objects." *J. Parapsychol.*, 1951, 15, pp. 40–48.

The number order of the target was usually first the six spaces, and so on around the die. The subject threw four times consecutively for each of the six face numbers, each throw with its 24 dice thus being the equivalent of one run. By the time he had thrown four times for all six numbers, he had made 24 runs of 24 die falls.

The results of 480 runs made in this way were positive and encouraging, but not high enough to be statistically significant. Cox then tried using spherical objects instead of cubes. His idea, one that had frequently been advanced (and had been approached in the unreported attempts to see if round-cornered dice would give higher scores than square-cornered ones) was that spheres should be more easily influenced than cubes because they roll readily, while square-cornered cubes do not. Accordingly now, for 144 runs, 24 air rifle shot were substituted for the dice. But the results did not prove the thesis. The score was −8, practically a chance result. It seemed to mean that the fact that spheres roll easily is not necessarily an advantage, for, by the same token, they do not *stop* rolling as easily as cubes.

Cox then went back to the 24 dice, and again in 96 runs got a positive, but not significant, over-all total. This time, however, he introduced what was meant to be a comparison between place and face. On each throw not only the number of dice on the numbered place was designated as target but also the number of die faces uppermost of the same denomination wherever they were. Thus if the throw was for the places marked six, the number of dice with the six face up was recorded, too. However, one of the two objectives was made the primary one; the other, the secondary. The two types of objectives were alternated, each being primary or secondary in half of the throws. Although the subjects knew that the count for the secondary objective was being made it was not stressed, and they were only asked to concentrate on the primary one.

The results were intriguing in that they brought out a comparison between the effect of the primary as opposed to the secondary objective rather than solely one between place and face as targets. In fact, the difference between the scoring on place and face was negligible, but that between the total scores on the primary and secondary objectives (192 runs each) yielded a $CR_d$ of 3.44; $p = .00058$. The total deviation on all of the primary runs was $+58$ and that on the secondary was $-87$.

This result, of course, called for further experimentation and so another similar series of tests was carried out. In this, the trends were in the same direction as before. The difference between place and face scores was again negligible. However, the score on the primary objective (864 runs) was only slightly positive (38), but that on the secondary objective (864 runs), still negative (200), was so great that the difference between it and the primary was a quite significant $CR = 3.60$; $p = .0002$.

By this time, the results of all these experiments of Cox's indicated that dice could be *placed* by PK too. Face targets were not the only kind on which it could operate. He had also shown that a real psychological difference existed between a primary and a secondary objective. The only counter explanation to this conclusion that was suggested was based on a possible flaw in the way Cox had counted the hits. Naturally a die occasionally landed only partly on a target square. It was then necessary for him to judge whether a hit had been made or not, and if his judgments had been biased, the number of hits—or misses, for that matter—would have been exaggerated. To answer this possibility, Cox decided to make still another series of tests and this time to take steps to eliminate the chance of error in his judging of hits.

Accordingly, for his third series, Cox raised the lines in his box by stretching fine wires over them so that dice falling on cross lines would tilt toward the square they favored. It would be obvious where they belonged, and he would not have to make any delicate decisions.

With nine different subjects, he then made up another series of 576 runs. The results this time were similar to the earlier ones though the values in general were lower. Once more the difference between place and face was negligible. While the total primary objectives yielded a chance deviation (+4), the secondary objectives yielded a significantly large negative (−139; CR = 3.17; p = .0015), but the difference between them did not reach a significant level.

In the total experiment one value that was highly significant if taken alone, curiously enough, was that of the die *face* target when it was a secondary objective. It came up so much *less* than would be expected by chance (816 runs = −167) that the deficit yielded a significant CR of 3.20; p = .001. This meant that for some reason, face hits when they were the secondary objective were suppressed to a significant degree, a result (involving about half of the data) that indicated PK, operating however in an oddly obscure and negative way.

At the time of these tests (the late 1940s), a negative deviation like this was still more than a little baffling. Today it can be recognized as the differential effect mentioned in Chapter 10 in connection with Betty Mc.'s opposite deviations when she was comparing the external conditions of light and darkness. The effect carries with it the fact that the difference is likely to be represented by psi missing on one or the other of the alternatives, usually the less preferred of two items. In this present instance the consciously stressed target yielded positive scores, and the less consciously stressed, negative ones.

The differential effect has been studied in connection with ESP scores much more than with those of PK; but results like Cox's show the same general tendency in unconscious mental processes regardless of whether ESP or PK is involved, which is still further evidence that the two abilities are parts of the same process.

In his discussion of his experiment, Cox remarked that he had undertaken the placement test only with the idea of showing if PK could be demonstrated in this manner, too. However it was suggested to him that his results could have theoretical im-

portance on the question of the way PK acts on falling objects.
For it seemed that they could offer a possible means of distin-
guishing between the two hypotheses (the kinetic and the loading), since tests could be performed under the conditions of
placement that would exclude the loading hypothesis.

### THE CORMACK PLACEMENT TESTS

During the middle forties, several persons wrote to the laboratory because of their interest in the then recently published reports of PK experiments. Two of these began series of experiments
that eventually were completed and reported. One of them, Forwald, in fact did so many that they will be reported separately in
the next chapter.

The second experimenter was a retired businessman, George
Cormack of Minneapolis.[3] Originally he carried out standard
types of PK tests, throwing various numbers of dice for specified
target faces and pairs of dice for high and low combinations.
From time to time he reported extra-chance results to the laboratory, but his work on faces did not make a unit for publication.
In the summer of 1949, however, it was suggested to him that he
try the placement idea introduced by Cox.

In the meantime, however, the Cox checkerboard technique
had been modified. When Cox had explained his idea of testing
for placement to those at the laboratory after he had started,
but had not finished, his experiment, the consensus there had
been that while the placement idea should certainly be tested,
the technique he used might be impossibly complex. It seemed
likely that a subject might well be discouraged if asked to will a
number of dice falling at one time to be guided to six single
squares imbedded in matrices of other numbers. Even in the
realm of psi where those who knew the history of the discoveries

[3] Pratt, J. G., "The Cormack Placement PK Experiments." *J. Parapsychol.*
1951, 15, pp. 57-73.

had become somewhat used to results that proved the seemingly impossible to be possible, this task might fail because it looked so complicated. If so, it would not actually show whether or not dice could be placed by PK. A fairer test to start with, it was argued, would be simply to see whether the falling dice could be deflected by will power from their normal path to one of two specified locations.

Since a number of those at the laboratory were interested in testing for placement PK, an apparatus was built with a simple two-target arrangement. This device utilized the same principle as earlier ones for face-testing. It involved a centered V-shaped trough container for the dice fastened above a roughened inclined plane down which they could fall (Figure 6). But now the table onto which they fell was divided down the middle by a line (later a wire) into a right and left side, either one of which

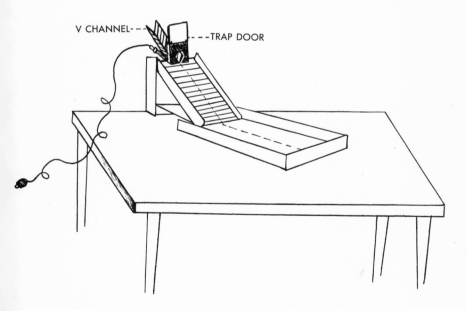

FIGURE 6. Typical placement apparatus, trap door raised.

could serve as the target area. With this arrangement, the earlier bugbear of possibly biased dice shifted to that of probably biased equipment. But here, too, the effect of bias could be controlled by the built-in procedure of always throwing an equal number of times for each side as target so that the biases would cancel. This type of arrangement or testing device became the typical one.

Cormack was then advised to use an apparatus like the one at the laboratory. He therefore constructed a similar one, and eventually reported nine separate series of tests in which he contrasted different sizes and weights of dice thrown in various combinations and alone, and with variations in the testing apparatus as well. In all, he reported 31,104 die falls from which he secured a total deviation of +690. This, over so many trials, yielded the huge CR of over 10, a probability of millions to one.

Spectacular results like these coming to the laboratory as they did from a private individual who was not personally known to anyone there and who had been his own subject throughout raised the same old question of what to do about "unwitnessed" work. The laboratory policy had always been necessarily conservative. But here insignificant results in some of the series Cormack had reported were mixed in with significant ones, and the very "perverseness" of some of the results seemed to speak for the honesty and reliability of the experimenter.

For instance, the results in different series with their variety in number, size, and weight of dice, fluctuated from series to series. The way they did so seemed to have nothing to do with the physical characteristics of the cubes. Instead, in a very general way, they seemed not out of line with the PK idiosyncrasies familiar in tests for dice faces.

In one series, for example, contrasting different weights of cubes of the same size, Cormack threw lead and light plastic cubes at the same time and got significant results on the heavier lead cubes, nearly significant ones on the plastic. But in a following series, he contrasted the light plastic cubes with still lighter wood ones, and got a significant deviation on the lighter kind, the wood cubes, and insignificant on the plastic. The wood ones were the more novel of the two. Later still, using all three kinds together, he got significant results only with the wood cubes but did not repeat the earlier success with the heavy lead cubes. These fluctuations seemed in line with those that had marked some of the comparisons of conditions in tests for face because they seemed to be connected with the varying psychological aspects of the tests rather than with the changes of physical characteristics of the dice.

Because of these internal fluctuations, then, it seemed that the Cormack results could be accepted as bearing on placement PK and showing, even by this placement method, the familiar tendency for psychological rather than physical aspects to be effective.

On the basis of this successful demonstration of placement PK, the inference was that the PK influence on the object must be a temporary one. In other words, it was easier to conceive of a placement result as produced by one "push" in the desired direction then as a longer term loading at the start of the fall. In a checkerboard situation, like Cox's experiment, it presumably would take the application of the "push" toward the end of the fall. The final statement of the discussion in the report of the Cormack experiments is, "This would pin the matter down to what we now think of as a kinetic hypothesis of PK, though it would leave open such advanced questions as that of exactly *how* PK acts on the dice." A "push" of course is only a partially descriptive word to cover an unknown.

### COX'S COMPARISON OF SPHERES AND CUBES

Sometime after his checkerboard experiment Cox decided to try another, also with a primary and secondary objective, this time to get a confirmation of the effect with the two conditions he had gotten earlier. The report of this experiment was published about two years after the first. In the meantime, several other experimenters, including Cormack, had obtained evidence of placement PK, and so Cox's interest was no longer centered on a comparison of place and face. However, remembering his earlier unsuccessful attempt to get placement results with spheres on his checkerboard arangement, he decided now to make another comparison of cubes and spheres. In the earlier experiment, he had used the two shapes separately. Now he decided to release them both together.[4]

However, this time he did not use the checkerboard arrangement, but instead he constructed a device similar to the one at the laboratory. He equipped his apparatus with a mechanical push button for releasing the dice, thus mechanizing it one step farther. He used 24 dice and 24 marbles at each throw and threw the same number of times for each side of the target area on which the objects fell.

He asked his subjects to concentrate for eight throws on one of the shapes (cube or sphere) as a primary objective, making the other secondary. Then for eight more throws, the shapes were reversed as primary and secondary objectives.

The result was an insignificant total deviation of −60. The distribution of hits on the dice versus spheres for 672 runs each was +102 on the spheres, and −162 on the dice. The $CR_d$ was significant, 2.93; $p = .003$, the more novel shape, the spheres, with which earlier Cox had failed to get significant scores, here yielding the positive deviation. On the two objectives, the result on 448 runs each, the primary was an insignificant −29, and on the secondary a still larger negative (−98). The $CR_d$ was insignificant, 1.21; $p = .23$.

The question, of course, is why did the change on spheres occur? The subjects used here were all different from and ignorant of the earlier results, although Cox himself knew them. If he had been the subject, one might suppose that his attention

[4] Cox, W. E., "A Comparison of Spheres and Cubes in Placement PK Tests." *J. Parapsychol.*, 1954, 18, pp. 234–239.

was focused on the marbles more than the dice, since he had already obtained positive deviations with dice, so that to him the marbles were more of a novelty. Whether or not the subjects preferred the marbles or whether Cox's special interest in them was somehow communicated to the subjects, or whether he (as the experimenter always present) could have been in some sense the subject himself, are all possibilities. The situation raises the same question of "Who does it?" asked by Mrs. Dale and others. It is still an unanswered one, but at this stage, it was not of central importance.

The effect of the dual objectives was not a clear one as before, but the comparatively large negative on the secondary objective was in line with the earlier result. The author suggests that this test with its own comparison of shapes also involved a "double dual aspect" (both the comparison of shapes and of primary and secondary objectives), while the first experiment had involved only a single one for in that one cubes and spheres had not been released together, as here. They were used in separate sections of the experiment instead. Whether this could explain the change is hard to say. It would appear that a faculty which could produce results on a checkerboard matrix as was suggested in Cox's first experiment should not be nonplussed by two such objectives as those employed here, but as already observed, the logic of unconscious mental processes is not necessarily the same as that of conscious ones. The questions, therefore, must be left unanswered. At least it seemed clear that both dice and marbles could show the PK placement effect, and since the deviations on both were roughly comparable, it looked as if the "ease" of affecting them was probably not radically different.

COMPARING CUBES, COINS, AND MARBLES

Soon after Cox's first introduction of the placement idea and the construction of the placement machine at the laboratory,

I, myself, undertook an experiment with it, one that ran from July 1948 to April 1949.[5]

I began before either Cox or Cormack's results had been reported, and when the idea was strong that Cox's checkerboard target complex was too intricate to give the possibility of placement PK a fair test. But my experiment did not prove that a simple two-target area would necessarily be better. The over-all results secured involved 113,100 trials, but the total result was not significant. This could have meant that the two-target placement idea was not a good one, but in view of the results achieved by Cormack and Forwald, some of which had been reported before I finished, this explanation obviously was not correct.

The explanation for the failure more likely lay in the over-ambitious nature of the experimental plan. Instead of using only dice for experimental objects, other shapes too were included for the sake of comparison and because I thought it would make the tests more interesting. And so, along with 10 dice and 10 marbles, 10 coins (quarters) also were used. Each kind was thrown separately five times for side A, and then five times for side B. All three kinds of throws thus made a set which included 300 objects. The plan was further to have each subject throw 24 such sets in each series of which there was a total of 15.

Two kinds of subject groups were used. One was made up of a small number of relatives and friends who understood the experiment and were interested in it and available so that they could complete the 24-set requirement. These were considered, therefore, as special subjects. The other group was made up of miscellaneous persons, mostly visitors and casual individuals who knew little about PK or the experiment and who could be present to take part in it only once or for a few sessions, but who had no enduring commitment to it. The results of the special subjects in the first chronological period were significantly positive, CR =

[5] Rhine, Louisa E., "Placement PK Tests with Three Types of Objects." *J. Parapsychol.*, 1951, 15, pp. 132–138.

3.01; p = .0026; but then a decline came in and the total gave only a slight positive deviation (CR = 1.37; p = .17). The total scores of the miscellaneous group were practically at chance.

In the comparison of shapes, the deviation of the coins was largest, but none of the three shapes yielded significant results nor results significantly different from the others, although different subjects expressed different preferences.

As the subjects did their tests, their results were recorded in columns 1, 2, and 3. Since the shapes used were staggered, each column then included an equal number of throws with each shape. The greatest statistical value secured occurred in connection with the columns and specifically with column 3. The results were: column 1, CR = −.07; column 2, CR = −.753; column 3, CR = +3.19; p = .0014. Although statistically significant by itself, the value for this third column of course could not rightfully by given full weight statistically because it was just one selected from the three, the total of which was not significant. Still it showed a familiar pattern beginning with Margaret P.'s results on doubles. Various other experimenters over the years had gotten inclines rather than declines as their tests progressed. For instance, Betty H. got an incline in her high-versus-low tests (Chapter 8), and Mrs. Dale got an incline over her entire first experiment (Chapter 9) as also did Nash in his second distance test (Chapter 10). In all such cases, the circumstances seemed to show the possibility that the subjects took the initial part of the experiment, as it were, to warm up to the task and only by the last part exerted a PK effect. This effect in this experiment was stronger than any difference coming from the shape of the objects thrown.

Other than this column difference, a chronological decline across the sets was suggested, for when all of the 24 sets per individual subject were divided chronologically into four sections, the first one only was significant, having a CR of 3.01; p = .0026. The rest irregularly declined, but the $CR_d$ between the first and last was not significant, CR = 1.37; p = .17. This seemed to show a gradual loss of interest or novelty value, just as was shown even in Steen's long series of baseball "games."

The lesson of this experiment was mainly that, in long drawn out experiments, subjects lose their ability to score successfully and that reasons for failure are not necessarily those that register on a conscious level. If conscious ones were prohibitive, Cox would have failed with his checkerboard experiment, for consciously the task seemed much more complex than any of mine. Cormack showed that a simple two-target area plan would work. But in asking my subjects for 24 sets, the task appears to have been too long. After the first six, the subjects ceased to score above the chance level. Another lesson, too, that these results suggested was similar to that given by Nash's captive subjects: that casual subjects, as most of those in the miscellaneous group were, are not likely to be sufficiently motivated to produce definitive results. Special subjects, well indoctrinated and really interested and determined are more likely to succeed.

### AN ATTEMPT TO COMPARE THROWING SURFACES

Further PK results were not reported from the laboratory for quite a time, as the trend of interest turned to ESP experiments rather than PK. (It is a curious fact that more parapsychologists have preferred to work with ESP than with PK.) But in 1956 a collaboration occurred between Dr. G. L. Mangan, whose initial PK test was reported in Chapter 6, and Dr. L. C. Wilbur of the Duke Department of Mechanical Engineering. In December 1955 the two conducted an experiment to compare some of the physical conditions that might influence PK in placement tests.[6]

Their selection of the one they decided to test began with a consideration of the effect of the shape of the test object on the PK result. In spite of Cox's final success using marbles, the

[6] Wilbur, L. C., and Mangan, G. L., "The Relation of PK Object and Throwing Surface in Placement Tests: I Preliminary Series." *J. Parapsychol.*, 1956, 20, pp. 158–165.

general impression was still that cubes made better PK objects than spheres, both because the latter in uninterrupted rolling tended to have more inertia and because PK would probably be more effectively expressed when the objects used were subjected to interruptions in their fall. The reasoning was that when interrupted, the object would be in a transitory state of unstable equilibrium, and so particularly susceptible to an external force like PK while a sphere would not offer any opportunity of that kind. Therefore if results were really better with cubes, it must be either because of the shape of the object and so ascribable to physical forces, or because the subjects preferred them. It seemed then that further research was called for to see which reason was the true one. This question was the one behind the research the two men undertook.

They decided it would be easier to test it by varying the roughness of the surface over which the objects fell than by altering the shape of the objects. In fact, if the surface roughness provided the necessary points of interruption, then spheres could be used and the same point tested that a contrast between spheres and cubes would have provided.

The experiment consequently began with a first series in which glass marbles (⅝ inch in diameter) were used on a medium rough, sloping runway. An apparatus was constructed in which 10 marbles could be lined up in a V-shaped trough, from which they could be released to roll down a glass surface roughened by sand imbedded in a coating of varnish. At the foot of the slope 12 chutes were placed into which the marbles would fall to be counted. The first six were on the right, the second six on the left. The trough above was, of course, aimed to deliver the marbles down the center of the runway, but to control for possible bias, the throws would be balanced in number between the two sides.

Ten marbles were used per release throughout, and 10 releases (five with each side as target), making 100 unit trials in all as constituting a set. Four subjects took part, and each one released 10 sets or 1,000 balls.

The total deviation for the four subjects (4,000 single ball trials in all) was +31. This was not significant. However, the test had started off well, for the first half had given a deviation of +64, which meant a CR of 2.86; p = .004. But then the rate of scoring in the sets of the second half of the experiment declined and yielded −33. The CR of the difference between the first and second halves of the experiment was 3.07; p = .002. A significant chronological decline is characteristic enough in psi-testing to take as a basis; it seemed here to show at least that the marbles could be influenced by PK. The decline, of course, would have to be interpreted as a psychological, not a physical effect.

The plan at the start had been to test various degrees of roughness and compare results in a second series of tests. However, it was decided that the same effect could be achieved by reducing the size of the objects used, as it could by using a rougher surface. Since it was easier to use smaller objects than to construct another, and rougher surface, a set of ⅜-inch steel balls was used in series 2. But the result was not significant. It was concluded, however, that this did not necessarily mean that the conditions were adverse from a physical standpoint. It could have been the result of changed psychological attitudes just as was true in Mrs. Dale's two succeeding experiments. In order for the comparison intended here really to be made, the conditions would have to be interchanged at intervals instead of one simply following after another. The test, therefore, was taken only as showing the need for further work with a better experimental design.

The two then continued their experiment. This time, however, they prepared three glass surfaces of differing and graduated roughness.[7] Each was first covered with a coat of varnish, and then fine sand was sifted on one, medium coarse sand on the second, and on the third, sand that would not pass a 16-mesh

[7] Wilbur, L. C., and Mangan, G. L., "The Relation of PK Object and Throwing Surface in Placement Tests: Further Report." *J. Parapsychol.*, 1957, 21, pp. 58–65.

sieve. Thus surface A was like fine sandpaper; B was fairly uniform with small voids caused by the clumping together of the particles; surface C was very rough and irregular.

With these surfaces, a new problem presented itself. If all runs were made at a similar degree of decline, the balls would drop very quickly down A and very slowly and even stall on C. It was, therefore, necessary to tilt the surfaces differently so that the time of falling would be approximately equal. This meant from about 15 degrees in A to about 45 degrees in C. The ⅝-inch glass marbles were again used.

Four subjects took part and the three conditions were alternated. Each subject released 1,800 balls. But again the results were not significant, nor were the declines. The best results—though not significant—were secured with medium surface B.

Still another series was then undertaken, and two new subjects were used. Since the speed of the balls had been held constant in series 1, it was possible that the chosen speed had been unfavorable, and so now the most favorable surface, B, was used and three different speeds of falling compared.

The apparatus was the same as before, but the tilt of the incline was varied, so that the fast speed would be about one and a half seconds; the medium about three seconds, and the third just fast enough so the marbles did not stall. But again no significant results were obtained. The medium and slow balls, however, yielded positive scores; the fast ones, negative; slight declines occurred, but they were not significant.

The experiment thus ended with inconclusive results. There was a suggestion that a degree of interruption favored success and possibly, too, that slower speed did also. But the only fairly clear result was to show the well-known tendency for chronological decline. It settled nothing about the physical factors involved. Unfortunately, neither experimenter was able to carry the inquiry farther. Like so many experimenters in PK research, since it was more in the nature of free-will contributions than of an organized and professional effort, Wilbur and Mangan had to leave still essentially unsolved the question with which they started.


### COX AND HIS THREE-TIER EXPERIMENT

Cox, however, was able to continue, and if the questions he asked one time were not completely answered, he restated or revised them in the next and went on into new experiments, usually, too, with a new apparatus.

Cox's next experimental report concerned a departure from the previous one, but his line of thought can be traced from that to this new one.[8] In the previous one it will be recalled, the two conditions he had contrasted had both yielded total results below the chance average, one of which was large enough that psi missing was significantly indicated. This phenomenon of streaks of negative deviation when positive deviations were desired, which for so long had plagued so many experimenters like himself, was still on his mind. He therefore wondered if such periods of missing the target necessarily occurred only in obvious streaks noticeable enough and great enough to be evaluated. It might very well be, he reflected, that at times when neither perceptible hitting or missing occurred and a subject appeared to be getting only chance results that both types of PK response might be occurring in such close and short sequence that neither could be detected in the final scores.

Carrying the question still further, he wondered if it might not be possible that hitting and missing by PK would occur in the same throw and so give no over-all deviation to indicate that PK had occurred. In fact, as he considered the matter, it seemed even possible that certain dice might somehow have a regular tendency to respond negatively while others had the reverse tendency. Cox does not say whether he thought of this possibility

[8] Cox, W. E., "Three-Tier Placement PK." *J. Parapsychol.*, 1959, 23, pp. 19–29.

as a kind of "loading" hypothesis, but in effect that is what it was. It was, however, in trying to think of a way to test the possibility, that the idea for some new test apparatus was born.

The essential idea was that the apparatus should have several sets of A and B target areas, and that if some of the dice were inherently negative in one set, they would be retained there, while others that might be inherently positive would be left free to go on to another target area.

The apparatus he then built was designed to test this idea (Figure 7). Gently sloping target areas were arranged in tiers staggered one below the other. Dice placed in the upper one when released would be able to divide into the target and the nontarget areas A and B, as before, but it was so arranged that those in the latter would be retained, while those that went to the target area would fall free into a chute that would deliver them centrally onto a second area divided into target and nontarget sides. There the same situation would exist and again the dice that fell on the target side would be delivered to the third and bottom tier, this one divided checker-board wise into target and nontarget areas; labeled alternately A and B, an arrangement designed to control against any tendency of the cubes to go to the left, since they had all come from the left side of the middle tiers (or the right depending on which was the target). On this third tier their positions would be counted and recorded.

As the apparatus stood when completed, the upper tier was six feet above the floor so that the subjects standing by the device could not see the dice in it. The bottom one was on the floor, however, and the second one was midway between; 20 subjects were used in the test. The target sides were alternated to avoid the effect of possible bias in the apparatus. The subjects were asked to think of all the target areas, designated as either the As or Bs before the test. However, it developed naturally that their attention came to be directed mainly to the bottom tier because they could watch the dice as they came to rest there, and that was the place where the definitive record was taken.

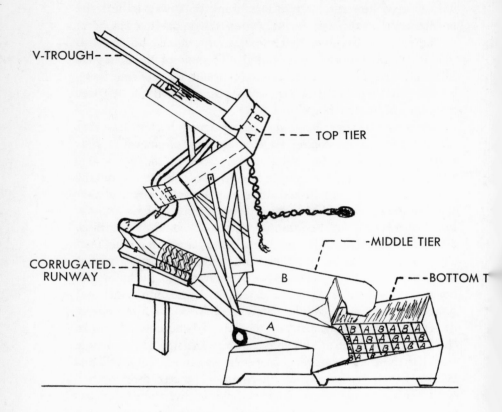

FIGURE 7. Cox's three-tier apparatus. From V-trough, cubes fall down runway into top tier; those on A continue through corrugated runway to middle tier; those on A fall onto checkerboard surface of bottom tier.

Cox, the experimenter, handled the dice and took the records. He recorded the numbers of dice retained on tier one and two as well as the position of those on tier three, and thus he could calculate the number of hits at each level.

According to the hypothesis that some dice could be negatively influenced at the same time that the others were positively influenced, the expectation would be, of course, that a large proportion of the "negative" dice would be retained on the first tier, while the "positive" dice would fall on down to the second level. Here again the same separation would occur. Presumably by the third level, most of the negative ones would have been retained and the proportion of each at the bottom level should be much higher for positive dice than for negative. In other words, the deviation on the bottom tier should be strongly positive, while on the upper one it might very well be negative.

The results bore out this expectation. Twenty-four thousand dice, 24 at a time, were released in all. On the first tier, 129 more than the 50 per cent expected had been retained, an insignificant negative deviation. On the second 35½ fewer than expected were retained, an insignificant positive deviation. On the third the deviation for the target squares was 118½, a quite significant CR of 3.07; p = .002. The bottom tier thus was the only one where the difference between the two target areas was significant.

However, although these results were in line with the hypothesis, they could not be interpreted as necessarily confirming it. The bottom tier could be seen to have a psychological advantage over the others and especially over the upper one in which the subjects could not even see the outcome of their throws. Instead, both subjects and experimenter were more concerned at the lower level. Also, the task there was the more novel one involving the checker board instead of the ordinary left-right division. This created a situation not too different from the one frequently observed in other experiments when runs are grouped in sets of three and when the tendency often is for the score on the third run to be the highest. My own experiment described previously is the most immediate example of this effect, but instances not too unlike it are scattered through the reports going back even to Margaret P. when throwing for doubles. Since any of these counter possibilities might have given similar results no conclusion could be drawn, and while this experiment gave one more demonstration of placement PK, it did not tell whether or not certain cubes are definitely set for hitting or missing the target on a given throw, nor help decide whether the loading hypothesis of PK action was more likely the correct one, than the kinetic.

### COX AND HIS FIVE-TIER EXPERIMENT

Dissatisfied with the ambiguous result of his three-tier experiment, Cox began to think of an apparatus by which he could further test his hypothesis of "negatively and positively imbued" (or loaded) dice.[9] Since the more favorable psychological situation of the lower tier had made the results uninterpretable, the new arrangement would have to be such that the subject's interest and involvement would be the same at all levels. If it was, then the proportion of hits should increase regularly as the cubes fell from one tier to another. The deviation at the lowest level would be highest, and it then could not be supposed to be so because the subject was most highly motivated on that last level.

With this in mind, Cox constructed a new apparatus. It occurred to him that the result might be more clear-cut if even more than three tiers, or separation points, were provided, and so he increased the number of tiers to five; the top one was lowered to four feet, and a chair mounted 18 inches above floor level was provided for the subject so that all tiers were quite visible. The release was mechanized, metal balls ($\frac{5}{32}$ inch) were substituted for the cubes and the count was also made automatically by having the balls fall into calibrated receptacles.

The plan was to release 100 balls per throw onto the upper tier, and by chance alone 50 should pass through to the second tier, 25 to the third, $12\frac{1}{2}$ to the fourth, $6\frac{1}{4}$ to the fifth.

Four experimental series were carried out with a number of subjects. Each series consisted of 25 sessions, 2,000 balls were

[9] Cox, W. E., "Five-Tier Placement PK." *J. Parapsychol.*, 1962, 26, pp. 35–46.

released per session, of which by chance 125 on the average should reach the bottom, and the A and B target sides again were alternated to take care of any bias in the apparatus.

The result was not a steady increase of proportions of hits as would have been expected if the hypothesis were fulfilled. Instead the first and second and fourth tiers gave somewhat negative deviations; the third, an insignificantly positive one; and only the last, the fifth in this case again, was significantly positive. The deviation on the fifth was great enough to yield a CR of 2.95, of which p = .003.

The results thus, in a general way, were similar to those obtained with the three-tier apparatus. In both experiments the top tier gave a negative deviation; in both, the bottom, a significantly positive one. However, the negative deviation above was not significant and since the only tier that did get a significant deviation was the lowest one in both experiments, it still seemed likely that in spite of precautions against it, the subjects' main interest had continued to be centered on the final tier where the objects were counted. But the fact that this was the place where the objects would be counted may not have been the only reason for the better scores on that level. At one point, Cox thought that perhaps seeing the dice there was causing that tier to be too interesting and so for half of certain sets he had the bottom tier shielded from view. But then the rate of scoring immediately decreased. It looked, therefore, as if the visual evidence, too, was part of the necessary condition contributing to the success on that level. It seemed very likely then that his attempt to equalize the appeal of all the levels had not succeeded, and that still the outcome was the result of the psychological situation. At any rate, it did not compel the view that certain cubes had been inherently repelled to the negative; others to the positive side. Instead, in both experiments, only the basic placement principle was confirmed.

Cox's curiosity about PK was in no way satisfied by his tiered experiments and their results. He next investigated a different area. In fact, he now departed so far from his earlier line of thought that the two papers which follow can hardly be said to be studies of placement. However, since that element is not entirely lacking in them they can be included in this chapter.

## COX'S ELECTROMECHANICAL SYSTEM

### The Clocks-Machine Number 1

The line of thought Cox now developed concerned the number of "events" in PK experiments and the way they are usually measured or counted. When a single die is thrown for a specific face, he considered that only a single PK event is involved. If six are thrown, six events are involved, and from all the experiments in which one or six objects had been thrown at a time, the total results with the six had usually been higher than with only one, although not necessarily six times as high. The difference thus did not appear to be caused by physical factors, but rather because the larger number was more interesting or for other, mainly psychological, reasons. But still, whatever the cause, the over-all value of the PK evidence secured with the large number of events per unit test was greater than with the smaller number. Presumably then, a still larger number of events than any yet tried should yield a still larger total result, whether or not in proportion to the number of events involved.

The logic of this line of reasoning led Cox to try to contrive an experiment in which the PK effect as measured would be "stepped up" by increasing indefinitely the number of events that would be provided on which the PK effect could be manifested. It occurred to him that one way to test the idea would be to use a spray of water.[10] Each droplet could be an individual PK event, and it would not matter that the number of them was uncounted and uncountable, if the total amount of PK that would be shown was an increase over that secured in the conventional

[10] Cox, W. E., "The Placement of Falling Water." *J. Parapsychol.*, 1962, 26, p. 266.

kinds of experiments in which the separate events were comparatively few.

Cox made an arrangement then with a bathroom spray mounted above a small grid whose narrow slits were connected with two vertical glass tubes. The droplets were to be collected in these tubes, one of which was the experimental or target tube, the other a control. They were used alternately as target and control, each an equal number of times. The subject was to will the experimental tube to fill faster than the control which would mean that some droplets would have to be deflected so that more than half of them would enter the experimental tube. He arranged a timing device to record the difference between the two. The test would thus still be one of placement but with water droplets rather than dice.

Cox obtained encouraging results with this arrangement, but the device was improvised and unsatisfactory, and so he rebuilt it on a larger scale, this time using an old automobile radiator as a grid. With this he reported 53.53 per cent of the trials he made to be hits, in that the water was higher in the experimental tube than in the control.

The apparatus, however, was still unsatisfactory in several ways, Cox thought, and so he proceeded to work out his idea differently. It occurred to him that clock timing techniques might be adapted to other forms of PK measurement. The water filling tubes were comparatively slow working, and so he decided to use an electrolytic saline solution and to pass an electric current though it directly. He reasoned that the sodium and chlorine ions, like the dice or the water droplets, would be the units on which PK would operate. The idea was that the effect of PK on the ions would change the fluid's resistance to the current. He thought he could measure the effect of such a change more sensitively with the timing device he had used in the water drop experiment than with a galvanometer.[11]

He used two electric stop-clock timers. One was connected in

[11] Cox, W. E., "The Effect of PK on Electromechanical Systems." *J. Parapsychol.*, 1965, 29, pp. 165–175.

series with four low-voltage relays (through which three pulses would pass each time the current was on) and the salt water. This was the experimental clock. The other was a control and its connections bypassed the relays and the solution.

Each clock had a sweephand that measured the time the switch was open, and in the difference between them the effect of PK could be shown. The experiment was set up to be performed in runs of 16 trials each; in half of each the task was to will the hand of the experimental clock to sweep out clockwise faster than that of the control, and then as the experimenter threw a reversing switch, to will it to return counterclockwise slower than the other so that the difference between the two would be as great as possible. In the other half of each run the task was reversed in order and the subject was to will the experimental hand to go slower and then faster so that its ultimate reading would be less than that of the control.

Target order cards were prepared in advance, eight printed with "fast–slow," eight with "slow–fast." These were shuffled by the subject who used the first one for the first trial, and so on, keeping the order concealed from the experimenter so that he could take the score "blind." He did this by recording at the end of each two-part trial the relative position of the two hands and the difference between them, indicating by a plus or minus sign the direction of the difference. At the end of the 16-trial series the experimenter's record and the order of the targets was compared, and hits were credited on those trials when the experimental clock hand differed from that of the control clock in the expected direction.

Before the subjects began their task, they were told about the saline solution and that when they wanted the hand to sweep longer to will the ions to cling to the electrodes; when shorter, to stay away from them.

Some of the subjects were members of the Parapsychology Laboratory staff. Some were visitors. The two groups were considered to be separate ones, however, because previous experience with staff members had shown that they usually reacted differently in psi tests from naïve subjects. In general, and according to a preliminary test Cox had made with some of them, they were likely to be analytical about the test, rather than spontaneous, and so to get negative deviations, if any. As it turned out, this kind of difference was shown again. The method-conscious staff group averaged below the number of hits expected. In 32 runs of 16 trials, only 46.48 per cent of their trials were hits. The visitors who made 40 runs all together averaged 56.72 per cent hits. This percentage yields the very significant probability against chance of .0007. The naïve subjects thus appeared to show that they had affected the system according to their desires.

With this success, however, the question was raised whether the PK effect had actually occurred *in the solution* according to the hypothesis, or elsewhere in the system, say, for instance directly upon the relays. To settle it, Cox then short-circuited the saline solution, or, in other words, cut it out functionally while still leaving it in place. Consequently, the device still looked the same but the current did not pass through the solution. Without changing the directions given the subjects, the tests were repeated; the results of staff and visitors still being kept separate.

Again the results for the staff were below chance; for the visitors, above; and at a rate comparable with the previous one. And so it was not the ions after all that had been affected by PK. The question now was, was it the relays?

In order to further test this question, Cox decided that if the PK effect somehow occurred in connection with the relays and the electric pulses through them, and if he increased these "PK opportunities," the result should be a higher deviation than before. Accordingly, eight pulses instead of three were sent through the four relays. Sixteen subjects, all of them visitors, did two runs apiece (a total of 512 trials). For the first, the subjects' attention was centered on the clock hands; for the second, the relay box was opened and the subjects told of its working. The result was better when the subjects' attention was only on the clock hand as the target, but neither set of runs alone yielded a significantly positive deviation. However, all the trials taken together gave a significant probability of .007. It looked as if somehow PK had operated in the system, and it seemed that it may have been in the relays, though other alternatives remained. The experiment thus was inconclusive, and it had not confirmed—or probably even tested—the initial hypothesis that a greater number of events taken collectively would yield a more significant result.

## The Clocks-Machine Number 2

A sequel to tests with the clocks-machine developed later when Cox turned the device over to other investigators to see if they, too, could get evidence of PK with it.[12]

The new experimenters were Mr. and Mrs. V. V. Akolkar from India, visiting research fellows at the Parapsychology Laboratory at the time. Their objective, besides simply getting evidence of PK, was also to test a method of evaluating results that Cox had found more sensitive than the count of all deviations he had made before. In looking over some old data he had noticed that more hits seemed to occur in the trials that had yielded a large rather than a small time differential. It seemed likely that most of the "noise" of the system would produce short time differentials rather than long ones and therefore that the long ones would be more likely to be caused by PK than the short ones. He wanted the Akolkars to use this method of evaluation, therefore, and he set the time differential below which trials would not be counted at .01 second.

The procedure followed by the new experimenters was the same one Cox had used in his experiment, except that two experimenters were involved in place of one. This meant only that the ar-

---

[12] Cox, W. E., Feather, Sara R., and Carpenter, J. C., "The Effect of PK on Electromechanical Systems. II. Further Experiments and Analysis with PK Clocks Machine." *J. Parapsychol.*, 1966, 30, pp. 184–194.

rangement was changed so that neither experimenter could see both clocks. Their independent records thus were a precaution against inadvertent errors in recording the positions of the hands. However, after 175 trials, the Akolkars were forced to terminate their experiments because it was the end of their stay in the United States. On these trials, they had secured 52.57 per cent hits which was encouraging, but the number of tests was too small to give a significant value.

After the Akolkars left, two student experimenters, Sara R. Feather and James C. Carpenter, continued with the tests, completing 964 trials in three series of tests. They used the same procedure the Akolkars had used. They also divided the data into two groups; one, the trials that showed a difference between clock hands longer than .01 second; the other, the shorter ones. They had 581 in the longer group; 383 in the shorter. The results on the 581 long differential trials were significant ($p = .01$), but the short trials did not exceed MCE. The Akolkar data showed the same effect. This result showed that this method of evaluation that took account of the length of time difference did in fact give a truer estimate of the PK involved than the earlier method of counting had done.

Feather and Carpenter carried out one other series of 228 trials with the clocks-machine. It yielded no deviation. But this series cannot properly be included with the rest of their work because of a change in conditions. In this series, which came between two of the foregoing, Cox removed two of the four relays. Although the experimenters felt that "something was different" in the way the apparatus worked, they did not know until afterward that the change had been made. The lack of results with the two relays then could have meant that the possibility of PK had been reduced so much that it no longer registered. Or it could have meant that the experimenters' feeling that "something was different" affected their attitude and, consequently, their subjects too were affected. Since, in Cox's earlier work, increased results were not secured when the number of pulses per relay was increased, and now none when they were decreased, the interpretation was still ambiguous. It was still unclear just *where* in this electromechanical system PK had operated. The possibilities had not been exhausted, nor the influence of concurrent psychological effects excluded. The main thing shown by the several clocks-machine experiments was that PK had been effective. The method of counting hits by using only those that fell into the longer time periods was shown to be a sensitive one. But since Cox soon discarded the machine in an attempt to produce a still better kind of apparatus, no further work was done with it.

On the question of *how* PK operates in electromechanical systems like the clocks-machine, not much light was shed by these experiments because the place where it operates was left undecided. Probably the best guess on that question possible now is that the actual method may vary according to the situation. Possibly if a "push" is needed (psychomechanical pressure), a push is given; if a current needs to be accelerated, or slowed down, PK does that, and perhaps if a clock hand needs to be manipulated, that kind of effect, too, can be produced. It looks as if the ability somehow is equal to the task, whatever its specific form. It is already clear that the various tasks that are involved in the different experiments vary too much to be covered by a single formula. The placement research threw enough new light on the old question to show that the answer is more complex than it looked at first. The range of possible answers is greater than can yet be envisaged.

Cox's efforts to construct a device by which the statistical significance of PK experiments could be "stepped up" did not stop at this point, although no further full reports of results have appeared. However, several preliminary ones have since attested to his continuing efforts to find a mechanical principle on which to construct a device that will give his idea a fair trial. Several more arrangements "along the way" to a final one have been tested in a preliminary way.

One of these Cox called a "multiple ball machine."[13] This was a device by which up to 200 steel balls in batches of 50 each could be released to tumble through a random distributing arrangement and disperse into six calibrated collecting chutes in a row at the bottom. Three of these were on the right of center; three on the left. The subject's task in the first half-trial was to will more balls to go to the left three or the right three, according to the preset target side, and those in the second half-trial to the reverse side from the first half. This split-target arrangement of course was a control for any bias that might exist in the apparatus. If more balls were recorded in the receptacles on the target side than in the other, the trial was scored a hit.

In preliminary tests a total of 39.5 runs yielded 57 per cent success, which Cox felt was enough higher than the success with any other arrangement to lend support to his idea that a "cumulative" method of measurement would yield a higher level of success than that of measuring PK "events" individually.

Later, the machine was tested by Robert Morris, a Duke graduate student who used high school and college students as subjects.[14] Morris reported no significant difference in the total number of balls that fell on the target as opposed to the nontarget sides. He did find, however, that the number of trials in which the majority of balls were on the target side rather than the other was not at chance, but instead sufficiently greater to yield a $p = .01$. This result seemed to mean that PK had been involved. It was sufficiently pronounced to fulfill Cox's objective of producing a higher CR than that obtained by considering each individual ball as one trial, but not high enough to prove much better than other devices might.

Again, Cox appeared not entirely satisfied with this machine. He continued to try out other ideas and with different devices

[13] Cox, W. E., "A Cumulative Assessment of PK on Multiple Targets." *J. Parapsychol.*, 1965, 29, pp. 229–300.
[14] Morris, Robert, "Further PK Placement Work with the Cox Machine." *J. Parapsychol.*, 1965, 29, p. 300.

has made preliminary reports with some of them, as having achieved more than 50 per cent success. Still, apparently no final "perfect" contrivance has been invented to permit a completely adequate experiment to be made to his satisfaction, by which he can measure PK more efficiently than has heretofore been possible.

This chapter has covered all of the work on placement except Forwald's. It has shown that objects can be "placed" by PK under a variety of circumstances—from the apparatus which simply lets cubes (or other objects) fall down a runway to spill out on either side of a table, to an unlocalized effect hidden in an electro-mechanical device. The research as reported opens new lines of investigation without deciding or closing any of them, for to a large extent this placement research is still at the early stage of finding the most effective technique. The psychological aspects as they apply here have not yet been as widely studied as they were when the targets were faces of the die rather than the place where they fell, but certainly those aspects are as effective here as there.

# CHAPTER 12

# Placement Experiments: Forwald

🙚

A VERY prolific producer of experimental PK reports, Haakon Forwald, a Swedish engineer[1] (in Ludvika, Sweden), has already been mentioned several times, particularly in Chapter 8. There an account is given of three experiments he made for die face targets after completing a record number of placement experiments. His placement experiments are sufficiently numerous and voluminous that they require a separate chapter in order to do them justice.

Forwald's research began about the same time as Cormack's but it loses nothing from being taken out of its chronological order in relation to the rest of the placement research. Nor is that affected by the deferment of Forwald's contribution. From the first, this experimenter to a large extent followed his own line of inquiry, one experimental project leading to the next with a kind of systematic logic, independent of the work of others.

When, in the late 1940s, Forwald first wrote to JBR at the Parapsychology Laboratory, he reported that with a group of fellow engineers some table-tipping manifestations had taken place which, although they could not be statistically evaluated, he thought gave evidence of psychokinesis.

JBR then suggested to him that he substitute dice-throwing techniques for the cumbersome and uncertain experiments with table levitations because the dice experiments could be conducted

---

[1] Mr. Forwald, an electrical engineer of exceptional attainment, for years (until his recent retirement) was employed by Sweden's largest electrical manufacturer, ASEA, and was at times sent abroad as a consultant. A prolific inventor, he holds more than 500 patents in various countries.

in laboratory conditions and also were amenable to statistical evaluation. The idea of placement PK, then newly introduced by Cox, was recommended as one in need of testing and further development.

Forwald quickly accepted the suggestion of transferring his efforts and using a more reliable and assessable technique and soon started PK research of his own. It began in 1949, and reports of it have continued to appear at intervals over the years up through 1968. With his engineering background, he was, of course, accustomed to experimentation in the physical sciences, in contrast to the psychological. In the physical sciences, the main verities with which the researcher has to deal are relatively fixed and stable; an experiment made today will yield the same results tomorrow if conditions are controlled and the same both times. Not so, however, in parapsychology. There the repetition cannot be guaranteed to produce the same result, because the conditions are not all controllable. When human beings are involved, situations are inevitably more complex than in the so-called exact sciences. In a psi test the subject is never exactly the same the second time as he was the first, the mere fact that it is the second time being one irreversible difference. This situation alone creates a natural gap between the fields and makes it especially difficult for physicists and physically oriented scientists as a group to appreciate the problems of parapsychology.

It is small wonder then that the path of Forwald's endeavor has been a tortuous one. It is an endeavor, however, not without its bit of drama, once one can see it as a whole. It has been a quest pursued with tireless determination that has produced an unprecedented number of series of tests (each including hundreds of die falls), each of which instead of bringing a final answer to the question toward which it was directed, brought instead only partial or contradictory answers and so raised further questions. However, once a perspective of the entire endeavor is attained, his contribution is valuable both for what it did and for what it did not show.

In trying to present Forwald's work a difficulty arises because his articles are confined largely to an objective report of procedures and results. Very little is said to indicate his psychological attitude toward the elements of his various projects, or to the logic back of them. On that account interpretations suggested here must be tentative, and very well may not be those that Forwald himself would make.

## 1. SUCCESSFUL PLACEMENT

For his first project, Forwald built an apparatus similar in principle to the one at the Parapsychology Laboratory.[2] It consisted of a dice container that was a shallow, flat-bottomed channel just long enough to hold a row of 10 dice (or cubes) and just wide enough to allow them to move freely. It was fastened at the top of a sloping runway, with a push button release on a cord (so that the releasing operation itself could not jar or affect the dice as they fell) The release then allowed the trough to drop and free the cubes to fall by gravity down the runway. The runway was made of fiberboard, rough side uppermost. It curved out and lengthened, horizontally, into a flat walled-in dice table.

The table was divided longitudinally first merely by a central line then after series 2 by a wire, into two target areas. To one standing behind the runway, A was on the right, B to the left. With the wire the question of doubtful "line" positions was decided objectively. The apparatus was set on a cement floor to insure stability.

In the first experiment 10 wooden cubes per release, precision-made by Forwald himself, were used instead of commercial dice. The experiment was divided into two series: series 1, exploratory; series 2, confirmatory. Two control series were also included in this first experiment. In these he merely released the cubes, while

[2] Rhine, J. B., "The Forwald Experiments with Placement PK." *J. Parapsychol.*, 1951, 15, pp. 49–56.

taking a neutral mental attitude, not consciously trying to direct their fall in any way.

The matter of controls calls for a few words of comment at the outset, since Forwald, who was his own subject, was also running his own controls. Much experience of other parapsychologists has shown that in psi experiments, controls made by the person who is both the experimenter and the subject are not likely to be reliable, for unconscious influences can affect and therefore contaminate the outcome. An instance of this, for example, was Harvey Frick's attempt (Chapter 4) in which his control series yielded results just as far from chance as his experimental series did, in spite of the fact that he did not consciously try to influence the dice at all. Naturally persons trained in the physical sciences are used to making their own controls in experiments in their field and so are unlikely to question whether they can do the same in this one. Forwald's controls, at least for a time, yielded chance results. In releasing the cubes in his experimental series, he said he always hesitated until he got the proper *feeling* that he had made a mental contact with the cubes and with the task. But on the other hand, as he released the controls, he did so at once without thought or time for thought.

In the first series, Forwald made five releases of the 10 dice for one side of the table and then five for the other. The 10 together were considered a set; each five, a half-set. Beginning with series 2 (below) a definite pattern of releasing for the two sides was established, which was A then B (one set), followed by B then A (the next set). This ordering of the sides later came to have a degree of significance not anticipated at first. In this series, 150 sets (15,000 cubes) were released, and a significant deviation of +147 was secured, CR = 2.40; p = .016.

Thus encouraged, Forwald undertook to confirm his results in series 2, and the series turned out to be really confirmatory, for in 250 sets it yielded a deviation of +353. The result was a very significant CR = 4.46, p = .00001. The two control series he made in this experiment yielded a chance result. When this experiment was published in the *Journal of Parapsychology* in 1951, along with Cox's checkerboard experiment, and Cormack's strongly suggestive results, the case for the PK placement method could be taken as fairly strong.

## 2. A REPETITION WITH UNEXPECTED OUTCOME

With the encouragement of these highly positive results, a second experiment followed soon after.[3] It seems to have been a logical outgrowth of the first.[4] In the first one, the indication was that the cubes had been deflected by PK. Obviously it took energy to deflect them, and it took as much as would be necessary to move that much mass the distance these cubes had been deflected from a random chance position. It followed logically that with a given amount of psi energy an object would be deflected according to its weight or mass: a heavier object would be moved less than a lighter one. This, of course, would be true if the amount of energy expended and other conditions were the same. Now in the second experiment the main purpose was said to be to inquire whether scoring levels would be affected by different kinds of cube materials and to try to relate them to the gross mass of the objects. Nothing was said about the kind of results expected.

Forwald then made cubes of as widely different mass (but the same size) as possible by using materials of differing weights. The materials selected were wood, paper (hollow), aluminum, Bakelite, and steel. With the same device as before in this second experiment, he used six cubes at a time throughout (instead of

[3] Forwald, H., "A Further Study of the PK Placement Effect." *J. Parapsychol.*, 1952, 16, pp. 59–67.

[4] NOTE: In 1950, JBR and I met Forwald in Sweden and conferred at length about his research. His main interest as an engineer was in the energy that must be involved and the question whether it could be measured. JBR encouraged him to attempt to make actual physical measurements.

10 as in the first experiment), releasing five times for each side in the same order as before: AB–BA; AB–BA.

This experiment included nine separate series (series 3–11) and several control series at the end. In some of the experimental series, one kind of die was used alone, in some three of one kind and three of another, while in one series two each of three kinds of dice were involved. But the total results, 27,000 cubes in all, and also the individual results of the separate series were all disappointingly insignificant. The differing materials, too, all averaged near the chance line, and the controls also were at chance. However, after four of the nine series of this experiment had been completed, Forwald noticed that the results of the AB-order sets were higher than those of the BA-order ones, even though the only difference between them was that the AB-order sets had been thrown for first.

Forwald then turned back to the data of the second series of his first experiment and found what he had not noticed earlier: that there, too, the results of the AB-order sets were higher than those of BA. When, just to see how strong the trend was, he added those results to these of the four new series in experiment 2, the deviation on the AB-order sets was significantly positive; on the BA ones, it was insignificantly negative. The $CR_d$ was a significant 2.56; $p = .0104$. This effect then could mean that PK was operating but in this unexpected fashion, in these four new series too, even though they did not have a significant over-all deviation.

As mentioned, Forwald had not been conscious before this point that the AB-order sets were giving higher deviations than the BA ones, but now he began to watch for the effect as he released the succeeding series. But when he turned his attention on it, the effect disappeared. "It was apparently some subtle little unconscious effect that was dissipated as soon as it became the object of conscious attention," he observed in his report. This described the situation, and in reverse it also described the circumstances under which the effect later reappeared.

Another analysis, too, was made, and this one too disclosed signs of PK in these apparently insignificant data. It will be recalled that each half-set was made up of five releases for a given side. Now Forwald analyzed the half-sets of the first experiment similarly. He found in it a general tendency for high scoring on the first release of the five, a decline on the second and third, and a recovery on the fourth and fifth. A graph of this tendency made a striking U-shaped curve for the releases of the half-sets. It was so pronounced that when evaluated (by chi square), it had a significant p-value of .007. In the second experiment, the same tendency was shown but not to a significant extent ($p = .11$), yet it was sufficient to add to the general impression that the PK effect was not entirely absent in the second experiment.

However, even a few encouraging signs like this did not remove the question as to why the results in this series were so much lower than before. The tentative parapsychological explanation would have been that the difference could have been due to a subtle change in motivation. Here, the main objective was not necessarily to repeat the high scoring of the initial series. Instead it was a more analytical attempt, directed specifically to trying to determine whether the different materials of which the dice were made would yield different levels of scoring. The change thus very well may have had a psychological cause, something like that of Mrs. Dale's second experiment.

### 3. INFLUENCED AND UNINFLUENCED CUBES

Forwald then started his third experiment.[5] This one included three more series (12, 13, 14) of 3,000 die falls each. The controls this time as before yielded chance results.

In this third experiment, Forwald used cubes of different mate-

[5] Forwald, H., "A Continuation of the Experiments in Placement PK." *J. Parapsychol.*, 1952, 16, pp. 273–283.

rials. However, he did not compare them as in the previous experiment. If he had done so he possibly again would have failed to score significantly. Instead, he introduced a novelty in procedure of a psychological kind. He continued to use six dice per release, usually of two different kinds, but he attempted to influence only one of the kinds and to give no "conscious consideration" to the other.[6] The kind of cube selected to be influenced in each combination was the one that appeared to be the more difficult to control. Thus in series 12, three steel cubes were used with three aluminum ones, the heavier steel ones being selected for influencing; in series 13, three rough and three smooth surface Bakelite cubes were used, the rough being selected for influencing; and in series 14 the influenced cubes were of wood, the others hollow paper cubes.

In all three series 4,500 die falls were "influenced" and the same number, of course, uninfluenced. The influenced cubes gave a deviation of 134, which yields a highly significant CR of 4.0; $p = .00006$. The ignored cubes apparently had not been influenced, for they gave an insignificant $-10$. The difference between the deviations of the two was significant, the $CR_d = 3.04$; $p = .002$. The change in method had worked, for with results like this, one can suppose the idea had been correct that the failure in the second experiment had occurred because the subject's attention had been divided when the target involved a conscious comparison between two kinds of dice.

The position effects on the five throws of the half-set of this experiment again showed a high result on the first release; the next, lower, and so on, as in the first experiment, but the effect $(p = .17)$ was only suggestive.

However, when the same analysis was made on the results of the uninfluenced dice, it was not so certain that no effect what-

[6] NOTE: This idea is the same as the one introduced by Cox in his comparison of cubes and spheres. Both investigators seem to have used it at about the same time. It is not clear if one suggested it to the other or whether each thought of it independently.

ever had been exercised on them. They showed variations in results in the releases of the half-set similar to those of the influenced ones and to a somewhat greater extent (p = .06). The suggestion thus was that PK had been operating in the uninfluenced dice, too, but in a less obvious fashion. If so, of course, the effect must have had an unconscious cause, since Forwald had not intended to influence those cubes.

But stronger evidence that PK was hidden in the results of the ignored dice was found when the "order effect" (AB–BA) was evaluated. By the time of this experiment, Forwald had practically forgotten about it after his failure to find it in the final three series of the second experiment. But now when it was no longer in his conscious attention, the effect came back again. He found it in the results of both the influenced and the uninfluenced dice —even stronger in the latter for the difference between the AB- and the BA-order results (in favor of AB) in the influenced dice was +48, but in the uninfluenced, +88. A difference of 88 between the AB and the BA sections of the uninfluenced dice results yields a significant CR of 2.62; p = .0087, a figure that, even though selected from the whole, still seemed to suggest that unconscious processes were influencing the cubes even in the "uninfluenced" section.

The deviations of 1,500 die falls each, or 60½ runs of the three kinds of dice used—steel, rough Bakelite, and wood—were +23, +39, and +72, in the order of their mass but hardly in proportion to it. Curious irregularities, however, had occurred in some of the series. For instance, in series 14, wood and paper cubes were released together, and the expectation would have been that the lighter paper cubes should be deflected more than those of wood. But the wood cubes had given a deviation of +72, and the paper ones had actually gone in the reverse direction (−12). This could have meant possibly that PK could not affect paper cubes, but in one part of an earlier series in experiments, a significant rate of scoring had been shown for the paper cubes when they were released with the wood cubes. Therefore, the failure here could hardly be supposed to mean that PK could not operate on paper. It suggests instead some difference in the circumstances of the two experiments. However, in neither case is enough information given in the reports to indicate what Forwald's attitude toward the two kinds of cubes was.

Another interesting effect was found that can best be laid to possible unconscious mental influences. At the end of the experimental series, Forwald, as was still his custom in spite of the doubts that any subject experimenter could make reliable controls himself, made three control series using the same kinds of dice respectively that had been influenced and uninfluenced in the experimental series. But now, as Forwald noted, there seemed "to be a carrying-over of the effects of the placement series into these control series," for in the first control series he reports without citing the figures that he got a relatively high positive deviation with the influenced kind of dice and also relatively high AB–BA declines with both, in spite of the fact that he had made no conscious attempt to influence the cubes, merely releasing both the "influenced" and "uninfluenced" kinds together. These position effects in the control thus, like those in the experimentally "uninfluenced" dice, can be interpreted as showing that here, too, influence was spreading beyond the conscious intention of the experimenter.

In the succeeding two control series, however, these effects faded out. The result strongly suggested that the specific mental set which the subject had as he performed the experimental series unconsciously carried over into the first control. This is not too hard to imagine. He had been engrossed in getting results on the influenced cubes and that no doubt became an unconscious as well as a conscious objective. The AB–BA effect, unconsciously produced in the experimental results, was unconsciously produced in the control, too. A peculiar circumstance about it, however, and one which tended to make that explanation less than convincing to Forwald, was that the control series had not been made until nearly two months after the experimental ones were finished.

By that time, it might well have been supposed that a specific mental set would have faded out. The situation thus still left much room for question as to interpretation.

#### 4. THE LIGHT OF CONSCIOUS ATTENTION

Forwald's next experiment, his fourth, probably was made more for social reasons than logical ones for it was one of the exceptional cases in which he used subjects other than himself. From October 1951 to March 1952, two engineering colleagues of his were his subjects. With them, 10,000 die releases were made under the usual placement conditions and with the initial objective only of trying to get significant total deviations. As usual the work was done in series, and, as it happened, almost from the start Forwald noticed that his subjects were scoring positively in the first half of the subseries and negatively in the last. After 3,800 die falls, both subjects contributing to the observed effect, they had a +41 in the first half and a −86 in the second. While their total deviation was not significant, the difference between the first and second halves of their subseries was. It yielded a CR of 4.0, which has a probability of .00006.[7]

Forwald, realizing this significant difference, was satisfied with the results his subjects were getting, but the subjects were discouraged. They only knew that their deviations were a disappointing low negative. It became necessary then for Forwald to encourage them. He did so by telling them about the significant trend their work was taking.

But once the subjects knew about the trend, it was like Forwald's own AB–BA decline. It ceased to appear. Instead their first halves now went slightly negative, and the second, mildly positive. Although not significant, it was a reversal, and appar-

---

[7] Forwald, H., "Chronological Decline Effects in a PK Placement Experiment." *J. Parapsychol.*, 1954, 18, pp. 32–36.

ently the result of the conscious knowledge the subjects now had of the effect.

Forwald considers the possibility that he himself may have been the effective influence in this experiment since he alone knew about declines, reversals, and the like; and he well may have been, but there is no way to tell. In this particular case, the subjects' own attitudes, whether or not in conjunction with Forwald's unexpressed one, could well be expected to have produced the reversal. Either way, it was neither the first nor the last time when the light of conscious attention seemed to change the direction of a trend of which the subject had been unconscious.

### 5. MEASURING THE ENERGY OF PK

After the project with his fellow engineers, Forwald in his fifth experiment made an attempt to measure the forces involved in placement.[8] He said earlier that in his successful tests he felt as if he exerted a side force on the cubes that diverted them in the desired direction as they fell. The next logical step then was to see if such a force could be measured, and in his fifth experiment, he set about to try to do it.

When a number of cubes roll down an incline onto a table below as in Forwald's tests, they move forward, of course, and also tend to spread somewhat in a lateral direction. But Forwald could only try to measure the energy expended in the movement in one direction at a time. He decided on the lateral direction. If he could measure the distance the cubes moved off their normal course to the right or the left side of the table, which he called the Y direction (in distinction to the forward, which he called the X direction), he could compute the number of dynes of force that had operated in their lateral movement.

[8] Forwald H., "An Approach to Instrumental Investigation of Psychokinesis." J. Parapsychol., 1954, 18, pp. 219–233.

The first step then was to calibrate the table so that the position of fallen cubes could be recorded. This he did by marking off the table surface into 1-centimeter-wide squares by lines running parallel with the sides and ends. (Figure 8.) Since it was 80 centimeters wide, he numbered the Y rows from zero to 80 beginning on the right, or A side, and the opposite lines, the X direction, from zero to 100 (the end of the table).

However, with this new arrangement, the objective of the experiment was changed. It was no longer simply that of getting

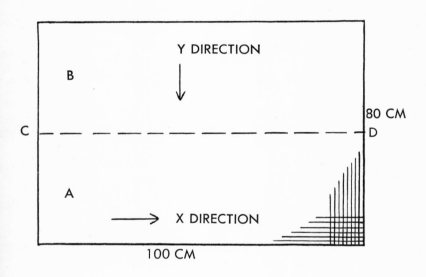

FIGURE 8. Forwald's calibrated table top. Surface marked into 1 cm. squares. Dice released from a V-trough over C to roll in X direction and deviate from C-D in Y direction.

as many cubes as possible to fall on the target side. Now the task was to get all of the cubes to fall as far to the right as possible when the A side was the target; and when B was the target, to get them all to fall as far to the left as possible, so that the number of centimeters of displacement for each target side could be recorded.

This meant that the positions of all of the cubes of a given release would have to be averaged to get a single representative position to be assigned to that release. First the averages of the five releases for one target side would be determined and then the averages for the opposite side. For instance, one might say that if those for side A in a single half-set averaged on the 35-centimeter line and those for the B side on the 42-centimeter line, then the difference between them of seven centimeters would be the average displacement. If 40 was the median and if the table were not biased, then a displacement of five centimeters would be shown on the A side and of two centimeters on the B. From figures like this, with the proper formula, the number of dynes required to move an average cube of a given weight that far could be calculated.

In the ensuing experiment, two series of tests (10 sets of wood cubes each, 630 cubes per target) and a control series (10 sets, 330 cubes for each target) in between were completed. The average position of the controls was at 38.89 centimeters instead of 40, the midpoint, showing a bias toward the A side. This however was controlled for since each side was the target an equal number of times.

All of the cubes released for the A side averaged at 36.26 centimeters, all for the B side, at 39.48 centimeters. The difference in average positions between the A side and the B side thus was 3.22 centimeters. The deviation on the A side of the average control position thus was 2.63 centimeters while that to the B side was only about .6 centimeters, showing as usual the greater effect on the A side. When the readings for the two sides were evaluated by the proper statistic (the student's T test of the difference), the difference between them was found to give a highly significant p-value of .0003, a definite indication that the cubes had been deflected beyond the position they would have taken by chance alone and in the intended direction.

However before making his calculation to convert the observed displacement result into dynes Forwald noticed that an unusual number of dice in his first release for the A side seemed to go as willed, to the far A side and stop within the 0-20-centimeter area. When the results for this release alone were tabulated separately he found that their average displacement was so much greater than that for the rest of the releases of the half-set that they accounted for practically all of the significance shown in it, a finding reminiscent of Pratt's in his analysis of the Pegram and the Gibson data in Chapter 5. It will be recalled that Pratt found that the significance there was limited almost entirely to the first throws of the runs. Here, Forwald's was concentrated in the first releases of the A side half-set.

The realization that the first releases for the A side gave results so much higher than any others raised the question if it could have been caused by some flaw in the apparatus. Forwald checked all possibilities carefully but could find no explanation of that kind. The only explanation had to be that it was the result of PK, which for some reason was concentrated especially in that particular part of the test procedure. Forwald's explanation at this point is that the aberrations "must be attributed to a physical influence of an unknown kind." A parapsychologist, however, by this time, would have been ready to suppose the influence to have been of a psychological kind, a combination of novelty effect and natural preference for A-side releases. Forwald then calculated the amount of force that would have been involved in the first A-side releases in this experiment and found that it must have been about 1,800 dynes, or 300 per cube on the average.[9]

---

[9] To arrive at the data for the calculation he first found the difference between the average reading for the whole series (37.91) and the average in the first release for the A set (28.50) which was 9.41 centimeters. The cubes weighed 2 grams apiece, and he estimated it took them .5 seconds to fall. With this data, by the formula given on pp. 230–233 of his article he was able to calculate the above result.

Forwald named his attempt at measurement the scaled placement method. One of its advantages he found was that it was
much more sensitive than the old method of simply counting the
cubes that fell on the target side. For instance, in his first series
here, he had secured only a deviation of 17 hits, which by the old
method yielded an insignificant CR of 1.33; p = .18. But in the
same series by the new method, p = .001.

It seems likely that to a physicist or engineer, a good reliable
numerical energy value like this would give a feeling of reliability
that the old method of counting cubes could never quite
give. At any rate after this experiment, Forwald at last could say
that these results "justify calling the effect a psycho-physical one;
and it is convenient to refer to it by the previously introduced
designation PK (psychokinesis.)"

From the point of view of a psychologist or parapsychologist,
too, it gives a certain satisfaction to be able to cite a numerical
value of energy expended in a PK operation. It helps in making
PK seem like a normal and legitimate force. Beyond that, however, it is far from clear that knowing such a value adds any
fresh insight into what goes on in placement PK. By getting an
average value for all the throws in a special section of a series,
the real puzzles and uncertainties that after all may be meaningful
hints to be interpreted, are merely covered up. Underneath the
average values here, there still remain facts like the concentration
of PK on the first A-side throw, the U-curve of the five-throw
half-sets, the greater effect on the AB than the BA-order throws,
even the indication of PK in position effects on uninfluenced dice,
and so forth. All variables such as these remain to be explained.
Since the effects vary in these different situations, obviously the
amount of energy expended in them varies, too. Since the amount
does not correspond to the physical realities of the test objects
the inquiry must go back to the psychological situations that do
vary with each experiment. The attempt, therefore, has to be one
of finding evidence of lawfulness in the complex and shifting
mental states, both conscious and unconscious, that obviously

are involved; but they, unfortunately, are difficult to measure, and in the reports under study are rarely even mentioned.

## 6. THE "CONTROL" PROBLEM

Forwald's next experiment with its unexpected outcome shows yet again the complicated interplay of conscious and unconscious mental processes.[10] In this one, his sixth, his main attention was centered on his control series. Although he does not expressly state the reason for the plan of procedure he used, presumably it was designed to give more information on the old question of whether his controls were true controls.

In this experiment then, each experimental series was followed immediately by a control series. The control series of course were marked by the *absence* of any conscious intention to influence the cubes. Thus all conditions were the same in them as in the experimental tests except Forwald's mental attitude.

Four more scaled placement experimental series (300 throws of 6 wood cubes each) were carried out, each followed by a control series of the same size. In the first of these Forwald worked alone as usual. In the second he had a subject. In the third and fourth he had two subjects. He attempted to stage a competition among them. The attempt did not succeed, however, and so only the first two series were of interest.

In these two series scaled placement tests were made as before. The result showed that the total average difference between the A and the B sides was 3.46 cm; p = .005. When the half-sets were analyzed, they showed the familiar U-curve; i.e., higher at the ends than in the middle.

The real interest of the experiment, however, of course was in the controls. Would they show signs of PK, too, and if so, would

---

[10] Forwald, H., "Experiments with Alternating Placement and Control Tests." *J. Parapsychol.*, 1955, 19, pp. 45–51.

they reflect the mental set of the experimental series just preceding?

They did show signs of PK for the half-sets, and did show a U-curve. But it was in reverse! The end throws were low and the highest scores were in the middle. By now a reverse was something to be expected when conscious attention was focused on a trend, and Forwald said that he did expect it.

This again, however, was an effect for which nothing in the physical situation could account. Forwald attempted to explain it by saying it was as if an unconscious state of "physical opposition" had built up, due, he suggested, probably to the monotony of the experiments.

To an extent he was correct. A state of opposition was indicated, but whether physical or psychical is the question. Also it probably was not so much because of monotony, for the effect of that would hardly have begun just in these tests. Instead it suggests that more was involved in these control series than Forwald was prepared to take account of. Naturally he, like anyone running control experiments, would certainly have preferred all along that his controls would yield purely chance results. Even on the conscious level, and still more certainly on the "lower" unconscious one, he would not want to see repeated here a reflection of the position effects that he had obtained in his experiments. The outcome thus could well have been the result of a mental set against effects like those in the experimental series. Whatever may have been Forwald's attitude, and he does not indicate in the report what it was, the reversal suggests so strong a motivation *not* to follow the pattern of experimental results (however unaware of it he may have been) that an avoidance reaction resulted. If so a reversed pattern would be expected.

The record shows that as Forwald's placement experiments continued he was faced with the fact that he was getting results the extent of which he could measure in terms of physical energy and yet they did not appear to fit familiar physical theory. But of course not everything had yet been tried. It was still possible that not all physical variables had been tested.

It will be recalled that in his second experiment Forwald had tried to compare the PK effect on different kinds and weights of cubes but that the experiment had not yielded significant results, and that when in his third experiment he took the types of cube that on a physical theory should be the most difficult to move, the heaviest and roughest, and gave them his primary attention, merely throwing an "easier" kind at the same time, he got extra-chance results with the more difficult ones but not with the easy ones. This did not make sense on a physical analogy, but at least it showed that PK could affect the rougher and heavier kinds of cube.

Whatever may have been the reason for inconsistencies like those, Forwald, having computed by formula the force in dynes that would have been involved in the 10 best throws of his experiment with two-gram wood cubes, now extended the inquiry into several other areas.

### 7. COMPARING ROUGH AND SMOOTH SURFACES

Long before the stage of Forwald's seventh experiment he of course was aware that his own and the parapsychological way of looking at his results were different. In the introduction to his seventh report he took time out to discuss "some general considerations which may facilitate the appreciation of the results on a recognized physical basis."

He briefly characterized the basis of the ideological conflict between the concept of PK (that physical effects can be caused by *mental* influence), and the general view of physicists on the topic. That view in a word was that since the mind is not a physical system, it cannot interact with any physical system.

Still, Forwald thought that it would be granted (by physicists, presumably) that if an experimenter specified in advance that he was going to look for a specific effect and then got it, such a result would have to be considered as "knowledge" even if it did mean that a mind exerted an influence on a physical object.

Possibly an explanation for the seeming anomaly of such a result, he suggested, could be found in the light of quantum mechanics. It is possible that the mental control may occur when the objects happen to be in a state of equilibrium, and then only a very slight force, one of "microphysical magnitude," (perhaps no more than the pressure of a light beam) might be required. As he says, "The mechanical laws of nature then would not be violated, since macrophysical causality would be maintained."

However, Forwald did not lean on this interpretation. He was an experimentalist, and this was a possibility that could not be tested. Also, he said it seemed unlikely that a sufficient number of such microphysical positions would occur to explain the results.

The only procedure then appeared to be to establish a physical *measure* that would permit a reliable comparison of results under different conditions, as is regularly the order of procedure in physical experiments. He called it a positivistic procedure and felt that the research was still at a stage too early for explanations. He concluded, "this kind of careful proceeding is without doubt the most promising way in so difficult a matter as the present. We have to build up our knowledge gradually, at no stage losing contact with *established physical facts*." [My italics]

In the ensuing experiment Forwald planned to measure the dynes involved in influencing heavier cubes than those used before and also to test the effect of varying degrees of roughness of the cube surfaces. He used 16-millimeter Bakelite cubes the same size as the 16-millimeter, two-gram wood cubes he had been using. These, however, weighed 5.6 grams.[11] Some of the cubes were left with their natural smoothness, some were covered with a network of fine depressions, and the roughest were covered with

[11] Forwald, H., "A Study of Psychokinesis in its Relation to Physical Conditions." *J. Parapsychol.*, 1955, 19, pp. 133-154.

glue mixed with fine sand. Friction coefficients were worked out for these cubes and for the wood ones used earlier. For the wood and roughest Bakelite the coefficient was nearly the same, .47 and .49 respectively. The other two Bakelite types were closely similar to each other, .38 for the smooth and .39 for the medium.

A number of series were run as usual. In the first series, three smooth and three medium rough cubes were released simultaneously, the attempt being to influence them all in like fashion. But for some reason, no significant results were achieved, and a control, run similarly, was also at chance.

In the next series, the roughest cubes were used with the smooth ones to make a greater contrast. Again three of each were released each time, the attempt again being to influence them all in the same fashion. But the results on the two kinds were quite different, and quite baffling to interpret. On the rough cubes in 600 throws, the average difference between the A and B sides was 2.45 cm. This gives a significant probability against chance of .014 in the expected direction. But the average difference between the A and B sides for the smooth cubes was −.48 which was, of course, not significant. On the first releases of the sets the differences as usual were very pronounced. With the rough, the average A–B difference was 7 centimeters, for which $p = .00027$; for the smooth it was −3.67, $p = .06$. The suggestion thus was that the smooth cubes, on the first throws were not merely at chance, but influenced in the direction opposite to intention.

According to expectation on a physical basis, of course the smooth cubes with a friction coefficient of .38 should have moved farther than the rough, with a coefficient of .49. On a physical basis, too, the smooth cubes should have moved in the same direction as the others.

The results, to say the least, show a strong favoring of the rough cubes, but no statement from the author is made to indicate whether he had a preference for one kind or any psychological reason to discriminate between the two types. However, the rough ones may at least have had a bit of added interest, for he had had to work on them to roughen their surfaces, but had had to do nothing to change the smooth-surfaced ones.

The difference between the results on the rough and smooth cubes was particularly pronounced when the A side was the target. In fact, taking that part of the series alone, it was great enough to yield a highly significant p = .00005; but even when the A and B side data were combined the difference was still a very significant p = .00011.

By this time, this favoring of the A side over the B was so regular an occurrence in Forwald's data that it might look as if it was caused by a bias perhaps resulting from the fact that Forwald usually stood on the A side of the table. But the floor was cement and so his physical weight could not have caused it. He had observed, however, that it seemed easier to "pull" the cubes toward him than to "push" them away. In this kind of situation, when no external condition interferes, it seems that even the slightest inclination or preference of the subject is likely to be reflected in the scores. It seems likely, therefore, that it was this feeling of Forwald's that led to an unconscious favoring of the A side.

About the tendency shown for the smooth cubes to go in the opposite direction from the intention Forwald said, "The smooth cubes—which were supposed to veer off to the same side as the rough ones—and conscious attempts were made to achieve this— show a different aberration pattern." When the A side was the target, the value of the difference between the rough and smooth was p = .00005, although when B was the target, it was not significant (p = .11).

Naturally enough, this anomaly was confusing, and Forwald was in the position of trying to harmonize the conflicting physical and psychological explanations. As he said, "the general opinion nowadays seems to be that ESP and PK have nothing to do with physics," but he argues that no crucial test has been carried out to show that there is no interdependence between the two. His opinion was that it was practically hopeless to control the psychological conditions quantitatively, but by his measurement method it was possible to measure the physical relations at least, and to see what similarities existed between them.

When he calculated the number of dynes of force involved in moving the Bakelite cubes it turned out to be 241, about the same as he had calculated for the wooden cubes in his first measurement experiment. Other similarities (too involved and detailed to enumerate here) had also impressed him, so that he felt he may have found a degree of basic physical lawfulness.

Then, too, from results like the opposite effect on first throws on the A side for the rough and smooth cubes, he arrived at the idea that there may be a sort of "oppositional behavior" between the two kinds of cubes. In other words, he suspected that they may tend to *repel* each other, perhaps particularly when "high" PK forces are operating, as in the first A-side throw. This then could be a possible physical relationship which could be tested by further research.

However, in turning attention only to these results that seemed to him possible signs of physical lawfulness, he had to leave unexplained others, such as the fact that more energy was apparently expended on the A side than the B; and the fading out of unconscious effects under conscious attention. Nevertheless by the end of this experiment he apparently had at least a suggestion of agreement in his estimates of the dynes of force involved in the wooden and Bakelite cubes, and it must have been an encouragement.

### 8. COMPARING LIGHT AGAINST HEAVY CUBES

In his next experiment, Forwald enlarged the range of kinds of cubes to test to see if he could continue to get results that would make sense, as he explored further the "psycho-physical" problem.[12] In the first new series, he tried throwing simultaneously three rough Bakelite cubes (5.6 grams per cube) with three heavier cubes made of aluminum (10.3 grams per cube). The aluminum cubes were smooth, like the smooth Bakelite, and could well be expected to act similarly and go in a lateral direction the reverse of that of the rough Bakelite cubes.

Again a surprise. By now it was coming to look as though when Forwald turned his attention to an effect that seemed to be developing, he thereby triggered off a reversal. And so here the aluminum cubes did not veer off in the opposite direction from the Bakelite, but they too went as intended. They showed an average difference between the A and B sides of 4.6 cm.; the Bakelite, of 6.36. With the number of trials involved, deflections as great as this give p = .014, which could scarcely be taken as a chance result.

The number of dynes involved in moving the two kinds were even farther from what might have been expected if the forces involved were operating with the regularity their physical properties should have produced. In the preceding series Forwald had found that the Bakelite cubes required a force of 241 dynes. And now, in this new series, the force involved was nearly the same, for it came out as 237. This result was of course reassuring. But the aluminum cubes had required 692 dynes for their movement, which was very upsetting; even though they had moved on the average 1.76 centimeters less than the Bakelite, their distance of movement was quite out of proportion to their weight. (Their weight was taken into account in the formula used to calculate the dynes.) The aluminum cubes weighed about twice as much as the Bakelite but the distance they had moved showed that about five times as many dynes had been expended on them as on the Bakelite cubes. In other words, they would not have moved so far if the same force had been expended on them as on the others. Up until this result Forwald had been able to maintain

[12] Forwald, H., "A Continuation of the Study of Psychokinesis and Physical Conditions." *J. Parapsychol.*, 1957, 21, pp. 98–121.

the idea of an amount of force expended per throw that would affect the objects in proportion to their physical characteristics. But now he was convinced that a different explanation was called for.

The main reason for the high value on the aluminum cubes from a parapsychological viewpoint could well have been a psychological one. These cubes were a novelty. (At least Forwald had never used them in a main experiment before.) Also, because of physical characteristics (brightness, smoothness, and medium weight,) they are usually liked by subjects in general. The same novelty value of the aluminum cubes could have been one reason they did not reverse sides, but went in the same direction as the Bakelite. Another reason could have been that even while Forwald was willing their direction, he half expected them to reverse. His conscious expectations, in conflict with underlying unconscious ones, have already been shown to be a likely cause for reversals. Again, there is no way to exclude the probable psychological factors. PK tests, after all, are tests of mental influence.

However, to one bent on finding a physical explanation, the result on the aluminum cubes could suggest again that not all of the physical possibilities had been exhausted. In any event, Forwald's next test concerned the material, the aluminum itself. He tested whether it was responsible for the high number of dynes involved in the movement of the aluminum cubes for it was possible on a physical principle that aluminum might have some peculiar quality of its own on which PK would operate in a special way.

In the second series of this experiment, then, Forwald threw six aluminum dice alone to see if he could get a confirmation on the large number of dynes that would be used, and he did; although a decline effect chronologicaly came in, and the number of dynes at the end was reduced to 485. That, however, did not disprove the possibility that the aluminum itself might be the special feature in the test that caused the unusual result.

If so, however, then Forwald's earlier explanation for the differing results he had gotten on rough and smooth Bakelite cubes needed reconsideration. He had supposed that the difference he obtained on them was the result of their differing friction coefficients (.38 on the smooth, .49 on the rough). But now the aluminum cubes, with about the same surface coefficient as the smooth Bakelite ones, had behaved very differently. However the rough cubes had been covered with glue and sand, the smooth ones with Bakelite varnish. This could mean that special attention should be paid the *surface material* of the cubes.

Forwald's next step was to coat wood cubes with aluminum. With thin aluminum coating, he got an increase in the dynes involved as the cubes moved in the desired direction, but it was still so much lower than the aluminum alone that it was possible that the interior too played a part. And so he thickened the coating and the dynes increased, this time to 430; but still it was not as high a number as that on the cubes made entirely of aluminum.

As the amount of force increased with the thickening of the coat, Forwald began to question the role of the surface material per se. And so he next covered the aluminum cubes with paper, expecting that if the surface were the effective part, then the number of dynes would be reduced from that with the uncoated aluminum alone.

Again—a surprise. The number of dynes increased instead, rising to the highest figure yet obtained with anything, 1,035. He then made a control series with these paper-covered aluminum cubes by throwing them quickly without consciously trying to influence them. But this time the control showed the reverse effect on the first throws of the sets. It was contrary to the experimental throw. This time, it showed to a significant extent, that as a control it was "contaminated."

The reason for this effect on the controls again could be a point of issue between a physicalistic and a psychological viewpoint. Forwald said of it that "it lends support to the opinion that the effects on these paper-coated aluminum cubes have been unusually strong and consistent." By this he apparently meant that something in the paper-aluminum combination itself caused a strong reaction even in the control, although even so it would not explain the reversal of direction in the control. The possibility that again it was an effect of unconscious mental influence *not* to secure results like those of the experiment is not mentioned, and neither is the possibility that his experiments themselves might also be "contaminated" by psychological influences, for Forwald still continued to try to follow the trail of possible physical relationships, while he disregarded psychological ones. However, in these various tests with aluminum, both uncoated and coated, the novelty effect may have been involved each time. It could have been a "contaminating" factor all along, added to his more or less unconscious expectations and desires. Just as he had said, these psychological factors were impossible to quantify. But that did not mean they were not operating. The main catch in all the effort to bypass his own psychological attitudes was that he was the subject himself, and as designer of the experiment he always knew what his intentions were. He had no way to insure his PK results against his own psychological processes. Although he seems to have recognized psychological effects when they came in consciously and intentionally, it was obviously very hard for him to recognize unconscious ones. The difficulty is shown by the long time it took to overcome his resistance to the idea that the making of his control series might not be a purely objective operation, and now he returned again to an argument that seemed to him to bear on it. That argument came up in connection with the difference he found between the nature of his results on the Y (lateral) direction of the table, and those he now got for the X (forward) direction.

The table had originally been marked off in both directions, but not until he began his scaled placement work had the X position, as well as the Y been taken into consideration. Now he turned back to the raw data from which he could determine and average the X positions, too, and evaluated the dynes of force their aberrations would have required. He found them at chance. A PK effect in the X direction, however, had never been part of any experiment, and so there was no reason to expect any evidence of it to have been produced there, either consciously or unconsciously. But the fact that none was shown apparently had implications for him in regard to possible unconscious effects in other connections. His conclusion was, "that the efforts are effective only in the intended direction."

In fact, at various times along the way, Forwald appears frequently to have found strength for the idea that his results followed his conscious intentions and not some hypothetical unconscious variable.

He continued to rely on the fact that the results of his calculations of the dynes of force expended on the rough Bakelite cubes were reasonably comparable from series to series, to show that the variations he got in the aluminum and coated cubes must have physical causes and not psychological ones. He does not elaborate the argument, but it would seem to be that if the psychological aspect with regard to the rough cubes is similar in different series, then there must be some equivalent variation, too, in the reaction of other kinds released with them. Such logic of course might be good in physics, but it is entirely fallible in psychology. The human mind with all its complexities and its hidden unconscious aspect is much too sensitive to every nuance of feeling or meaning for that.

Baffled as he obviously was by the conflict between the two kinds of influence in which he found himself entangled, Forwald now said that he would cease trying to make logical conclusions or to follow any "special" hypothesis and simply collect more data, the procedure he had referred to as a "positivistic" approach; and he made an earnest attempt to do just that. But the logic of the successive series of this experiment still shows the basic physicalistic orientation of his inquiry.

It is proper, of course, for an intelligent experimental plan to be oriented toward a "special hypothesis" as a tentative working model. The research is designed to test its validity. In this case, obviously no conclusion was reached, since the report of this, Forwald's eighth experiment, ends with a seemingly contradictory statement which appears to reflect his bafflement. He says, "It looks as if it is no longer correct to talk about PK *forces*— but rather of *mental effects.* The new experimental material suggests that the PK forces are not dependent on the subject's efforts alone, but also on the cube material."

### 9. FORWALD AT DUKE

It was after this report, which was in a degree climactic, that a novel interruption in Forwald's work came about. For all the years of his PK research, he had been working in his spare time at his home in Sweden and he almost always worked alone. His work thus was nearly all unwitnessed. The general tenor of it and of the man, too, had from the first been such as to excite confidence both as to carefulness and as to honesty. Although JBR and I had met Forwald in Stockholm in 1950, just when his placement work was getting under way, and though the meeting had done as much as such a meeting could do to confirm the confidence in him that Forwald's correspondence had engendered, still it was felt by all concerned to be highly desirable that a "confirmation," a two-experimenter experiment, be performed. Consequently, he was invited to the Parapsychology Laboratory in 1957 to demonstrate his PK ability and his technique.[13] Both Forwald and JBR felt that it would strengthen his case with the public in general if he would repeat some of his experiments in the presence of another person as observer. He accepted the in-

[13] Pratt, J. G., and Forwald, H., "Confirmation of the PK Placement Effect." *J. Parapsychol.*, 1958, 22, pp. 1–19.

vitation and spent October and November 1957 at the Para-psychology Laboratory.

Everyone recognized what a great psychological change it would be for Forwald to come to a strange country and to work in the presence of another person when for so long he had worked alone. With an ability as delicate as PK had shown itself to be, the change might very well prevent him from being able to pro-duce results. Therefore, the program scheduled was designed to give him every possible opportunity to adjust gradually to the new conditions, rather than to court disaster by trying at once to pro-duce a definitive experiment.

It was agreed by all, including Forwald, that he should begin alone and work by himself until he found himself sufficiently at home to be able to obtain significant deviations again. Then an observer would be introduced who would sit quietly and not interfere until the adjustment to that change too was made. Only then would he attempt a confirmatory test. And since it had developed so unmistakably that Forwald's significant results were concentrated in his first throws for the five-throw sets, it was de-cided that the objective of his work at Duke would be to secure significant results of the same limited type. The plan was fol-lowed closely, although it had to be somewhat more hurried than had usually been the pace in Sweden in order to get to the confirmatory stage before the end of Forwald's time in the United States.

When the first observer was introduced, scoring was almost at chance. Forwald said the presence of the other person made him self-conscious and interfered with his concentration. However, several different observers were tried and with one, Mrs. Peggy Murphy, he found himself sufficiently at ease that his scoring rate returned to normal. He had worked out with her a system in which she acted as cosubject and entered into the spirit of the test with him, while also keeping her own record of the scores.

Mrs. Murphy, the wife of a Duke graduate biology student, was a young secretary in the laboratory and had had experience assisting in experiments. She knew that her role in this one was to observe all that occurred and that the strength of Forwald's case might rest in part on her testimony. And since the significance of his work had come to be concentrated so much on the accuracy of reporting the first releases per set, she knew she should observe them particularly. She needed to be certain that the starting point for the first release of the sets was actually designated in advance. (The possible alternative to be guarded against was that Forwald might make releases "off the record" until a favorable result came up and then consider it the first one of the set.)

Twelve preliminary series (300 die falls each) were carried out using an apparatus similar to the one Forwald had used in Sweden. Then on November 12, the two started a confirmatory experiment, which consisted of two 300-die-fall series. It was concluded on November 21, just before Forwald had to leave for Sweden. It was a complete success for the average difference secured between the A and B sides was +21.47 centimeters, the $p = .00015$. This was not only the largest average of all the various preliminary series Forwald had done at the laboratory, but it was equal to the highest rate of scoring he had ever achieved at home. For the other series the average difference was 8.80; $p = .093$; the two probabilities combined give $p = .0002$. It was all the support and corroboration any PK experimenter could ask for, and Mrs. Murphy could attest to the fact that his first releases actually were first releases. She could corroborate his statement that he never made "off the record" releases but counted every one he made, and in every other way carried out his tests in a strictly scientific manner.

The trial thus ended successfully and Forwald could return to Sweden secure in the knowledge that his long and untiring research on PK would be accorded all the respect possible for the parapsychological community to give.

### 10. PK AND THE NUCLEAR CONDITIONS OF MATTER

After Forwald returned home he undertook another experiment that in size and scope probably represented the greatest effort yet. He outlined the reasoning that led him to it in the introduction of his report.

Going back to his seventh experiment in which he had tested cubes of different degrees of surface roughness, the results he said had supported the opinion that PK operated better on rough than on smooth surfaces. But he had to change this opinion later when (experiment 8) he tested light against heavy cubes it appeared that it was the *material* itself instead that seemed to effect the results.

In experiments undertaken at the beginning of the present study, new materials were introduced in the coating of the cubes and the thickness of the coatings were varied until, in his words, he "was led to a theory suggesting that there must be an exponential relationship between the measured energy and the thickness of the metal layer on the cubes. Experiments with copper and silver as coating materials gave support to this theory. The results further indicate relationships between the energy and certain *nuclear conditions* of the metal which is used in the cube coating."

The present experiment therefore was one to test out the nuclear hypothesis.[14] Later on in the paper when Forwald discussed his approach to the problem he explained that he did not intend to explore the "causal interaction between the subjects' 'will' and the physical system but the causal chain of events set in motion by the 'act of will' in the physical system, which events in turn are responsible for the observed effects."[15]

[14] Forwald, H., "An Experimental Study Suggesting a Relationship Between Psychokinesis and Nuclear Conditions of Matter." *J. Parapsychol.*, 1959, 23, pp. 97–125.
[15] *Ibid.*, p. 118.

This seems to be a rather clearer statement than he had made before that he considered the "will" only the influence that started the action, and that still, in spite of the irregularities and reversals in his data he felt that the "chain of events" was governed by the physical characteristics of the test objects. Since he had not found evidence of it when he tested the more obvious physical properties of the cubes, then others as obscure as the atomic structure of the molecules of the different materials must be investigated.

In the course of the resulting experiment at least his indefatigable persistence was demonstrated. For all persons not deeply versed in atomic physics, the rationale back of the details of his ensuing long series of experiments, the types and kinds of cubes he used, the measurements he made, the dynes, the ergs he computed, and the physical and mathematical equations that were involved, would make a complicated maze of reading matter. Those who are so versed can get the details from the report itself. Suffice it here only to enumerate the different kinds of cubes he tried out: beechwood, aluminum, and zinc (hollow) and then beechwood covered with various metals, each in three or four different thicknesses including aluminum, copper, cadmium, silver, lead and hexamethylene-tetramine, a compound with about 40 per cent nitrogen. In general the energy values he derived increased with the thicknesses of the coatings and decreased again when the coatings were removed. From this and other results Forwald found support for the opinion that he was approaching closer to a reliable physical constant.

As he worked, he said it was necessary to amend his tentative hypothesis as to the source of the energy involved in the placement results. According to his original supposition it was derived from the outside but then he was forced to consider that it might in some way be *liberated* within the material itself. According to this idea he explained it could be that "the mind action is of a relaying kind that is able to start an energetic process within the atom but does not convey energy to it."[16] Leading on from that idea, the next question was, if so, whether or not the energy is evenly distributed over the layers of coating.

However, although no final clear conclusion could be drawn after the enormous effort of all the tests reported here, Forwald thought his results did give strength to the hypothesis that PK involves *micro*physical processes. He still thought it possible that a "neutron emission" from the cube material might be the answer.

Then he says he discussed the results with several atomic and theoretical physicists who pointed out that such emission would have to be comparatively strong to be adequate to account for the observed deviations. If so, it should be easily possible to detect secondary radiation effects resulting from it by investigating the surface of the cube with a Geiger counter immediately after the experiment.

Accordingly, Forwald followed this suggestion under a number of different experimental conditions, but in no case did he observe unusual effects. His final remark after that attempt is, "At present, therefore, it looks as if the hypothesis of neutron emission must be abandoned."

One more attempt to find an answer, or at least a fruitful lead, was made. The possibility that some kind of magnetic effect might be involved led him to put the cubes through an induction coil in which any electrical effects could be measured by an oscilloscope. But nothing came to light to indicate that magnetic forces were involved in the placement results.

Thus it was that after all of the efforts leading off from the initial measurements on the wooden cubes, the record, at least to a parapsychologist, looks a lot as if the trail Forwald followed was a will-o'-the-wisp, ever beckoning on and on but never to be captured. This tenth report is the last one along this line of thought that Forwald has made to date, but from indications in it not the last research he intended to undertake in order to follow

16 *Ibid.*, p. 119.

further the *physical* vistas of exploration that he seemed to see opening up before him.

If further investigation of this kind should be reported by Forwald or any others who feel that the physical possibilities have not been exhausted, the results will be received with interest by the parapsychological as well as any other community—with one provision. That is, that naive subjects be used in order to rule out the possibility of contamination of the results by unconscious mental influences. Possibly however it was because of the baffling situation into which his "nuclear" theory and the unsatisfactory results of testing it had driven him that Forwald's succeeding reports for the following years, 1961, 1962, and 1963 were no longer on the topic of placement PK. Instead, he turned to *face* targets, and the three reports reviewed in Chapter 8 resulted.

### 11. MCCONNELL AND FORWALD

In 1959 a new player came on Forwald's stage. With his help, some further reports of Forwald's placement work appeared in 1967–68. The new player was Dr. R. A. McConnell of the University of Pittsburgh, whose earlier contributions to PK research were reviewed in Chapters 6 and 10.

McConnell, as a physicist, had been much impressed with Forwald's research and naturally felt that the world of physics ought to recognize and take account of it. A revolutionary principle like that of a mental effect on a physical system ought to be of supreme interest in the very field whose dogma it challenged. McConnell felt that if he could bring the work to the attention of the profession, and if he could show that it was sound, surely it would have an effect and lead at least some of the scholars in the field to take it seriously and investigate it. McConnell, however, knew from his own earlier experience that no journal of physics would be likely at this stage to accept an article on the topic of PK by Forwald, himself, or anyone else. Still, if he could get the material published even in the *Journal of Parapsychology*, he could privately distribute a sufficient number of reprints to strategic physicists and other scholars to make the attempt worthwhile.

And so McConnell invited Forwald to visit and work with him in Pittsburgh. Forwald accepted and spent a little over two weeks there in September, 1959.

At the University of Pittsburgh, in preparation for the visit, McConnell had constructed a device basically similar to the one Forwald had used at home but with several additions, particularly two motion picture cameras arranged to operate every time a button was pushed that released the cubes.

The cameras were introduced to afford a check on the possibility of recording errors and also to allow a detailed kinetic study of the way the cubes were pushed and bounced as they fell. Another check on accuracy was included, too, this one built into the cubes to be used. For the purpose, six precision-made maple cubes were marked individually. Hitherto in Forwald's experiments, cubes were placed in the trough in random order. Now they were to be placed in the same order and position each time. McConnell's objective was to remove every possibility that anything but PK could explain statistically significant extra-chance results. One possibility of criticism he thought might be that the falling cubes could so influence each other as to produce a spurious effect, but if the original order and position of the cubes was always the same, then variations in the results would be free from the possibility of such an artifact.

In fact, the main idea of McConnell's proposed collaboration with Forwald was increased precision. Since precision was a characteristic of both men, they apparently agreed entirely on the procedure by which a flawless experimental series should be made.

McConnell's reports of this collaboration began by a reexamination of Forwald's Durham experiment.[17] In his report McConnell reanalyzed the significant series Forwald had done there and came to the conclusion that it was substantially correct as earlier reported and that Forwald had demonstrated PK in his test series there when he had worked in the presence of Mrs. Murphy. McConnell even checked on the character of Mrs. Murphy (no longer at Duke) and added his certification that she appeared to have been an honest and trustworthy person.

Then, upon Forwald's arrival in Pittsburgh, but with no time for "warming up" to the new situation as he had had when at the Parapsychology Laboratory, Forwald began a series of experiments with the equipment McConnell had ready for him.[18] Using the six cubes placed in the same order and position on every throw, and with five releases for each target area per set as before, he ran 14 preliminary test sessions (without the camera) with eleven different cosubjects. But presumably the situation was too strained and unfamiliar; for no significant results were obtained. Two formal series (with cameras) and, in addition, a session with McConnell himself as cosubject, were carried out before Forwald had to leave, but they too yielded only insignificant results.[19]

After Forwald's return home from Pittsburgh, one question in his mind naturally was whether perchance he had lost his PK ability. In the first seven weeks after his return he carried out four experimental series on his familiar apparatus and with the cubes he had been using before going to Pittsburgh. The results

[17] McConnell, R. A., and Forwald, H., "Psychokinetic Placement. I. A Re-examination of the Forwald-Durham Experiment." *J. Parapsychol.*, 1967, 31, pp. 51–69.

[18] McConnell, R. A., and Forwald, H., "Psychokinetic Placement. II. A Factorial Study of Successful and Unsuccessful Series." *J. Parapsychol.*, 1967, 31, pp. 198–213.

[19] NOTE: It may be recalled that Forwald was at Duke over a month before he had been able to secure positive deviations there. The time at Pittsburgh almost certainly was too short for the delicate readjustment necessary.

well renewed his confidence in his ability for they were highly significant, and as before, the major part of the significance came from the first throws of the five-throw half-sets.

After these four series, Forwald was ready to make such special studies as he and McConnell might agree upon. They hoped, of course, to prove beyond cavil the primary fact of the reality of the physical influence of mind or will on the placement of the fallen cubes, and not, as in so much of Forwald's earlier work, to show *how* such placement is accomplished. The point still to be established in McConnell's mind apparently was to show that statistical results, if obtained, did not depend upon the equipment, design, or method of use.

In consequence, Forwald then made 10 more series of tests using four different release methods, in all of which the dice were always placed in the same order and position.[20] The first method of release was the customary one in which the pivoted trough swung downward when the release button was pressed, and the cubes tumbled out by gravity to fall down the inclined plane. Four of the 10 series of releases were made with this. In the second method the cubes were held in place in a sloping trough by a gate that was removed upon pressing a button so they could slide out and fall onto the inclined plane. Two of the 10 series were made with this. In the third and fourth methods the cubes were held in a horizontal column by pressure at the ends and, when released, all fell at once to the sloping runway below. In one case the horizontal column pointed to the center of the table; while in the other, the column of cubes was crosswise to the direction of roll. Two more series were made with each of these. While Forwald did not have the automatic camera arrangement that had been provided at Pittsburgh, he did secure professional motion picture photography of the effects of the different kinds of cube-releasing devices so that the paths of the falling cubes could be studied.

20 McConnell, R. A., and Forwald, H., "Psychokinetic Placement. III. Cube-Releasing Devices." *J. Parapsychol.*, 1968, 32, pp. 9–38.

In each condition, the results were highly significant, and, because of the variety of methods, the possibility of an artifact introduced in releasing the cubes was eliminated. As McConnell and Forwald jointly concluded, the results were either PK—or cheating. Fortunately for the progress of science, however, points are ultimately established by independent confirmations. The question of personal honesty can thus be bypassed. In this case the occurrence of PK has been independently confirmed by many experimenters.

Forwald has contributed a total of ten papers on placement PK besides those coauthored with McConnell. In addition are the three on dice tests for face targets of Chapter 8. Along with this record for numbers goes a record too, for diversity of results.

By testing the effect of PK on various kinds of materials, Forwald practically proved that the *kind* of material is not important. By testing cubes of varying mass he has shown that the *physical variable* of mass in the range he tested is no limiting factor. But besides all that he is the only investigator thus far to attempt an actual measurement of the force involved in a PK operation. His results at least give a general idea of the amount expended in regulation placement tests like his. His work opens the way to refinements of methods on psi energetics. In his attempt to find an amount of energy constant according to the mass of the objects, he showed that no such constancy exists. Instead, the record indicates that the amount of energy utilized varies according to the work to be done. If the task is to move 2-gram cubes, enough energy to influence cubes of that weight is called out. But if aluminum cubes that weigh twice as much are to be influenced, then even five times as much energy can be mobilized, if for some unconscious reason the task calls for that much more.

The question all this raises is not only how much energy is expended in a given PK operation, but whether there is any limit to the energy that can be called out. Even if Forwald's supposition were correct that the necessary energy is somehow released *within* the physical material (on the assumption apparently that this operation would not require energy input, which still would seem to be an anomaly in the physical world), the question would remain as to why it was unequal at different times and under different circumstances. If, on the other hand, the energy expended comes from a subject as parapsychologists have generally supposed, then presumably its source is the human organism. If so it would surely be expected to have lawful relations including an upper limit, and eventually this could be determined.

Obviously the answers to the questions that Forwald's work raises must await a new stage of research. It must be one in part oriented, like his, to an attempt to find all the physical principles involved. But it must not be limited to physical principles alone. The human volition that affects the objects is the new factor in the equation, and the central unknown to be determined is the nature of the interaction between the two.

Even though the problem of the source and method of operation of the energy involved is still unsolved, Forwald has made a truly pioneering beginning. The light his work throws even on the kind of difficulty that confronts an experimenter can help the next investigator who tackles the problem to an advanced point of departure, whether it be Forwald himself in research yet to be reported or someone else who has not as yet identified himself. Forwald's extensive work, too, has called attention to the problem in an unmistakable way that should lead to its investigation on a wider front than that of parapsychology alone.

# CHAPTER 13

# States of Matter and the Application of PK

✣

ONCE the evidence for PK is recognized and its occurence is granted, a natural question follows: Where and how has it and can it be applied? Of course nature must have been unobtrusively applying it all along, to fulfill some function of its own. Like the rest of the natural universe, including man and his potentialities, the operation of the PK ability certainly did not wait until it had been discovered to serve its purpose in the human personality. Like the New World before Columbus, it was "there" whether the civilized world knew about it or not.

The question, now that it has been discovered, is whether it can be applied consciously and intentionally? What need can it satisfy? What use can be made of it?

In a way, however, these questions are premature. The occurrence of PK is still sporadic and unpredictable. An experimenter may or may not be able to get evidence of it. And the evidence if he gets it may not follow the lines of his expectation. Like Forwald, he may constantly get surprises. It is not that his results do not show lawful effects, but that the laws they seem to follow are still at least partially obscure. Before the ability can be consciously applied, it will be necessary to know the answers to questions experimenters have long been asking, but to which they have only slowly been finding the solutions.

It will be necessary to know, for instance, not only the strength of the force in given situations, but what limits it has, and what psychological attitudes foster or suppress it. It will be necessary to find out how the subtle and unstable unconscious mental factors can be recognized and controlled. Besides this it will be necessary for definitive research to succeed in influencing stationary objects. Thus far, PK has been successfully demonstrated only on objects that are already in motion. In all of the tests described in which dice faces were targets and in all of the placement tests, the motion was initiated by the experimenter who threw or released the objects to fall by gravity, and the PK influence affected them when they were already in motion. No laboratory experiments have been reported as successful when the objective was to cause static objects to move. Until these various remaining objectives have been achieved it cannot be very profitable to try to foresee future uses for PK.

However, instead of looking ahead too soon, it can be both revealing and profitable to look at some of the areas in which the attempt to apply PK has already been made. For whether so regarded or not, some of the practices of the past can now be recognized as attempts to apply it. Three outstanding areas are worth discussion at this point, for they are areas in which one can now see that the attempt has been to influence matter by a mental effect only. These three areas are very widely different in kind, in importance, and in objective effect; one involves certain kinds of gambling, those in which PK on moving targets is involved; one involves an aspect of photography, which is matter in a state of rest; one involves the healing of disease, which, of course, involves living tissue.

In each of these areas, a desire or a need existed for physical realities to respond to human will. The fact that the uses for PK, or the practices that developed, have not been so successful that they have become dependable, and hence orthodox procedures show that they were but blind gropings for a method, the principles of which were still mysterious. But on the other hand the fact that they have persisted over long periods of time and differing cultural settings probably means that a valid principle was in operation at least sometimes. Consequently, the practices, although never dependable, always had believers, and hence never quite died out.

However, when today one pauses to compare these more obvious areas of attempted application with the results of PK research that have been secured in the laboratory, the still remaining gaps between the two stand out very clearly. The comparison shows where bridges must still be built; where the research of the future must be centered if this still primitive natural capacity is ever to become a useful and consciously applicable human adjunct.

## 1. PK IN GAMBLING

One of the earliest attempts to apply PK seems to have been in connection with the unhallowed practice of gambling, especially when it took the forms that involved the manipulation of objects. Some of these gambling techniques are apparently practically as old as the human race, but if nothing but blind chance had been involved in them it is a question whether they would have held sufficient fascination to have been promulgated through the ages. Games devised today (usually they are for children only) seldom hold interest long, if only chance and nothing else can play a part. The PK force, like "chance," is also "blind"; but it is not impersonal. The old saying is that chance plays no favorites. But PK does. Along with chance it could much enhance the game.

Whether so recognized or not, devices for testing "luck" with dice and similar objects were attempts to apply the principle of mind over matter. Ancient Chinese records show a game of chance in use in which marked sticks were thrown in order to reveal the thrower's destiny. While this may have involved a precognitive ability, the psychokinetic, too, could have been a factor. References are made in Dante's *Divina Commedia* to a three-dice game of chance. Down through the centuries further references can be found to gambling practices of many different and specific kinds. They show the timelessness of the human urge to challenge the mysterious influence known as luck; a capricious principle of "good streaks" and "bad streaks," for which no reason whatsoever was known.

Practically from the beginning, along with the desire to win by a lucky throw, went the need to know how lucky a given chance, or the next one, might be. And so, as a byproduct of the gambling urge, the need to evaluate the chances caused the theory of probability to be developed. Galileo made a contribution to it and Pascal, also, when gambling friends brought problems to them. And thus it was that the mathematics of probability were developed because gamblers needed to know the odds they faced.

This mathematics makes it possible to evaluate results in science generally and in parapsychology particularly. It will only be a kind of elemental justice then if parapsychological results help to clarify the idea of luck and bring it at least a bit within the bounds of rationality. It can now be considered a practical certainty that parapsychology can do just that.

The findings of ESP and PK certainly have a definite bearing on the luck an individual will have in winning and in losing. With PK and the rules that govern it, the good and bad luck streaks are no longer so unexplainable as they have seemed. The concept of PK as an ability which may operate either to produce a hit (psi-hitting) or a miss (psi-missing) can explain many of the lucky or unlucky streaks that beset those who would stake their fortunes on the turn or fall of a physical object. Once a real understanding of both the hitting and the missing phenomena is achieved, and of the circumstances that cause them, such streaks will no longer be simply inexplicable luck, but they will be seen to be psychological realities as predictable, let us say, as that low spirits follow failure; high ones, success. As predictable, but not as obvious, for the secret here has taken millenia to be discovered, while the other was no doubt observed even in the caves of our prehistoric ancestors.

An indication that the contribution of parapsychology to gambling is coming into a bit of recognition has recently appeared in book form (a contribution that can conceivably have a sting—at least for gambling houses). The book is titled *winning at Casino Gaming* ("gaming" is a word considered here to be more respectable than "gambling"!)[1] According to the flyleaf, this book has "The latest scientific information on how to improve your casino gaming." The objective is probably not unusual in books of this type, but in attaining it the authors (or author) apparently informed themselves in a surprisingly thorough fashion of the general experimental results of both ESP and PK. They also performed experiments of their own, and though no formal tables of results are given, they obviously learned at first hand some of the cardinal facts about the effect of attitude and atmosphere on a person's likelihood of success in parapsychological tests. There is even a list of requirements for successful ESP and PK experiments that have been confirmed by successful play in the casino. These requirements read as if they were taken almost directly from Thouless' suggestions on the psychological influences affecting PK. They concern mainly the attitude to be recommended which is characterized as relaxed, and almost playful in contrast to the negative ones of tension and anxiety. Better results are secured, it is said, by those who consider themselves lucky than those who think they are unlucky (sheep versus goats?). The tendency is recognized for a "process of inhibition" to set in in the course of casino play which may lead to negative results (psi-missing?). The authors have added, too, that PK seems even more easily influenced by unfavorable conditions than ESP (a comparison that has not been made in the laboratory, although Thouless made a comparable suggestion) because they think proper conditions free from anxiety are hard to achieve in the casino environment, but as in the laboratory they find that

[1] Staff of "Rouge et Noir." *Winning at Casino Gaming* (Glen Head, New York; Rouge et Noir, Inc. 1966), p. 341.

number, size, shape, color, and even the distance of objects show no relation to success.

A section is devoted to the procedure for applying ESP and PK to the casino and it is recommended that a prospective player make a pregame evaluation of his attitude, feeling of luck, and his psychological condition. This then should be followed by a record of the kind of results achieved. This kind of record should give the player a basis on which to predict whether or not he will win or lose and consequently when to play and when not to. The authors also promise him that such a study of the application of the known principles of parasychology in gambling can be very interesting and exciting.

Perhaps for the first time, the discussion is one in which an attempt is made to apply to the gaming table the understanding of PK that has been gleaned from research. To the extent that such understanding can be applied even now, some of the "blindness" should be taken out of the idea of luck and a degree of rationality substituted. Proper attitudes for winning may still be difficult to define and to attain, but knowing that they exist is at least one step nearer to the point of bringing games of chance that involve luck in relation to the manipulation of objects, under a measure of conscious control.

This information in general should be of benefit to players rather than the house or casino. The house already knows that a certain few individuals do win consistently, even though quietly and without fanfare. The house, therefore, certainly must hope that, like the bearers of contagion, the knowledge of how these players do it will be confined. It is just possibe that sufficient application of principles like those advised in *winning at Casino Gaming* could eventually put casinos out of business, or at least reduce the "take," as more patrons learn about ESP and PK and when these abilities can be expected to operate in one direction, when in the other.

In distinction to the approach of the authors of *winning at Casino Gaming*, who obviously undertook their PK tests with a learner's attitude, another quite different volume, designed for a somewhat similar purpose, has still more recently appeared.[2]

This book, by a statistician of the Hughes Aircraft Company, also takes note of parapsychology and the author also says he performed some tests himself "with an open mind"—but nothing but chance results were obtained. Under a chapter on "Fallacies and Sophistries," he gives a short, superficial, and almost totally *incorrect* rundown of parapsychological claims. Dedicated to the idea that only cold statistics govern the luck of players in gambling games, this author concludes satirically that advice like that given in the first book mentioned is offering only a *dream* of beating the game through the exercise of "personal psychic powers." His presentation undoubtedly is one to please the house and in making it such, he quite conveniently sweeps under the rug hints that can make more perceptive individuals into highly probable winners.

So much for gambling and the bearing of PK on some of the practices connected with it. It looks as if those with the gambling urge have long tried, and sometimes successfully, to find a way across the chasm from their desire to win on a lucky throw to a reliable practice. With the recognition that PK is possible and of the effect on it of psychological attitudes, it just may be that the beginning of a bridge in that area is coming into sight.

### 2. PK AND PHOTOGRAPHIC FILM

The attempt to apply PK to static matter shows up unexpectedly in the field of photography. However, almost from the beginning of the photographic art, now more than a century ago, certain claims have been made, which if valid would be instances of it. They consist of cases in which pictures appeared on film or photographic plates which it was said could not have been pro-

[2] Epstein, Richard A., *The Theory of Gambling and Statistical Logic* (Academic Press: New York and London, 1967), p. 492.

duced in the ordinary way by the action of light on light-sensitive substances. Instead they must have been produced by human thought or desire.

The claim had no traditionally established practice to suggest it, and almost no spontaneous occurrences attracted attention to the possibility of such a phenomenon in nature (maybe because photography is not a "natural" phenomenon but one produced by man). If in a very few widely scattered, possibly analogous instances, someone reported that a piece of jewelry, usually silver, a necklace or a ring had tarnished suddenly, "overnight," at the time the person who had given it was killed, the report was so impossible to verify that it fell not only into the category of the least frequently reported kind of possible PK occurrence but also that of the most poorly substantiated.

The reasons the photographic effects in question came to attention thus was not because of a traditional background of any kind, or of a motif of personal gain or the will to win as in gambling. It was instead a quite other-worldly reason, the human desire to know what follows after death. The earliest claim of "unorthodox" photographic effects depended on the supposition that they gave proof that the dead still live, for the evidence took the form of spirit "extras" on photographs of sitters whose relatives had died. The result was known as spirit photography. Today analogous claims are more likely to be known as psycho-photography.

Just who first made the claim of photographing a spirit, the available records do not tell. But the idea originated in the early days of spiritualism, when photography itself was in its infancy. It originated in connection with the spiritualists' belief that apparitions of the dead are in some way "real" even though immaterial. Therefore, when a face appeared, usually placed at random on the sitter's photograph, which he often recognized as the likeness of a deceased relative or friend, it could be taken as evidence of the survival of that person.

Whatever the actual origin of the idea of spirit photography may have been, the taking of pictures with spirit "extras" early became a commercial enterprise. One of the earliest records of it goes back to 1862 when a photographer in Boston, William Mumler, sometimes credited with being the originator of the idea, claimed to be able to get extras on photographs of his sitters. He appears to have been doing a good business, but eventually (and on this account, his case is on record) he was charged with fraud and brought to trial, and his business at least temporarily interrupted. (It was proven in one instance that one of his extras was the face of a man still living, and that man did not appreciate the situation.) However, the business must have been a fairly profitable one, for other photographers, too, in this country and in England became "medium-photographers," and records in police courts show that Mumler was not the only one charged with fraud. In general, the easiest explanation for the extras that skeptics advanced was that they were trick photos, made probably by double exposures. The recognition of the likeness by the sitter, while seeming like proof to him, was not convincing to outsiders. The world in general paid little attention to the unlikely claims.

In 1882 the Society for Psychical Research was formed in London by some of the foremost scholars of the time. Its objective was to investigate claims that today fall in the field of parapsychology. But not until 1891 was the claim of spirit photography taken sufficiently seriously, even by this society, to put it among those investigated. Then, none other than Alfred Russel Wallace, codiscoverer with Charles Darwin of the origin of species by evolution, in an American periodical, *The Arena*, January 1891, challenged the society for not investigating spirit photography. He was convinced that spirits could be photographed for he had received an extra that he was certain was a likeness of his mother.

The challenge was taken up by Mrs. Henry Sidgwick, one of the founders of the society, and sister of Lord Balfour.[3] Her reply

[3] Sidgwick, Mrs. Henry, "On Spirit Photographs; a Reply to Mr. R. A. Wallace." *Proc. Soc. psych. Res.*, Part 19, 1891, pp. 268–289.

took the form of a review of the claims of spirit photography to date, and her conclusion was that it included much unquestionable fraud, and if anything genuine had been produced, the evidence for it was too weak to be taken seriously. She refused to consider that identification could be taken as proof that "extras" were photographs of spirits.

However, after this thoughful, but generally negative review, claims of spirit photography still continued to be made. Over ensuing years, controversy for and against their genuineness went on. In 1914 Dr. James Hyslop, research officer of the American Society for Psychical Research, published a report of the unusual photographic effects secured by a Mrs. Lee of Washington, D.C.[4] He had interviewed Mrs. Lee and seen her pictures. Mrs. Lee was a member of the wealthy DuPont family and had no mercenary motive; she apparently had no other motive than her own curiosity and satisfaction.

The story as told to Hyslop was that Mrs. Lee had become interested in automatic writing after the death of an Episcopal clergyman who had been a coworker in some of her charity work. Through her automatic writing, she was directed to try spirit photography. After a period of trying, she got an "extra" of the clergyman. In general however her pictures did not have a direct spiritistic bearing. Instead they suggested unusual photography of some unexplainable kind. Some of the pictures suggested double exposures, but she said no double exposures could possibly have been taken. The pictures leave today's reader, as they left Hyslop, puzzled.

Although his findings were not published until 1916 (with an introduction by Dr. Hyslop), a Reverend Charles Hall Cook, also an Episcopal clergyman, in 1901 had made a series of tests of spirit photography.[5] He worked in connection with a medium-

[4] Hyslop, James H., "Some Unusual Phenomena in Photography." *J. Amer. Soc. psych. Res.*, 1914, 8, pp. 395–463.
[5] Cook, Charles Hall, "Experiments in Photography." *J. Amer. Soc. psych. Res.*, 1916, 10, pp. 1–57.

photographer, Edward Wyllie. Cook used Wyllie's place of business, his camera and dark room, and took pictures in his presence, but without his assistance in any way. Instead, a trusted friend of Cook's handled the equipment.

The procedure was for Cook to purchase commercial plates, bring them to Wyllie's office where Cook kept them in his own possession and in his sight in the dark room where in the red light he and the assistant loaded them into the plate holder. When the camera was loaded Cook sat in the sitter's chair and his assistant took the pictures. The plates were then taken to a commercial firm to be developed. From the account, no loopholes for fraud can be seen; Cook watching the operation from beginning to end and Wyllie having no hand in it.

Extras were obtained including one supposed to be the face of a college girl classmate of Cook's. Her friends and relatives, as well as Cook, were convinced of the likeness.

In general, Cook's extras, like those of the medium-photographers, were located in random positions around his own photograph, and in general, too, as if in front of him, their edges overlapping parts of his photograph. The net result of this report, like that of Mrs. Lee, is to leave the reader baffled. To neither of the two, could an obvious ulterior motive be easily attributed, and both obtained pictures that are inexplicable under the conditions as given, unless they were genuine psychophotographs. But no conclusion need be reached of course. If these effects were real, then further research under more strict conditions in time should tell.

A few years later came another report of successful spirit photography and this, again, stirred up considerable interest.[6] This was the appearance of an extra on a photograph taken of an American couple, Dr. and Mrs. Cushman. Their daughter, age 16, died very suddenly, and they went to England unannounced to try for a spirit photograph with the well-known spiritualist medium-

[6] Cushman, Allerton, S., "An Evidential Case of Spirit Photography." *Jour. Amer. Soc. psych. Res.*, 1922, 16, pp. 132–212.

photographer, William Hope. (Hope never worked under controlled conditions and much fraud has been charged against him.) Taking care to conceal their identity and their mission, they found Hope inaccessable. But they accepted instead an immediate sitting with Mrs. A. E. Deane, another and less well-known medium-photographer (also sometimes charged with fraud).

The extra they obtained bore a strong resemblance to a photo of their daughter, but was not identical with any they possessed. The claim to validity in this instance depended on the identification of the picture, and on the success with which the Cushmans had kept their identity and objective secret. Again an indecisive situation that can only call for suspended judgment.

Meanwhile, in Japan in 1910–11, the first attempt was made to conduct controlled experiments on the effect of thought on photographic plates. This was by T. Fukurai, professor of psychology at Tokyo Imperial University.[7]

Fukurai's studies involving photographic phenomena began quite fortuitously after he heard of the apparent clairvoyant ability of a young woman, Chizuko Mifume. He was interested in the possibility of clairvoyance and at the beginning had not even thought of a photographic test. Even the idea of clairvoyance at that date in Japan as elsewhere was revolutionary enough, for as Fukurai said, "Scientists in general were against clairvoyance on the ground that such a phenomenon was opposed to the established scientific conception."

He began experimenting with Chizuko and considered he had succeeded in demonstrating clairvoyance when, among other tests, she correctly identified three Japanese characters written on a paper and enclosed in a hollow leaden pipe, soldered shut at the ends. However, in spite of the evidence, Fukurai's work was criticized in the public press, and Chizuko, apparently thrown into depression by it, committed suicide by taking poison. It was a great setback to Fukurai.

[7] Fukurai, T., *Clairvoyance and Thoughtography* (London: Rider & Co., 1931).

Meanwhile, however, another potential medium for the investigation of his clairvoyance studies had come to Fukurai's attention. This was Mrs. Ikuko Nagao, whose unusual powers had been recognized after the shock of the death of her oldest child. With her, Fukurai not only was able to get evidence of clairvoyance, but in the course of the experiments for it, an incident occurred that gave him the idea of imprinting plates by thought processes. It came about after Mrs. Nagao also had succeeded in identifying characters concealed within the lead pipe. Fukurai, impressed by this evidence of clairvoyance, then made a test using undeveloped film to see if images he had tried to imprint on it mentally could be recognized clairvoyantly. Mrs. Nagao succeeded in identifying his message. Fukurai noticed later when the plate was developed that it came out much darker than a control he had imprinted but kept at home. The one on which Mrs. Nagao had concentrated appeared as if it had already been exposed, and so the idea was suggested to him that perhaps Mrs. Nagao's concentration had affected the plate.

From this, he began to ask her to transfer to undeveloped plates, certain images he designated. In the first experiment, it was a circle, in the second, a cross, and so on; and from the account as given, she succeeded in each instance. Experiments were carried out over a few weeks in December 1910 and January 1911, but before the end of January Mrs. Nagao died of pneumonia and Fukurai again was almost defeated.

In Fukurai's photographic work with Mrs. Nagao, he made a number of improvements in method over anything that had been involved in the Western world. Fukurai, of course, was making a scientific investigation, as the spirit photographers had not been. Whether he even knew of the western spiritualistic claims is doubtful, so that the research techniques he developed were his own. The spirit photographers had used cameras and regular sitters, but in his work with Mrs. Nagao, Fukurai used no camera, but only sensitive photographic plates. They were carefully wrapped in layers of black paper. A plate was held by the medium during periods of concentration in which she attempted to imprint on it the assigned image. Thus she was the first subject who herself as agent consciously and deliberately tried to produce an effect on the plate and without the camera. The spirit photographers (if any of them were genuine) presumably would not have considered that they were themselves producing the extras that appeared on their plates.

In a number of instances, the images that Fukurai set for his subject were Japanese characters, and sometimes they were secured by the "sandwich" method, another advance in method that Fukurai introduced. In this, three sensitive plates were wrapped together, the middle one being the experimental plate on which the image was to be imprinted. The two outside ones were controls and were to remain clear.

Striking successes were secured, but reports of the work got into public print and were received unfavorably. In fact, the adverse publicity hampered the research to an extent that today seems almost unbelievable. Reporters even forced their way into the house where experiments were being attempted. In one case they made off with some of the records and equipment in the hope of being able to prove that fraudulent methods were being used. Eventually the situation was so acute that Fukurai was forced to resign his university position. However, he continued his studies and finally, in 1931, his book about them and about the results of his experiments with several other mediums appeared in English.

Today, from this (poorly edited) English version, it is not possible to be completely certain just what went on. It is clear that although the experimental packets were carefully and adequately wrapped and sealed, at least some of the methods used were not as sophisticatedly rigorous against the possibility that someone cheated, as would be required today.

An obvious weak point in the method as it appears from the record is the fact that Fukurai usually carried out his tests at the home of the medium or of a relative of hers. When he arrived there for a test, he always left his briefcase containing the prepared "sandwiches" in an outer room unattended until time for the test to begin. (The reason for this, whether because of some local social custom or what, is not explained.) Sometimes the briefcase was unattended only for a few minutes, sometimes longer, but as far as the record goes, one has no way now of deciding whether or not plates could have been switched during that interval. However, the sandwiches were so carefully prepared in wrappings of black paper and various kinds of seals that Fukurai was convinced they could not be opened without detection. To have switched packets would have meant that someone else who prepared the duplicate knew the exact manner in which Fukurai had prepared his. While this seems unlikely, one cannot from this time and distance tell if it was impossible.

Fukurai himself appears as a transparently honest and unsuspecting person and also one brave and original enough to engage in an unpopular research even though it brought him only trouble. The real question then is whether his several mediums or, more important, members of their families, were equally innocent and unsuspecting. From the accounts, one has no reason to suppose otherwise but, on the other hand, no way to rule out such possibilities entirely. However, like any single experimenter's work in any area, Fukurai's can only be considered as suggestive until the work of other researchers confirms it. If thought can affect film, then sooner or later other experimenters under conditions that cannot be criticized will also obtain the effect.

After Fukurai's work, no further reports of experiments in psychophotography appeared for decades. The claim that it could occur was again relegated to the shadows of superstition. Recently, however, it has come to life again. It has been revived by a series of experiments reported in a book by a Denver psychiatrist, Dr. Jule Eisenbud.[8] Ted Serios is a unique character who, according to the book, can project thoughts on film, in this case

[8] Eisenbud, Jule, *The World of Ted Serios* (New York: William Morrow & Co., Inc., 1967), p. 367.

that of a certain type of Polaroid camera. The text of the book is a description in popular style of tests with Serios made under the control and supervision of Dr. Eisenbud, who has long been interested in parapsychology.

Briefly the situation presented in the book was that initially Serios had made the claim that he could produce thought effects on film in a Polaroid, and Eisenbud, hearing of it and after seeing a demonstration, felt it was a claim that should be investigated. According to the account Serios was an uncertain quantity, not always sober and often profane. Nevertheless, Eisenbud invited him to his home where Serios was provided with living quarters while tests of his ability with the Polaroid film were carried on.

Although Serios was temperamental and difficult to handle, in the course of many months, a large number of inexplicable pictures resulted. The method of procedure varied, but usually the camera was either pointed at Serios' face, close range, or set at infinity and pointed at the wall or at some object in the room. Serios, at his own request or at that of someone else, pushed the button, but when successful, the local object did not appear in the picture. As a matter of fact, Serios usually held pressed against the lens a short hollow cardboard tube which was blocked off by a piece of blackened exposed film at one end, clear cellophane at the other. This device presumably shut out light from the room and, when it did so perfectly, would account normally for the "blackies" that frequently resulted. This tube, which they came to call the "gismo," Serios explained was a gadget he had originally fallen into the habit of using to keep his fingers off the lens during an exposure. But he had become so habituated to it that now he was more comfortable using it than not, and so its continued use was permitted.

Among the pictures that were made, some were "blackies," the developed film showing no exposure, although exposed; some were "whities," apparently the result of complete exposure; others showed light spots and unrecognizable blotches and blurs. Many that were his most significant were likenesses of buildings or parts of buildings or other familiar objects (like an airplane or plane); some were recognized, some were not.

In later tests, some of the pictures were produced with Polaroid cameras and film supplied by outsiders with no contact by Serios allowed. Some of the pictures were secured in the presence of a number of observers, some of whom were quite skeptical. A number of the observers were from the University of Colorado science departments or medical school. According to the report, no one could see how such effects could be produced. No one reported any signs of fraud.

While the "gismo" was always an object of suspicion by critical observers, it became especially so after two commercial photographers, C. Reynolds and D. B. Eisendrath, spent several days watching the Serios performance (or attempted performance, for no effects were obtained in their presence). In an article published later[9] they described a gadget which exists commercially they said and could be concealed in the gismo. It was in the nature of a small tube with a lens at one end and a photographic transparency inserted in the other. Light from external sources could affect this and cause an image when the film was exposed. While presumably such a gadget could be used to produce results on the Polaroid film, no one present when effects were obtained ever saw anything to indicate that Serios used one. If he did, therefore, he must have exercised a high level of skill in the sleight-of-hand that kept him from being found out by the many observers usually present, some of whom at least thought they had the gismo under observation. However, it can be noted that the best effects usually came well along in the test period when the observers were certainly likely to be less alert than at first. But since it can also be supposed that it might take a number of tries— as well as a number of drinks—to put Serios in the proper state

[9] Reynolds, C., and Eisendrath, D. B., "An Amazing Weekend with the Amazing Ted Serios." *Popular Photography*, Vol. 61 (Oct., 1968), pp. 81–87, 131–140, 158.

of mind to affect the film, nothing can be learned from this argument. The method of presentation in the book, popular rather than scientific, sometimes leaves the critical reader uncertain whether or not the conditions were still well controlled when the result was obtained.

One reviewer of the book, William G. Roll, made an especially careful and detailed study of the evidence presented in it, from a number of different angles.[10] One strong line of evidence against fraud would have existed if Serios had produced a picture set as a target for him just before the session so that he could not have prepared for it in advance. The evidence on this point is not clear and involves the question of just how much latitude can be allowed in judging a hit. For instance, when asked to reproduce an etching on the wall showing buildings of a medieval town the resulting picture showed buildings that had walls and roofs but were not identical with those of the target. In some cases the target was unknown to Serios at the time of the trial. Out of about 23 such trials, Roll found one result that was obviously similar, ten in which similarities were claimed that he could not corroborate, and eight in which none was claimed. The verdict on this line of evidence thus is not conclusive, although no one would expect a PK effect to be obvious all the time. If only one case were so well substantiated that no question could be raised it might go as far toward proving a point as could be asked for under conditions which after all do not meet the experimental requirement for statistical evaluation. No one can say here therefore whether an outcome is or is not significantly different from chance coincidence.

Roll made a study of the time of day at which the images, usually of buildings, were made. He could do this mainly by noting the angle at which shadows showed in the Polaroid productions. He found that the images seemed as if taken in day-

10 Roll, W. G., "The World of Ted Serios." *Jour. Amer. Soc. psych. Res.*, 1968, 62, pp. 193–216.

light, regardless of the time of day in Denver when the test was made. Another feature too seems to show that Serios was not reproducing contemporary situations. This was in connection with scenes that were reproduced more than once and that contained aspects that normally would have moved in the interim. The images of persons, for instance, showed that they had not moved between shots, and the blades of a windmill are in the same position in two different pictures, although it appears that the angle from which they were taken changed from one time to another. And so the reviewer, Roll, although puzzled at many points, felt that the data did not support the idea that the images were perceived from the original objects by ESP. He feels that such facts as the prevalence of daylight scenes with shadows, and the lack of movement, indicate that the images originate from photographs rather than from the structures themselves. He also draws a further inference from the fact that nearly all the images are bordered by a curved outline, presumably the shadow of the gismo. Since the gismo was allegedly made of cardboard, the fact that it interfered with the images would then suggest that light in the visible spectrum was involved. These points tend to suggest a spurious origin of the phenomena, although conceivably a genuine effect might have these characteristics. The total result of Eisenbud's book certainly is to leave the reader perplexed. Some evidence seemed to indicate that an unusual photographic effect was produced that it is not possible to explain from the data as given, while on the other hand, the suspicion of fraud or deception cannot be entirely removed on the basis of this account.

The record of experiments with Serios does not quite end with Dr. Eisenbud's report, however, although the rest of the story to date still does not solve the puzzle.

In April and May 1967 Serios spent a month at the University of Virginia at Charlottesville, under the investigation of Dr. Ian Stevenson, again a psychiatrist, and Dr. J. G. Pratt, the parapsychologist formerly at the Parapsychology Laboratory.[11] Their studies began with the plan of imposing strict controls on camera, film, and gismo and in setting targets for Serios. Their tests, however, were interrupted before a conclusive stage was reached, by the unceremonious departure of Serios. The question whether the phenomenon he claimed to perform was real is still unanswered, and reports of later work, reportedly without the use of the gismo, are still unpublished.

As with Fukurai, the decision about the validity of Serios' claim to produce images on Polaroid films also awaits more definitive research. It is certain that much, and probably nearly all, that glittered in the days of spirit photography was not gold. It probably was largely a compound of deliberate fraud, credulity, innocent error, and artifacts of procedure. Certainly, too in a number of historical instances no explanation except PK seems possible with the facts as given. The question thus remains open and no decision is possible. However, since the discovery of PK, one can only remember that for all that is now known this area of sensitized film is one in which presumably PK *could* operate.

If PK cannot affect silver nitrate, or comparable chemicals, then no one will get incontrovertible evidence, and the claim of psychophotography will slip back again into the shadows. If it can, then in time evidence of it will be forthcoming under conditions that leave no question. If this development should take place, it would not necessarily be much of an advance for photography, which has done very well without "thought effects." It would not prove that spirits can be photographed either, but if it were shown that PK can thus affect a chemical reaction it would be a big step forward in the application of PK, one involving a static (chemical substance) condition of matter.

The question that remains for parapsychology on this topic is not only how to build a bridge from the established facts of PK

[11] Stevenson, Ian, and Pratt, J. G., "Exploratory Investigations of the Psychic Photography of Ted Serios." *Jour. Amer. Soc. psych. Res.*, 1968, 62, pp. 103–129.

to its application on film but whether such a bridge is within the realm of possibility.

### 3. PK IN HEALING

One of the most important areas in which the attempt to apply PK has long been made is that of healing. Even beyond the now well-recognized psychosomatic effects of mental states on bodily functions, in which for that matter the PK effect may also very well be a hidden factor, is the still further out area commonly known variously as unorthodox healing, spiritual healing, prayer therapy, and the like. These are all methods of response to the timeless need for physical health and for a way to control disease. They involve attempts to achieve results by mental influences. If effective and if suggestion is ruled out then results would indicate PK acting on living organisms.

Of course, with modern medicine at its present advanced stage, the urge to find unorthodox methods is much less acute than it used to be, but in every culture and every time, numerous illnesses remain that doctors cannot cure or do not cure. Witness to this fact is the prevalence of unorthodox methods, even in areas in which medicine is as advanced as in the United States and Western Europe, as reviewed recently by Dr. Brian Inglis.[12] With an urge so elemental as this one, it is small wonder that many claims of healing by unorthodox methods have been made. People do not wait for bridges of fact or logic when a life may be at stake, and when orthodox medicine does not fill the bill.

A small number of researches have been made in parapsychology to find if such action is possible. Investigation in this area, however, is still exploratory and none as yet has been adequately confirmed.

An attempt to affect living systems by will power was made by

[12] Inglis, Brian, *The Case for Unorthodox Medicine* (New York: G. P. Putnam Sons, 1965).

the Vasses, as mentioned in Chapter 9. In one experiment Mrs. Vasse tried to affect the rate of germination and growth of seeds, a very complicated process which if it were shown to be possible would raise the same question that Cox's electromechanical device raised. Just where did the PK effect occur?

Then in a second experiment Mrs. Vasse attempted to influence the phototropism, or bending toward the light, of seedlings. This effect depends on the different osmotic pressure of cells and in a way would probably be less complex as an experimental project than germination. But even so the two types of project can at least suggest the complexity of life situations that would be involved if PK effects were obtained on them.

## PK and a One-Celled Organism

The first published report of a research in which the attempt was to influence a living animal organism was made by Nigel Richmond in England in 1952.[13] It represents a sort of intermediate problem area, one of motility rather than a growth process. Richmond undertook to influence by concentration the movement of paramecia, which are single-celled organisms only about .01 inch long. Paramecia are common in all natural pond water and move or swim by moving hairlike cilia.

Since the organism is so small, Richmond's research on it was done by low powered microscope; a magnification of x75 proved the most effective. His objective was to see if he could cause the animal to swim in a desired direction.

The technique used was to divide the microscopic field into four quadrants by two cross hairs at right angles to each other. A drop of pond water was put on a microscope slide, a slip cover

[13] Richmond, Nigel, "Two Series of PK Tests on Paramecia." *Jour. Soc. psy. Res.*, 1952, 36, pp. 577–588.

over it. A paramecium was then centered under the cross hairs at the start of a 15-second period, during which it was willed to go in the target direction. The target was determined by assigning one of each of the four suits of a deck of playing cards to each of the quadrants. As the 15-second period began, one card of the shuffled deck was turned up, and it determined the quadrant toward which the organism was willed to go. At the end of the allotted time, the location of the paramecium was recorded.

Several situations were noted in preliminary testing which were taken into consideration in the planning of the procedure and in assessing the results. It was evident for instance that paramecia that were swimming in a straight line in a given direction were not good prospects for the experiment. As Richmond said, "They were moving too fast and it was thought that strong stimuli were already acting on them." (In other words, they were going somewhere.) This is reminiscent of the problem that concerned Wilbur and Mangan in their test in Chapter 9. It is the question whether situations that offer many "checkpoints," like square-cornered cubes or rough surfaces, are likely to promote PK. Richmond, with this possibility in mind, selected individual paramecia that were just then motionless or temporarily blocked (undecided?) by a mud particle. These he thought would be more easily susceptible to his will. He also found that for creatures as unstructured as these, backward motion was just as easy and frequent as forward. And so, for scoring purposes, the field was considered as made up of two diagonal sections, each including a forward and a backward opposite quadrant. The basis of evaluation thus became one-half, instead of one-fourth.

Two series of tests were made differing only in fine points connected with the noting and recording of responses. One of the fine points had to do with determining borderline results, the other with exactness of timing.

A proper correction for inexactness in both of these points was made in the second series of tests. It did not, however, reduce the level of scoring. Instead, the results on the second series were somewhat higher than on the first, so the details of these changes can be omitted here and the two series considered as one.

Along with the experimental tests, which Richmond refers to as "attempts," he also made a kind of control in which he merely recorded the position of the paramecium at the end of 15 seconds without having attempted to influence it. In a way it was a safer control than some of Forwald's, for instance, because Richmond observed the paramecium for 15 seconds *before* he turned up a target card. He, therefore, did not have a target consciously in mind, toward which to will the animal. He knew, however, that this was only a nominal control and could not be relied upon to be an indicator of the random behavior of the organism. He realized that unconsciously he might still exert an influence and by clairvoyance be himself guided by the card to be turned up next. But he felt that tests of this kind interspersed with the others would at least show a contrast between those made with conscious and those made with unconscious objectives.

The results covered a total of 1,495 experimental attempts and 1,500 controls. For the tests, the deviation in the forward direction was over a hundred; in the backward or opposite, about 70. The total gave a highly significant CR of 9.28, the p-value of which is well into the millions. It seemed to indicate that the mind of man had influenced a single-celled organism.

Something else had happened, too. The deviation on the controls was 57 which gives a CR of 2.94. On that, p = .003. But it was a negative response and meant that the organisms had to a significant degree gone at right angles to the experimental direction. At any rate, curves plotted on the data of the experiment and of the control diverge quite strikingly, that of the control group going below chance as consistently, although not as far, as the other goes above it.

Since the control thus was not at chance, it appeared that even though the experimenter did not intend to exert an influence, he had nevertheless done so. His result suggests some of Forwald's reverses, in which it appeared that the intention *not* to influence "backfired" or overshot the mark.

One can only say about this experiment, that it *looks* as if PK was operating and that the mind of a man influenced a living organism. But was it by PK? A living organism brings with it an unknown that complicates interpretation. Did the human being "do it," or did the paramecium? Does a single-celled organism have a "will"? In other words, is the paramecium the equivalent of the die in a dice experiment or something more? Perhaps this was a telepathy experiment rather than one of PK. The results raise the question.

Before the question whether the human mind is *that* effective (whether by telepathy or PK) can be asked, with full seriousness, experiments like Richmond's must be repeated and confirmed. However, in spite of the obvious importance of the question, only one other report of a similar attempt has come in. Thouless attempted a replication of Richmond's work[14] but reported only chance results. Richmond objected however that Thouless had overlooked the stress he had laid on selecting organisms that were momentarily at rest. He said he had used pond water and particles of mud often seemed to serve as interruption points, but Thouless had used clear water and Richmond thought the difference might have accounted for the failure. There the question rests. In science one failure does not cancel one success, but leaves the question open for further attempts at confirmation.

In this case, however, no more have been reported, probably because no other biologist has ventured into the parapsychological field, and no more parapsychologists have elected to do research along this line rather than the usual less biologically oriented ones toward which their own proclivities propel them. Even at the Parapsychology Laboratory priorities on research topics are still dictated largely by personal preferences and no doubt will be until a later stage of organization in research attempts is reached.

[14] Private Correspondence.

## The Laying-on-of-Hands

One of the age-old attempts to cure without benefit of medicine is that of the "laying-on-of-hands." Ever since Biblical times, individuals have existed who felt that they could cure this way. Not everyone, but a certain few, from "medicine men" in primitive cultures to "healers" in our own time, have claimed they could do it.

Orthodox medicine has paid scant attention to this claim; the cures so produced have generally been easily written off as the result of suggestion and overinterpretation. No medical school has set up a comprehensive research to test whether anything more is involved.

A controlled experiment, however, was made in Canada in 1961 by Bernard Grad, a biochemist of McGill University, in collaboration with Dr. Remi J. Cadoret, of the University of Manitoba, to test the claimed healing ability of a Mr. E.[15] The two investigators wanted to find out whether such an ability could be demonstrated and, if so, whether it could be shown to be anything more than the effect of suggestion. Since Mr. E.'s claim involved the laying-on-of-hands as the healing technique, Grad and Cadoret were not attempting directly to apply PK, or the power of thought on a living system, as Richmond was. Although they both no doubt knew of the PK research for both were interested in parapsychology, nothing in their reports suggests that they related the effect they studied to PK. However, any effect a healer could have on the physiological system of a subject by direct will power, other influences being ruled out, would by definition be an effect of PK.

In order to avoid the result of suggestion, these investigators

[15] Grad, Bernard, Cadoret, Remi J., and Paul, G. I., "The Influence of an Unorthodox Method of Treatment on Wound Healing of Mice." *Int'l Jour. Parapsychol.*, 1961, V. 3, No. 2, pp. 5–24.

decided to use animals rather than humans as their experimental organisms. And in order to be able to use a large number of individuals conveniently, a small and easily handled animal was necessary. Mice therefore were chosen.

In the experiment, 300 animals were used. Each was wounded by snipping out an oblong piece of skin on the back. Then under "blind" conditions, the animals were divided into three groups. One group was treated by Mr. E, one by persons who claimed no healing ability, and the other, a control, was treated by no one.

The method of treatment used was that the person giving the treatment twice daily for 15 minutes held a cage containing the animal between his hands. The cages were enveloped in paper bags so that the treaters did not see the animal, although they were permitted to put their hands inside the bag and directly in contact with the cage.

The animals treated by Mr. E. healed more rapidly than the others to a degree sufficient to warrant continuance. However, the experimenters did not consider the results conclusive, but only that they suggested that the effect was one that could not be explained in terms of "presently understood mechanisms." The topic was pursued, further, by Grad in subsequent studies.

THE LAYING ON OF HANDS: PLANT TESTS

## Number 1. Open Containers

In Grad's next attempt to test the healing powers of Mr. E. he reduced the elaborate investment of time, space and personnel of the initial experiment.[16] He did it by transferring the tests from animal to plant tissue. This was possible because Mr. E. felt he could work with plant material, too.

[16] Grad, Bernard, "A Telekinetic Effect on Plant Growth." *Int'l Jour. Parapsychol.*, Vol. V., No. 2, pp. 117–133.

Through a series of preliminary studies, several features of the technique later followed in general were worked out. For instance, germination trials were made with treated and untreated barley seeds, Mr. E. holding the treated ones in his hands for 15 minutes daily. No differences resulted. On the next attempts, the seeds were planted in pots, and Mr. E.'s treatment consisted of holding the pots daily. Some differences were noted, and it was further noted that differences were greatest when conditions for growth were rather unfavorable, as when the pots dried out considerably.

A method was therefore worked out in which the planted barley seed was subjected to conditions designed to be generally unfavorable to growth, but without entirely prohibiting it. For this, the seeds were first watered with a saline solution and then dried in an oven at 38 to 40 degrees C. for 48 hours. Initially, Mr. E. held saline solution as well as the treated pots in his hands. Later it was found that it was not necessary for him to hold the pots, for an effect was obtained if they were simply watered with the treated saline solution.

The experiment that followed involved 24 pots in each of which 20 barley seeds were planted. Double blind conditions were imposed throughout. These were much facilitated by the fact that Mr. E. did not have to hold the pots. Instead, he treated one of two beakers of water by holding it for 15 minutes, his left hand supporting it from below; his right, three or four centimeters above the surface of the water. In this way, the laying-on-of-hands principle was invoked.

This treatment was carried out in the presence of an assistant who then took the beakers and when alone marked one X and one Y and wrote down which letter signified the treated beaker, sealed the record, and hid it in a place known only to himself. He then gave the beakers to Grad, the experimenter, who had already, by a random code, marked the 24 pots into two groups. He then watered one group with water from the X beaker; the other, from the Y, using 25 milliliters on each. Thus, during the experiment no one person knew which group of pots was the experimental one, which the control.

Differences between the two groups of planted pots showed between the seventh and the fourteenth days after planting and were significantly in favor of the treated ones on three counts. The first was number of plants; the second, the height of plants; the third, the yield that was obtained from the total of all the heights of each plant in a given pot. Thus, the experiment seemed to show that the treatment of the water had somehow had a beneficial effect on the growth.

However, it was realized that a possible explanation could have been that Mr. E. might have added a bit of chemical favorable to plant growth during the time he held the beakers. A later experiment was then performed to guard against this possibility.

## Number 2. Closed Containers

In this experiment the conditions were all as before, except that the open beakers were not used.[17] The water to be used, both experimental and control, was kept in glass reagent bottles with ground glass stoppers. Four series were made in all, and in two, three, and four the reagent bottles were stapled into heavy paper bags. In experiment one and four Mr. E. held the experimental bottle between his hands. In two and three he only held his right hand on the bottle. In each case, the treatment lasted 30 minutes.

The results still showed a consistent favoring of the experimental pots. The author felt that it had been well shown that "something" passed from Mr. E. into the solution. The two solutions were then subjected to a number of tests to see if some alteration of the chemical properties of the treated water was detectable. The pH (acidity or alkalinity) was tested, the presence of a number of chemicals was tested for, and the absorption and trans-

[17] Grad, Bernard, "A Telekinetic Effect on Plant Growth." *Int'l Jour. Parapsychol.*, 1964, Vol. VI., No. 4, pp. 473–498.

mission spectra of both solutions were observed. No significant differences in any of these aspects were found. The only remaining possibility seemed to Grad to be that perhaps an electromagnetic change had been induced. On this supposition, he felt, further experimentation was needed. At this stage, the only deduction he had was that energy had passed from the hands of Mr. E. into the bottle and from the bottle to the plants.

### CHANGES IN HEALERS

Later Grad undertook a somewhat different aspect of the question of the effect of the laying-on-of-hands.[18] For this the same technique was employed that was used in the last experiment with Mr. E. Three persons in the role of treaters or healers were involved; one, J.B., a psychiatrically normal male of 54; the other two, patients from a psychiatric hospital. One of these, R.H., was a 26-year-old woman with a depressive neurotic reaction; the other, H.R., a 37-year-old male with a psychotic (delusional) depression.

Each of the three was asked to hold a sealed bottle of normal saline solution between his hands for 30 minutes after which an assistant took the bottles and coded them, according to the prescribed proceeding. Another person with codes for four sets of planted pots (one for each person and the fourth a control) watered the planted seeds accordingly. As before, the procedure was blind throughout.

The reactions of the three subjects when asked to hold the bottles were different. The normal subject, J.B., accepted the idea of the treatment of the solution matter-of-factly. Although he made no claim to being a healer, he was interested in the project, understood it, and had even tried to help members of his own

18 Grad, Bernard, "The Laying on of Hands; Implications for Psychotherapy, Gentling, and the Placebo Effect." *Jour. Amer. Soc. psych. Res.,* 1967, 61, pp. 286–305.

family when ill. The woman, R.H., however, knew nothing of the experiment. When asked to hold the bottle, she was amused and interested. When the idea behind it was explained to her, she showed a decided brightening of mood. The other man, H.R., was anxious, agitated, and depressed while holding the bottle, did not ask why, and expressed concern only over his own therapy.

The results of the test showed J.B.'s plants significantly better than the others. R.H.'s were better than the control and H.R.'s, not as good. While these last two were not significantly better or worse than the control, they did suggest to Grad that the mood of each of the two depressed patients at the time of the test may have had some effect on the plant growth.

In Grad's reasoning, the effect secured by the subject, J.B., as well as that of Mr. E. in the earlier experiments, must have been one transmitted through the bottles to the solution to the plants. As such, it could be nothing but an *energy*, he decided, and "inasmuch as both favorable and unfavorable responses have been observed, there must be a dual aspect to this energy."

The mystery of this "energy" then drove Grad to a consideration of studies that have been made on such physiological reactions as cell division, but he did not suggest that it might be the same effect that parapsychologists have been studying under the name of PK.

Apparently the flask of solution intervening between the hands of the healer and the living tissue to be affected seemed to Grad to be a block to the influence of PK, if he even considered it. He knew that work had been done showing a mental influence on dice but apparently did not appreciate the significance of it for his own results.

However, if the laying-on-of-hands principle can hasten the healing process, as was suggested in the experiment with mice, then the basis of that action would have been the influence of the healer's mind or will, not the actual contact between the healer's hands and the animal to be healed. He did not touch the mouse, but only held the cage in which it was confined. An experiment like this is obviously already once removed from actual laying-on-of-hands.

Then when actual holding of the pot of seeds was eliminated, another step of physical removal had been taken. But the report says that results were still achieved. The removal, therefore, was only on the physical level. On the psychological level the chain of cause–effect had not necessarily been broken because the physical one was interrupted.

As PK experiments, too, had shown, no vehicle in the sense of a physical mechanism is necessary by which to transfer the interaction of the subject to the object he wishes to affect. In this plant experiment, therefore, the treated solution must have been only the medium on which the healer's conscious attention could be focused, while unconscious mental processes came into operation.

But if PK was the energy involved in these experiments, it apparently operated in spite of all the "blind" conditions. No one, neither healer nor experimenter, nor any of the assistants knew which flask or beaker or which pots of seedlings were the experimental ones as the tests proceeded (a "blind" situation reminiscent of the blind PK targets of Thouless, Osis, and Fisk). Similarly, in an ESP test in which a subject calls a deck of cards in a test of clairvoyance, no one knows what the various symbols are. The fact that subjects can and often do identify too many of the symbols to be explained by chance coincidence is the basis of evidence for ESP. In the blind PK experiments, similar evidence for PK was obtained when the subject did not know the PK target but could only get it by ESP. In the same way here, psi, by a combination of its ESP and PK processes could direct the healer's will to the *proper pots*, regardless of the lack of conscious information as to which were tests and which control.

If the suggestion coming from the depressed patient, H.R., should be proven to be a valid one, then one more indication of PK would be shown. If his results actually were depressed *below* the control, then psi-missing would be involved. The *mood* of the moment would have been one to generate it, just as with the interested and amused R.H., the mood of the moment would have been conducive to psi-hitting. But no finality can be given to a single experiment or set of experiments by one investigator. Independent confirmation is necessary before conclusions can be drawn.

PK ON A FUNGUS CULTURE

Still another experiment on living tissue has been reported.[19] This one is from France, and was carried out by Jean Barry, M.D. Being a physician, the harmful effects of certain kinds of living organisms was on his mind. His experiment, for which he had the collaboration of the staff of the Institute of Agronomy, Bordeaux, to handle the biological technique, took the form of an attempt to *inhibit* rather than to accelerate the growth of the tissue involved. Because of this approach, a number of parasitic fungi, which are the basis of various diseases, were tried out to see which would be most amenable to the proposed experiment. For instance, mycelium colonies of Stereum Purpureum and of Rhizoclonia Solani were tried out, and the latter chosen for the experiment because a colony of it produced a sharper boundary, and therefore its amount of growth would be the easier to measure of the two. This is a polyphagous parasitic fungi which causes diseases known in France as "Rhizoctone Brun."

The procedure was, in general, the regulation one for the culture of *fungi in vitro*. Petri dishes containing a proper culture medium were inoculated in the center at 5:30 P.M. of the day before the experiment and placed in the incubator under constant heat and light conditions until time for the test.

The experimental plan was to have subjects attempt to inhibit the growth of the fungus by concentration. For this attempt, five

[19] Barry, Jean, "General and Comparative Study of the Psychokinetic Effect on a Fungus Culture." *J. Parapsychol.*, 1968, 32, pp. 237–243.

experimental and five control dishes were prepared for each subject. At the experimental session, all ten dishes would be brought into a room, and put before the subject. The preparation of all were, of course, identical, but the subject was to concentrate only on the five experimental dishes and pay no attention to the controls. Each subject was placed about 1.5 meters from the dishes and his period of concentration, usually about 15 minutes, determined by a timer.

In order to make conditions as comparable as possible from test to test and from session to session, special stress was put on the genetic purity of the fungus, the composition of the culture medium, the uniformity of humidity, heat, and light.

The method of evaluating the results was to outline on a sheet of thin paper the boundary of the colony at the moment of maximum growth (i.e., when the mycelium filaments touch the rim of the culture dish). The outlines were cut out and weighed. The weights in milligrams were then treated statistically.

The experiment that was carried out consisted of nine sessions of eight different persons, and two combinations of two persons acting as subjects, making in all, 11 subject conditions. A total of 39 individual attempts were made and in each one, the subject attempted to inhibit the growth of the fungus in his five experimental dishes.

In assessing results, the growth in each individual's control dishes was taken as the standard of comparison. All five of them were measured for each session and the average taken. The growth in the five experimental plates was then measured and averaged. If this result was smaller than that of the control, the session was considered successful and a plus sign was recorded for it. If the experimental growth was more than that of the controls for a given session, it was unsuccessful and a minus sign was recorded for it. On a purely chance basis, the expectation was 50–50 or that the number of plus and minus signs would be approximately equal.

The actual results showed that 33 sessions were successful, three were unsuccessful, and three were neutral. Both Barry and Salinas were successful in all sessions. Out of the 36 trials in which a deviation was secured, when by chance alone 18 would have been expected to be successes, and 33 actually resulted, the deviation was +15. The CR = 5; p = millions to one.

Other evaluations, too, were highly significant. Of all the subjects who participated, ten scored above chance, and only one at chance. Then when the individual experimental dishes were compared with the control dishes, the general result was consistent to a significant degree in that 144 of the experimental dishes showed less growth than their controls.

The experiment thus was a very promising one from every aspect. If these results can be validated and confirmed, the implications for "thought control," at least of the organism under study, would seem to be assured. And if this particular parasite is amenable to an effect by PK, it very likely is not the only one. It seems that the encouragement given by a pioneer study such as this one should quickly lead to others so that the possible beneficial effect of PK on disease-causing fungi—and other parasites—could be utilized more quickly.

The tests on living tissue to date end here, but at least some beginning has been made. If any healing PK has been in operation in these "parabiological" researches it will now at least be easier to follow up on this new trail. In physiological functioning, at least in the growth processes involved, PK may well play its almost unsuspected part. In psychosomatic effects of many other kinds, perhaps when the healer is no external figure but the owner of the organism himself, PK may be the instrumental factor of the phenomenon and conceivably could even have played a part in the mechanics of evolution, as suggested by JBR in an editorial in 1943.[20] Speaking of the unpopularity in biology of the Lamarckian view that acquired characteristics might be inherited, he comments that it has been aggravated by the lack of any

[20] Rhine, J. B., "The Significance of the PK Effect." *J. Parapsychol.*, 1943, 7, pp. 139–143.

known means by which such an effect could occur. But PK could give new plausibility to the Lamarckian concept of evolution.

The tentative results of these first explorations are suggestive; the question awaits comprehensive and exhaustive research. The bridge is started. The outlook is good. The possible outcome could be tremendous.

Research on moving objects is obviously much farther along than it is on either static or living matter. In one way it might look accidental that research at Duke began with moving rather than with stationary objects. The gambler brought his idea to JBR and it happened that his were moving targets. The reason the technique was accepted quickly too was because it was simple, easy to assess statistically, inexpensive, and it "worked." If stationary objects had been involved instead, but if the test had still possessed these practical qualities, no doubt it would have been accepted just as quickly.

But apparently nature had made it likely to happen just as it did, for the situation regarding stationary objects and PK is peculiar as will be discussed in Chapter 14. Few life situations (except those of gambling) offer an obvious instance of moving objects to be influenced. It therefore may have been no accident that the technique for a test should have come from a gambler.

Research on animate matter would appear to be much more complex than on inanimate objects. Yet results with living organisms are promising. Research in this area has been slow mainly because of practical obstacles such as lack of biological equipment and medical supervision. No dime store dice can do this job. But, given the necessary setting, no reason appears why PK should not be conclusively demonstrated in life processes, just as the first exploratory attempts, from Richmond to Barry, suggest that it can be.

# CHAPTER 14

# *Spontaneous PK*

❧

LABORATORY research on PK would never have been thought of if no one had ever reported a spontaneous occurrence that seemed to be a direct effect of mind on matter. It was on account of the accumulation of reports from persons who thought that a mind-over-matter effect had occurred, culminating in the young gambler's demonstration one day in JBR's office, that finally led to controlled tests to see if a principle like that of PK could possibly exist in nature.

And yet in spite of these reports the curious fact is that most persons will testify that nothing in their experience has ever remotely suggested that they have influenced a physical object by thought alone or that they have ever been aware of any physical disturbance that did not seem to be the result of ordinary causes. This means for one thing that PK in nature is not an easily recognized phenomenon. But then, if it were conspicuous, it would certainly have been noticed long ago. However, as the record shows, even in the laboratory PK was not successfully distinguished from biases and coincidence and all such obscuring factors until statistical methods for evaluating results could be applied.

In daily life statistical methods cannot be used, and so any effects that would call for them are certain to go unrecognized. Only those that are much more obvious can ever hope to be noticed. And even so, how can they be recognized with certainty and not brushed off one by one as only an odd coincidence, or an "I must have been mistaken" kind of impression?

In everyday life the situation is not like that in the laboratory when the experimenter knows what target is to be affected and, therefore, when and where he should look for results. The only sign of PK in life situations that can be registered in a noticeable way seems to be by the evidence of the physical effect itself. That effect then has to be one that calls attention to itself because it has no detectable ordinary explanation; and it also has to be one which seems to be related somehow to a human situation that could bring in the mental aspect necessary when PK is concerned.

As one would expect then, the occasional reports of events that suggest PK involve unaccountable physical occurrences that appear to be connected with the affairs of a human being. As it develops, too, the human being so involved is usually one who is undergoing a crisis at the time. JBR's student who said the clock stopped when her father died thought it stopped when not run down or out of order. Because the stopping coincided with the death, she wondered if it could have been connected somehow with that. If it was, of course, the stopping of the clock would have to be considered as a probable instance of PK in a life situation.

Persons who have observed a phenomenon like that of the clock are usually reticent about telling of it. The thought "What will people think if I tell this?" is a strong inhibitor. Nevertheless sometimes when circumstances are right, people are glad, even relieved, to tell about some experience of the kind which long has puzzled them. Apparently the situation around the campfire and the serious discussion that had gone on in JBR's class that night was right for that student, and the fact that a serious study of "psi ability" was being made at the Parapsychology Laboratory was right for many others, for over the years many reports of such experiences accumulated there. They were mainly of the type that can be referred to as nonrecurrent, because the effect that seemed to involve PK, like the stopped clock, only occurred once, or if the same person reported more than one episode, the different ones seemed to be unrelated.

Another type was reported too. It was recurrent. In it a series of effects that seemed to be connected occurred. These were the kinds of cases commonly known as hauntings and poltergeist phenomena. For all anyone can tell now the basic phenomenon of the recurrent and nonrecurrent types is the same but for convenience and, because the methods of study are necessarily different, the two types are best discussed separately.

One reason for the different methods of study is that the non-recurrent kind is much simpler and more specific. When a sufficient number of accounts of this kind of effect accumulate, they can be studied and compared and if basic similarities exist they will stand out and can be recognized. However, they will do so more clearly if a fairly large number of separate reports are on hand for comparison, for then details that are only individual or personal can be discounted. They are unlikely to add up, while any that are general will. But the situation with the recurrent kind is quite different for here the problem of the reliability of human testimony is more complicated. Usually there is no way to tell how much of the account is the result of suggestion or imagination, so that it is less a matter of collecting a file of reports than of trying to get at least a few reliable accounts. This could be done ideally only by firsthand study. For practical reasons, however, such studies are seldom possible; and even when they are, too often the situation is complicated by local publicity. This alone can make unprofitable the study of a subtle and unpredictable effect like the one presumably involved, if the situation should in fact have in it any veridical element. For all of these reasons no specific number of recurrent cases can be said to have been on file at the laboratory when, in 1963, the number of cases of the unrepeated type in the collection had reached 178. Since that number seemed sufficient to make a study and comparison of them profitable, one was undertaken.[1]

---

[1] Rhine, Louisa E., "Spontaneous Physical Effects and the Psi Process." *J. Parapsychol.*, 1963, 27, pp. 84–122.

## NONRECURRENT PK EFFECTS

The first question about a report of possible spontaneous PK effect is whether or not it is reliable. If it seems to have been reported in good faith, the next is whether under the circumstances as given, it would seem necessary to suppose the effect to have been the result of PK. These questions, of course, and particularly the last one, can never by answered with finality. It is always possible that a coincidence however rare may have been the explanation. The study of case material is therefore not on a basis as reliable as tests that can be evaluated statistically. Nevertheless it can contribute ideas that tests alone cannot. Hopefully the proper tests later can disprove or confirm them as the case may be, and understanding be advanced accordingly.

In nearly all of the nonrecurrent cases one or more persons noticed or observed the effect, and it seemed to concern another, often distant, person. The college girl and her mother, for instance, noticed the stopped clock and therefore were the observers, and the dying husband and father was the one whom the effect seemed to concern; the crisis of course was his death. While a crisis seemed almost always to be involved, it was not always that of dying, for in some cases the person concerned was already dead. In still others, he was living. By dividing the group according to whether the person whom the PK effect seemed to concern was dying, dead, or living, the characteristics of each group could be considered separately.

## PK EFFECTS ASSOCIATED WITH THE DYING

The person with whom the effect the observers noticed was concerned was sometimes at a distance, and sometimes not. In a case reported from England a distance from a home to a hospital intervened.[2]

In this case an elderly widow and her (adult) daughter were reading in their respective beds on opposite sides of the same room one night when suddenly the mother's but not the daughter's light went off. The bulb was not burned out, for moments later the light came on again. Both persons testified that the light did go out so that the effect could hardly be considered a hallucinatory one, for while still a possibility it is much less likely that two persons would be hallucinating simultaneously than that one alone might do so.

As it happened, a close friend, Philip, who had helped the widow through the financial crisis following her husband's death and had shown great consideration for her and her daughter ever since, was now very ill and in the hospital with uncertain likelihood of recovery.

As the widow reports it, "Our latest news was that he was sinking. We were in the high state of emotional tension and had been silently reading in our beds for some time when suddenly, just at 10:30 P.M. exactly, my light went out. It stayed out three minutes. Muriel's light remained unchanged and when my light came on again we simultaneously said, 'Philip!' "

Very soon after the light episode the word came; Philip died at 10:30 P.M.

Cases like this are commonly called "death coincidences." They made up about half of all the nonrecurrent cases in the collection. The kind of PK effect in the cases of the collection varied a great deal. Sometimes a clock or light was affected; sometimes a dish broke, or a picture fell, usually one associated with the dying person. In practically all such cases the episode easily led to the assumption that the dying person had sent word of his crisis by this "sign."

[2] Accounts from the persons who reported the cases given in this chapter are on file at the Institute for Parapsychology.

Yet very occasionally a different light was thrown on such an occurrence when the question "Was it a message?" appeared to get a different answer. A few years ago a report came in from a nurse in a Veteran's Hospital. She said she looked in at a certain male cancer patient at 4 A.M., and he was breathing normally. But at 4:20 an orderly called her, and she found the patient dead. His watch had stopped at 4:15. She added that this patient had been very conscious of his watch having used it to check his medication during his stay in the hospital.

The stopping of the watch hardly seemed to have been a message because no message to the nurse or orderly would have been necessary, and no distant relatives were apprised of the death thereby. If a connection existed it would seem more likely that the effect on the watch was somehow simply a circumstance concomitant with the death, the relationship not presently obvious.

### PK EFFECTS ASSOCIATED WITH THE DEAD

In about a quarter of the cases the observer knew that the person involved was dead. Naturally the "sign" then could not be taken as a message to tell of his own crisis. Instead, it seemed to be a response to an emotional need or situation of the living observer, sometimes a warning of danger but more frequently a message of comfort and reassurance.

An example of this kind of situation was reported by a woman in California. Her husband had been killed in a car accident in February 1966, leaving her grief stricken. Their youngest child was 2½ months old, and, as she told it, had been

a wonderful tie between us. After the accident, I felt dead inside myself and each time I looked at the baby, I died a little more. I have always been religious but now I even began to doubt because death seemed so final. So I began to pray and I asked that if there was life after death, that my husband be able to give me some sign, however small, just so I would know his spirit lived on and there was a chance of our being together again someday.

I got that sign a week later.

He was killed on a Tuesday and one week from the day of his death, I was in the nursery tending the baby. On the baby's crib is a mobile. It has little angels and bluebirds suspended from it. When turned by hand, there is a musical jingle and the angels and birds all flutter.

I had left the crib and was by the dresser with my back turned away from the crib when all at once the mobile began its musical jingle. I turned around open-mouthed. The music was playing and the little angels and birds were revolving at full swing as if an unseen hand was moving them. This kept up for what I would say was a full five minutes—then stopped suddenly and there was no more motion.

While this was taking place, I saw no one and heard no one, but I knew my husband was in the room with me. This was the exact place where I'd seen him stand so many times at the foot of the crib watching our small son sleep. The baby had been asleep all the time, so there was no movement from inside the crib to have caused the mobile to have swung around as it had.

After it was over, I felt that I was in the room alone again, but a new feeling came over me. I knew now that there was life after death and, sad as the days are to me at times, nothing can ever shake my faith again. My oldest daughter was in the next room when the mobile was turning. She heard the music and asked me about it when I came out, so I know it was not an hallucination.

This has not happened since. Apparently that was my answer once and for all, but the experience was so vivid and the feeling of him in the room so strong that I really don't need any other.

Cases in which the sign was associated with someone deceased, have also usually been taken as a message from the dead person, and an indication that he still "lives" and in this way is able to communicate.

When the PK ability of the living was still unknown and unsuspected, if the case was taken seriously the assumption had to be that after death—or even at the time of dying—a new power of mind was attained that could influence matter directly, and that the person involved, however distant he might be, could cause the effect that was observed. The "sign," then, was something in the category of the miraculous. The possibility that the normal living person had the power to cause such an effect and that therefore he might be the one who did it was not even suggested.

No doubt it is because of the interpretation that "signs" are messages from the dead or dying, as well as because of their emotional quality, that so many of the cases reported are of this kind, for they are unlikely to be passed over as only coincidences or forgotten and more likely to be reported than if less meaningful situations were involved.

## PK EFFECTS ASSOCIATED WITH THE LIVING

The limelight has always and quite understandably been so strongly on "signs" involving dying persons or those already dead, that it comes as something of a surprise to find that very similar occurrences are reported in connection with living persons, too. They are fewer however, and in the Duke collection made up only about a quarter of all. Either they occur less often, or they are less likely to be taken as extraordinary and noticed and reported.

However, when a living person was involved, the sign could be interpreted as a message from him just as easily as in the case of a dying person. It seemed to tell of some crisis that had befallen him. Such an occurrence was testified to by a man in North Carolina.

Living next door to his family in a small Carolina town in 1918 was an elderly couple named Walker, whose son Harry was a sergeant in the Army in France. One day that fall, Mrs. Walker came running out of her house, weeping and wringing her hands and sobbing over and over, "Something has happened to Harry! Something has happened to Harry! I know it, I know it." For no discernible reason some bricks had fallen from the chimney, and this was the "reason" she knew it.

Something indeed had happened to Harry. He was struck in the chest by a shell that destroyed his left arm, ribs, and nearly, but did not quite, reached his heart. He lived, later returned home, and it was confirmed that the time of his injury was the time when the bricks fell.

However, the inclusion of signs that involve the living, as well as the dying and the dead, and of such as the man in the Veteran's Hospital, make less tenable the idea that the PK effect was a message. In most of the cases like the one above, the crisis in which the person was involved was sudden, seemingly too quick for thought- or message-sending. Such experiences call for an interpretation with a wider meaning.

In fact, the "message" interpretation, natural as it is, begins to look like another result of the naïve assumption that the universe is arranged for the benefit of mortals. The ancients thought the lightning and the thunder were evidence of the gods' concern with man. Even in the Middle Ages, the earth seemed to be the center of the universe, the abode of man who was the highest of God's creations.

Slowly the advance of knowledge is showing this concept of a man-centered universe to be but evidence of man's presumption. He is not necessarily the ultimate creation, after all, and the universe in general seems quite oblivious of him.

However, a wider world view has opened in which man is no smaller than before, but only diminished by perspective. If in turn he learns to see himself in true perspective, a vaster universe opens up before him. In this matter of "signs," the advance of knowledge brought in by the PK research already shows that the real meaning here, too, is a less obvious, less immediately personal, but a wider, more challenging one.

Because now with the discovery of PK the emphasis must shift, experiences involving living persons, even though comparatively infrequently reported, become more significant than before. Earlier they were anomalies and almost had to be shrugged off as "just coincidence," because they did not fit easily into the pattern that made those from the dying or the dead seem meaningful. But now, since PK is a phenomenon demonstrated in the laboratory, it has to be expected to occur spontaneously, too. It has developed, therefore, that experiences involving the living must be studied carefully, without, however, forgetting that the actual number of cases is limited and the impressions they give quite tentative.

One of the first things that is noticeable when only living persons are involved is that in some of the episodes no second person is concerned. This fact too detracts from the idea that the occurrence the person noticed was in any sense a message. And since only one person is concerned the situation is more like that in the laboratory. In a few of the reports the difference between the life and the laboratory situation is not very great. Take for instance an occurrence reported by a young man who in 1959 had spent two weeks in the National Guard on military police duty. On the return home, circumstances had conspired to make him and a companion overly tired and hungry as they rode along on an army truck from Utica to Kingston. As he recounted it, it was a "long haul," and at one point he turned to his companion and said, "How would you like this truck to stop so we could rest and possibly get a bite to eat?" His friend just laughed as the truck was running smoothly with no sign of mechanical difficulty. But the man reports, "wishful thinking got the better of me. I closed my eyes and visualized the engine and began to imagine that the gas could not get through the carburetor. Within a couple of minutes the truck had to pull off to the side with the carburetor not working correctly."

As a result, the men had the rest they wanted, and later the engine again worked properly. The point of course is that the trouble with the carburetor came when the man was wanting it to. But was it more than a coincidence? The setup was similar to that in a PK experiment except for the essential part, a basis for judging the likelihood of chance coincidence. And of course in everyday life no PK effect has been recognized, and so the general reaction in a situation like this has had to be, "just a coincidence," whether it was something more or not.

If it was something more in the above case, at least it would have been a response to a conscious intention, as in the majority of significant PK effects secured in the laboratory. In real life, occasionally effects are reported, too, when, as in some of Forwald's experiments especially, only an unconscious mental process could have been involved. A woman in Philadelphia a few years ago was so mystified by a case of this kind at a time when she was in correspondence with the laboratory that she wrote about it almost at once, saying:

Something has really surprised me. I was reading an article on Jimmy West, a crippled orphan who did so much for child welfare when he grew up. His experiences as a child were so appalling to me that it made a deep impression, particularly his having a tubercular hip, and being accused of malingering instead, and then the hospital discharging him later as incurable and refusing him readmittance. I don't know whether my mind has ever been so stirred and perhaps that is why it happened. At any rate, as I put the magazine down, we heard a loud sound from the living room. There was no one in there, not even the dog or cat for I looked. The sound had been made by a book falling out of the book case *by itself*. When I picked it up, I was hardly able to believe my eyes, for it was a book on surgery for children. I wonder how that could possibly be explained.

The answer to her question could be "By PK," although there again, no CR or p-value of the probability against chance coincidence of such an occurrence is possible. If it were, it would no doubt be much smaller than in the case of the faulty carburetor, for as everyone knows, engine trouble is not too uncommon. However, books falling out of a bookcase "by themselves," especially significant ones, are certainly uncommon.

One feature of the above case that is common in nearly all of the spontaneous situations in which PK may be involved is the emotional aspect. This woman, like those in cases involving the dying or the dead, was emotionally stirred. But intense emotion, which for all one can say may be a *facilitating* factor in the production of a PK effect, is apparently not really necessary in life experiences any more than it has proven to be in the laboratory. A young man reports that one evening when he was telling his roommate how much he wished he would hear from a particular girl, he impulsively pointed at the phone suddenly and exclaimed, "Ring!"

"To my amazement," he continues, "the phone rang at the exact moment and because of my surprise I asked my roommate to answer, which he did only to find there was no one on the other end. Had there been someone there it would have been 'just coincidence.' "

Again one must say that the p-value against coincidence, if it could be computed, in a case like this would surely be a comparatively small one. However, that incident may not be a perfect example of a case involving only a slight emotion, for one cannot actually tell from the situation how emotionally involved the young man may have been. But in the following case, the circumstances may give better grounds for supposing that no very deep emotions were stirred.

In this instance a small boy of my own acquaintance who had been given a battery-operated "ack-ack" gun was upset because it would no longer operate when he pressed the trigger. (The gun had no bullet or projectile of any kind. It just made the ack-ack sound so dear to a small boy's heart.) Tearfully he brought the gun in to his father, the proprietor of a small country store. As it happened, the little boy's mother and 12-year-old sister and a customer were all in the store at the time, and among them they jokingly decided that the father could not fix the gun. He was no electrician, and what did he know about guns?

A few minutes later, in spite of the fun at his expense, the boy's father announced that the gun was fixed, "and if you don't believe it, I'll shoot that clock [electric] right off of the wall."

And he aimed, pulled the trigger, the gun ack-acked like mad—and the clock *jumped* off the wall.

"*Jumped*" is the word they all agreed on, for the joint testimony was that the clock did not drop straight down, but seemed to project itself out a foot or so, and then suddenly as if just released, fell, missed a shelf, and reaching the cord's length, swung back to the wall, and broke, glass flying everywhere.

No wind. No traffic. No airplanes overhead. As the report says, "Everything was still, including us—for a long time."

In these cases, obviously the effect that seemed very appropriate to the situation could have been the result of PK. They could have been cases as simple as those in the laboratory when the subject throwing for a one face gets it—by PK. Only there he must repeat his success sufficiently that coincidence is excluded. In life, it must be taken as a solitary case.

The list thus spreads out broadly and "signs" seem to have occurred that coincided with human situations ranging from death and bereavement to purely emotional ones, the latter even when the emotion involved was comparatively slight. This is the list as it was found in the 178 cases in the collection at the Duke laboratory. If these are a sample of the kind of life situations in which PK may occur in sufficiently conspicuous manner to be noticed, what can one make of it? What is the relation of such spontaneous occurrences and the experimental research?

## THE RELATION OF NONRECURRENT SPONTANEOUS PK
### AND EXPERIMENTAL RESULTS

The kinds of spontaneous experiences given above *could be* instances of PK operating in real life. Even if some of them—say, those like the carburetor that went bad—were only coincidences, still they took the form that PK in real life presumably might take, if it does occur spontaneously, a supposition one has a right to make. One therefore must try to answer the question: how would occurrences like these fit into the information about PK that has accumulated from the experimental work?

The first observation about the relation of life and laboratory is simply that the experiments have shown that PK is a reality. Without that assurance no report of a spontaneous effect could possible stand up against the sheer improbability of its occurrence. One after another, cases like these 178 of the collection could all be dismissed as the result of poor observation, over-interpretation, or coincidence. But if PK does occur, then for all one can tell by present knowledge, it could be involved in such situations as these. And even more than that, some of them can reasonably be expected to be PK in life situations, for processes in laboratories are basically only real ones confined, not invented, by laboratory conditions.

Several aspects of PK that have been observed in the research results can help a little in interpreting effects like these that are reported from real life situations. First of all, in the laboratory the unconsciousness of the process is unmistakable even though the subject is consciously trying to induce it. Still he does not know as he makes his trials in the test whether or not he will succeed. And next, if he succeeds, he has no idea how he did it. He may have been throwing dice for the one-face, let us say, and if that face comes up significantly more than it should by chance, how did he do it? He has no idea. Also, if he then becomes an experimenter and asks a subject to produce a significant score on the one face and the subject's results show that a significant score was obtained, another perplexity arises. Who did it? Was it the subject or the experimenter? The question, who does it, as shown in various experiments like Mrs. Dale's and some of Forwald's, comes up often in experimental results. Even though the subjects may give evidence that they exert their own effects, still the results often appear to show the influence of the experimenter too.

All of these points affect the way spontaneous experiences must be tentatively interpreted, even though no difference marks off the experimental from most of the spontaneous situations. In the experiment, the subject consciously sets out to get his one face. In the spontaneous one, the conscious aspect is lacking. But experiments with "blind" targets succeed, as tests by Thouless, Osis, Forwald, and Fisk have demonstrated. The difference in states of consciousness, therefore, seems not to be a prohibitive one. With or without conscious intention, the PK process obviously can go on. The woman disturbed about an incident involving surgery in children then could have produced a PK effect with neither conscious intention or knowledge that she did so. Standing alone, however, a case like that would probably be more easily ascribed to pure (uncaused) coincidence than to PK. But it does not stand alone. It represents one of the types of occurrence in which it seems as if the single individual involved is in a sense his own PK subject, just as in many PK experiments he has been.

If occurrences like the falling book are taken as an example, they can be revealing because they are more simple than cases involving several persons. In instances like that one, again the effect was clearly *not* a message. It was a sign, yes. But a sign of the emotional situation that engendered a PK effect. That effect then was a result; a product, not a motivated end in itself. Similarly it may well be that when two persons are involved, someone dying and an observer of an effect possibly caused by PK, the observer could be the one whose PK is involved. In these cases, too, the effect can be an indication that information about the distant crisis has registered by ESP at some unconscious level of his personality. It follows then that now with PK a known ability of living persons, it is no longer necessary to suppose that PK effects like these are messages from the dying or the dead. The miracle is no longer an unearthly one. It is instead something hidden within the normal living personality.

Does that statement mean then that the old interpretation in cases like the mobile on the baby's crib do not show that the dead survive? No, such cases simply give no final answer to the question. The living person can exert PK. Whatever energy may be involved, and however it may be applied, presumably it comes from the living observer. Unconsciously, unknowingly, it still is his. But the further question, whether it be a function stimulated at the particular time and place by one deceased, is still unanswered. The evidence of today tells only that living persons have the PK potential. It says nothing about the deceased. Whether they "survive" and can influence the living is a question still open and awaiting the type of crucial experiment that can decide it.

Thus the greatest result of all that the discovery of PK has on the status of PK in daily life, is that it puts the footing of possible legitimacy under cases that could be instances of it. As long as such occurrences had no possible explanation other than the miraculous, they had to be rejected as unproven by all who believe that the world is governed by natural law. It can now be said that PK in daily life *might be* expressed like this, and thereby the way to greater understanding of the natural universe, of man and his place in it, has been opened a little farther; an appreciation of the possible reach and ability of mind very much expanded.

### RECURRENT SPONTANEOUS PK

The kinds of reported occurrences that come under this heading of possible recurrent spontaneous PK, hauntings and poltergeist phenomena, are further instances of alleged happenings that have never been satisfactorily validated, and yet have continued to be reported in practically every time and culture. In the main they have been ignored by scientists as the stuff of superstition, and even the Psychical Research Societies in earlier times so often found evidence of fraud, suggestion, or overimagination in the claims that very little validity was given them.

However with the discovery of PK a different attitude can be taken. It is possible now to see that a kernel of truth may be hidden in the claims. It could be that PK has sometimes been involved and therefore that an element of veridicality was supplied that kept those concerned from being able wholly to dismiss the occurrence as pure imagination, or delusion of one kind or another. And if PK was involved in any such episode it is a certainty that it would have been unrecognized and misinterpreted just as it has been in the nonrecurrent cases. Now a more insightful approach to mysteries of this kind can be taken than the old spiritistic one could give.

### HAUNTINGS AND PK

The effect known as haunting usually is specifically associated with a place. Particularly houses are reported as haunted. In most cases this means that inexplicable events are reported to occur there which have usually suggested a "spirit" presence of some kind, and which involve things seen and heard that are not explainable in ordinary ways. Since these effects do involve the senses (mainly sight and hearing) for which no objective reason is ascribable, the experiences are hallucinatory at least, whatever further explanation may be necessary to account for them. As a matter of fact the experiences that most often suggest haunting seem to involve ESP rather than PK. But exceptions occur, and one of these may be in connection with inexplicable sounds. As a matter of fact the most frequently reported kind of phenomenon in so-called "haunted" houses is the auditory type. While the sounds heard are most often interpreted as footsteps or simple knocks or tappings, occasionally they are more specific and then can be related to some event that is said to have occurred there earlier. An example of this kind, from Ohio, has been reported in these words:

My husband, five-year-old son and myself moved into a strange town and rented a two-year-old home, very nice, at a ridiculously low rent, which we could hardly understand, unless it was because it stood in the center of three two-year-old homes—all empty, although all other houses on the street were occupied.

We also had a bulldog which my husband took to the basement and made a bed for under the stairs.

Hours after we were asleep that first night, we heard a loud crash and a "rolling" noise in the basement. The noise was terrific. I called to my husband in another room, and he said he thought the dog had become untied and upset the two metal wash tubs causing them to roll.

The next morning we found the dog still tied and the tubs still full of canned goods that we hadn't unpacked.

After a short time, I began to feel during the day that someone or something was evading me—a sort of "presence" that was always near, but moved faster than I could turn my head.

In the evening, my husband and I would be reading and I would feel that a gray shadow had just brushed by me—leaving a cool feeling—but I *never saw* anything.

My husband would go to bed early and he couldn't understand why suddenly I began to retire when he did as I was a "night hawk." He slept in the front bedroom and although we had three bedrooms, I slept with my little son in the back bedroom—I hated this room.

I'd wake up in the middle of the night—many nights—and feel that if I turned my head that I would see some monstrous presence in the dark room. (I never did.) It got so bad that I'd wake up "shaking" and cover my head with my sheet and push my son and myself to the further wall. Finally one night after three months of this, I woke up with the impression that something terrible was at the edge of the bed and I must escape.

I'll never know how God gave me strength, but I grabbed my son, jumped over the low foot of the bed, ran down the hall and landed in my husband's bed and lay there shaking, my son in my arms.

My husband was amazed, but all that I could say was that there was something terrible in that room.

We stayed there three more months—until the house was sold; and all that time I insisted on sleeping all in one bed in my husband's room. The night before we moved, the owner took my husband aside and asked if we had ever experienced anything *unusual* in the house, as it was haunted, and no one would stay over 30 days in it!

He said his first tenant was wanted by the police and when they were closing in, he (the tenant) stood on a *metal* tub in the basement and hung himself by *kicking the tub away!* Also, this man had occupied the room that had frightened me so.

My husband never saw anything or had any of the impressions that I had—except for the horrible noises that first night.

The case is at least typical of the majority of those reported in recent years in that it has no visual aspect. But here it seems as if "fashions" in haunting experiences change, as in other areas of human experience. Earlier, and especially, say, in Victorian England, hauntings more often seem to have involved apparitions which of course are hallucinatory experiences of the visual kind involving the human figure. As visual impressions, they involve ESP rather than PK. Even apparitions that spoke were not uncommon in the old collections (although of course one has no way of knowing how much the cases may have been selected). Today, only very rarely does a person report *seeing* a figure or "luminous object" or something of the kind, and apparitions that also speak are practically nonexistent in the Duke collection. Sounds of other kinds, however, seem to be reported perhaps as much as ever. Of course, they too can be hallucinatory and therefore not of the PK type, and many of those reported probably are just that.

A study of auditory psi experiences (either ESP or PK) made on the unrepeated cases of the Duke collection, showed that the sounds reported were of two general kinds.[3] One was the human voice. In instances of this kind, which were by no means infrequent, the person usually heard himself called and very often, in a voice he recognized, as in the following case from a woman in New Hampshire.

She said, "My youngest son and his wife were living in Japan. He was a lieutenant in the Air Force. We had received a cable-

[3] Rhine, Louisa E., "Auditory Psi Experiences: Hallucinatory or Physical?" *J. Parapsychol.*, 1963, 27, pp. 182–198.

gram saying a little son had been born to them. Three nights later, about 3:40 A.M., I was awakened by my son calling to me from our western window. I got up and was half-way down the stairs when I realized that Jim was in Japan. Then I thought about his call, Mother, Mother, Mother, Moooth-er! the last time so despairingly it still rings in my mind.

"The next day we received a cablegram saying the baby was dead. The difference in time zones made the call at the exact time my son was told of his son's death."

Nearly all of these "call cases" were hallucinatory and the possibility of PK not involved. They therefore could be so classified, both because the person whose voice was heard was not within hearing distance and because if a second person was present he did not hear the call.

But many of the sounds reported were not of the human voice. They were impersonal, as knocks or thuds, or else they were mechanical, as bells or musical instruments (similar to the case in Chapter 1, reported by Flammarion).

For instance, a woman in Illinois told of such an occurrence when her father died. He had had cancer and was on the terminal list and in a coma in the hospital. She and her mother were at home in their third-floor apartment.

At 5:40 A.M., the back door bell rang, awakening both of them. They sat up, wondering who it could be at that hour. Her mother went to the door. No one was there. She stepped outside onto the porch. No one was on the stair or in the courtyard below.

Twenty minutes later, the phone rang. Her mother picked it up, and said, "I know." It was the resident physician saying her husband had died at 5:40 A.M.

All such sounds could possibly have had a physical cause. Presumably the bell could have responded by PK. And just as in this case, in a large percentage of the entire group the sounds were heard by all persons within range. The facts as presented in such episodes then made cases with this kind of sound seem possibly to have been instances involving PK.

However, in the case of sounds heard repeatedly in houses, an explanation is more difficult, and the question whether they are hallucinatory or have a physical, and hence PK, origin is usually impossibe to decide. Often, as in the case above, when the sound of a rolling tub was heard, although both husband and wife were reported as having heard it, and although possibly it could have had a PK origin yet no regulation physical mechanism existed to produce it. In that case, the sound was eventually associated with an event that had occurred earlier, but it could not have been caused as that one was, by the tub. Any attempt at a further explanation must be given up at this point.

Occasionally, but rarely, an actual physical effect may be observed in connection with a haunted house, or at least the person so sees it, again whether hallucinatory or real, may be difficult to say. Such an effect was reported by an Ohio woman. It occurred in her girlhood when she says she lived in a "haunted" house. She went on to say:

We were warned that it was haunted before we moved in, but my father laughed about it—as did all of us. It was an old Victorian monstrosity, with two wings separated by a hall with stairs leading to the second floor.

My father and mother slept downstairs, while my brother and I had our rooms upstairs. At night my brother and I would hear footsteps pacing in the attic, but my parents would laugh and say, "We must have rats."

One night when my parents and brother were all gone away together to another part of town, I was sitting alone in the downstairs living room reading, when I heard footsteps in the hall. It was winter, so all the doors and windows were closed, including the door between the living room and the hall.

"Hey, you're home early," I called, thinking that a member of my family must have returned. There was no answer.

"Don't scare me," I called. "Who's out there?" There was no answer. I saw the knob on the door to the hall slowly begin to turn.

"Don't do that!" I called. "You're frightening me. For heaven's sake, answer!"

The knob continued to turn and then the door slowly began to open and it opened all the way until it was flat against the wall and, of course, there was no one there. It's the one time my hair has raised from my head, like you read about in stories. I stared for a long frozen moment at the empty doorway, and then slowly the door began to close. It closed all the way, the knob once more turned and the door clicked shut.

I leapt across the room and locked the door. My family got home a half hour later and they had all been together all evening, so it wasn't my brother playing a trick.

The difficulty of extracting a "common denominator" from accounts like these is obvious. A PK effect may have been involved in some cases, but the distinction between such and hallucinatory experiences induced perhaps by suggestion or expectation is impossible to make with assurance. And the question "Who does it?" is more unanswerable than ever. On that point, one can only say that not everyone, even in a haunted house, experiences the phenomena, and thus such effects undoubtedly depend on a combination of personal susceptibility and external circumstances, for usually those who report having lived in a haunted house have not experienced similar hallucinatory effects elsewhere.

### POLTERGEIST EFFECTS AND PK

It seems probable that spontaneous PK is sometimes involved in the incidents commonly known as "poltergeist" activity. The antiquity of the type is suggested in the name, which is a German term meaning "noisy or boisterous spirit." A better and more modern name could be "recurrent spontaneous PK," or RSPK.

In this kind of manifestation, more than in haunting cases,

the effects are likely to be unquestionably physical. But whether they are the result of PK, or have a normal explanation is the problem. They generally consist of some type of disturbance of objects in or near a dwelling and, usually in conjunction with a certain individual. More often than not the person about whom they seem to center is an adolescent.

Like haunted houses, reports of poltergeist activity have come down through the ages and from the four corners of the world. In some cases, fraud and trickery have been shown to account for the phenomena, but in many, nothing of the kind was ever uncovered. Usually, as with haunted houses, investigators, when they arrive on the scene of action, fail to witness the phenomena as reported, and therefore they are unable to reach a firm conclusion.

In recent years, a few cases in England and in the United States have been studied under somewhat better conditions than most, and have left the investigators with a little more than a negative conclusion. But in no instance has a final verdict seemed to be warranted. The completely experimental and controlled investigation is yet to be reported. A case in Scotland (1960) is reported by Dr. A. R. G. Owen, a Cambridge University professor of mathematics, who calls it the "Sauchie poltergeist."[4] While Owen was not an investigator on the spot, he interviewed all the main participants soon after (which is a circumstance only once removed for the ideal one of on-the-spot observation). From their testimony he wrote his book. Incidentally, in it Owen also gives an inclusive history of poltergeist reports.

The character of the witnesses in the Sauchie case, a minister, three physicians, and a teacher, besides the family and the neighbors, was above the ordinary, and the fact that Owen interviewed them very soon after the period of activity lends credence to their stories. The character and standing of Owen himself, too, is a large factor in making this case outstanding.

[4] Owen, A. R. G., *Can We Explain the Poltergeist?* (New York: Helix Press, Garrett Publications 1964).

The main individual in the case was an 11-year-old girl, Virginia, who, with her parents, had lived a secluded life in a remote locality in Ireland, but at the time of the outbreak of poltergeist activity had very recently come to Scotland to stay in the home of a much older brother while her father remained in Ireland and her mother lived at a distance. Presumably the change was a very drastic one to the girl. She had come into this entirely strange environment, leaving behind her only companion, a pet dog Toby, and her only friend, a little neighbor girl.

Virginia was put in school at Sauchie in October 1960. The teacher recalled later that Virginia and her mother who brought her, "gave the impression of people who had lived for a long time in a remote and isolated place."

On November 22, the family began to hear unaccountable "thunking" noises that ceased when Virginia went to sleep. They reported that articles of furniture—a sideboard, a linen chest, and the like—had been observed to move, and loud knocks to be heard. The preacher had been called in and he felt vibrations when he gripped the bed head on which Virginia was half asleep and felt vibrations when knocks were heard. Other movements, especially around Virginia's bed, were observed by many different people, especially an unaccountable rotating of the pillow, and at school a few unaccountable movements of her desk lid.

Later, other outsiders were called in and a movie camera set up in the child's room. Some unexplained sounds were recorded eventually. Then as the publicity was allowed to die down, the effects diminished in extent and by the end of the month had nearly ceased.

In his discussion of the case, Owen is convinced that inexplicable movement of objects must have occurred. They were, however, all such that they would have been within the energy capacity of a girl the age and size of Virginia, although she could not have caused them by ordinary means. He goes on to evaluate the situation by summing up the outline of the psychological situation of the girl and decides that her "transplantation" to

Sauchie created an emotional crisis, even though she suffered from no physical unkindness.

He considers the possibility that at her rapidly developing adolescent stage, the phenomena could have in part been motivated subconsciously as attention-seeking devices. However, nothing told about the girl suggests this trait, although the psychological upset the change must have created in her seems obvious. But, as Owen concludes, the "case is replete with suggestive possibilities. Firm conclusions of course cannot be drawn. But correlation with other cases might well provide some useful steps toward an acceptable theory of poltergeist genesis."

In the United States, one of the most thoroughly "researched" of the more recent cases occurred in the town of Seaford, Long Island, in 1958.[5] The family involved was that of a Mr. and Mrs. James M. Herrmann, which included besides the parents a 13-year-old daughter and a 12-year-old son, James.

On February 3, according to the report, disturbances began that consisted mainly of toilet bottles of various kinds moving "by themselves," their caps becoming unscrewed and falling to the floor. But other objects, too, including objects in the boy's room, and bric-a-brac and furnishings elsewhere fell, or were moved, some broken—all, according to the family, quite inexplicably. By February 9, Mr. Herrmann decided they needed help, and he called in the police.

Apparently the police arrived soon after being called, for their record stated, for February 9, "While Patrolman J. Hughes was at the complainant's home, all the family was present with him in the living room when noises were heard in the bathroom. When Patrolman Hughes went into the bathroom with the complainant's family, he found the medicine had again spilled." The patrolman had inspected the bathroom earlier and thought, but could not be sure, that the bottle had been upright then. However, if it had not been, he could not account for the noise

[5] Pratt, J. G., and Roll, W. G., "The Seaford Disturbances." *J. Parapsychol.*, 1958, 22, pp. 79–124.

they had all heard that had caused them to go in and find the bottle overturned, the contents spilled.

When the police continued to be baffled by the occurrences, and because the Herrmanns, too, wanted to find an explanation, the Duke Parapsychology Laboratory was consulted. Two members, Dr. J. G. Pratt and Mr. W. G. Roll went to the Herrmann home to investigate. These two men were able to isolate reports of 67 separate disturbances attested to by seemingly reliable people. A sufficiently large number of these occurred near the boy, James, to make it seem that he was somehow the "focus" of the occurrences.

Of the 67 disturbances five occurred when the Duke investigators were in the house. One was a lamp found overturned, and one was a bread plate with bread spilled on the floor. In both instances, the investigators were in other rooms and did not actually see the action. Two more cases were thumps apparently coming from the room where James was in bed.

The fifth case was centered in the basement when the family and the two Duke men were all on the main floor. All of them heard a "loud, dull noise" that was traced to the basement. There, as Pratt reported, "the bleach bottle (with screw cap) was in the cardboard box by the washing machine. It was standing on an overturned jar containing starch. The bleach bottle had lost its cap and was leaning against the side of the box. The cap was on the floor—the contents of the bottle had not spilled. . . ."

The cap of the bottle was found to be still wet inside and a wet spot was on the floor beside it, which seemed to show that the cap had arrived there recently. The movements of the family before the sound was heard could be traced, and it was certain that none of them had been in the basement for at least a half an hour before. James had been in the bathroom when the noise was heard, and so circumstantial evidence seemed to say he could not have produced the effect, although the possibility could not be absolutely ruled out that he could have made the noise and staged the bottle cap effect earlier. The wet spot, however, appeared to count against such a possibility.

The hypothesis the police and others entertained that some physical cause was involved in the disturbances in general included such possibilities as high-frequency radio waves, a stopped chimney, or structure defects in the house. But no evidence was found that any of these were involved, or could have produced the peculiar kinds of effects that had been evidenced.

After finding none of these possible explanations satisfactory, the authors of the report go on to outline some of the clues that seemed to point to a psychological, rather than a physical, origin for the phenomena. For instance, nothing occurred when everyone was out of the house, asleep, or when the children were both in school. James was practically always in the house when a disturbance occurred, and more of them occurred near him than anyone else. The fact that the effects apparently centered around an adolescent conformed to a pattern generally found in other cases. Also, it is a general rule that each case has its own distinctive characteristics, as in this case, the "bottle popping."

While this episode was by no means the most striking of the 67 reported at the Herrmann's, it was the one in which the investigators got the closest to making firsthand observations.

In discussing the case in their report, Pratt and Roll considered three possible kinds of explanation. One was fraud, but this could be fairly well ruled out, since no evidence of such could be found, and even James had been under surveillance at the time of some of the disturbances and could not normally have produced those specific ones at least.

The second possibility was called "psychological aberrations." This referred to such effects as group hallucinations, amnesia, and the like. But this kind of effect, too, could be dismissed since the police as well as the outside investigators could testify to the actuality of some of the effects.

In a summing up paragraph, the authors said, "The detection of such psychological correlations shows that we are not dealing here with a kind of impersonal physical force which perhaps sometime in the future will fall within the scope of physics although its operation is not now understood. If the Seaford disturbances are not fraudulent—and no evidence of fraud was found—they clearly make a proper claim upon the interest of parapsychologists." Or, in other words, they might have said, they appear to have been caused by PK. But to say more than that the investigation had to be considered as exploratory rather than conclusive would have been as unjustified as it would have been to have drawn the conclusion that PK had been proven after the first few statistically significant experiments had been made.

As the authors continued still further, "This is an inconclusive report. . . . It would be an improper application of scientific method to attempt to go further on the basis of such material. But science consists of more than reaching conclusions. One of its important functions is the appraisal of problems that might justify further study."

One of the points they foresaw that might develop from further study of such cases of possible spontaneous and repeated PK was a clearer understanding of the *modus operandi* of PK it might give.

An attempt was made to follow up some of the psychological implications of the case, but they were not very successful. It was ascertained, however, that James, like many adolescents, was undergoing some more or less repressed emotional strains. Even though the facts were somewhat conjectural, it seemed possible that in his case, as in that of Virginia in the Sauchie poltergeist, a state of inner turmoil must have existed when the effects broke out. In many other cases, too, not always with children as young as these, and even occasionally with adults, it appears that the "poltergeist person" is more or less emotionally disturbed. This is the general impression, but in no instance can it be said really to have been proved to have had a direct connection with the PK effect. It seems in line with the observation on the unrepeated spontaneous cases that they usually result when an emotional crisis is involved. And it can be said that even in the laboratory, where emotion in its more extreme forms, and even its more obvious forms is excluded, the effect of interest and enthusiasm is recognized as important even though they scarcely classify as emotion on a level like that of Virginia's and James's.

### THE RELATION OF SPONTANEOUS RECURRENT PK AND EXPERIMENTAL RESULTS

Just as with the nonrecurrent type of spontaneous PK, the recurrent type too, calls for explanation. In spite of all the superstition and imagination and other rubbish in which the topic of hauntings and poltergeist activity are immersed, the more recent investigations of these cases, especially the latter, leaves room for the supposition that a genuine element of PK is sometimes involved. If so, however, the situations from which these manifestations are reported are by all odds the most complex in which a spontaneous mental effect on physical objects can be suspected. And as with the nonrecurrent type of spontaneous PK, the main reason why they can be taken seriously now, more than at any former time, is that PK has been confirmed by reliable experimental tests.

Direct application of research findings to recurrent PK phenomena is no more possible than it is to the nonrecurrent type. Here too, only the unconscious aspect of its occurrence is comparable to that of PK in the laboratory. In both recurrent and nonrecurrent spontaneous PK the person involved has no awareness of his part in the effect.

In the spontaneous cases of both kinds a wide range of objects is affected. From the few examples given here, clocks and lights were mentioned, and the list could have been much extended. It could have included pictures that fall from the wall, dishes that break, doors that open or close, other furniture that moves, and similar phenomena—all, of course, without any ostensible ordinary reason.

These effects are in contrast to the laboratory work, both in their wide range of variety and because they all appear to show PK operating on stationary objects and causing them to move or to be otherwise affected. In the laboratory on the other hand, the PK effect has been shown to occur only to influence movement of objects already in motion. This difference however is the result of the emphasis of the observation. In spontaneous cases it is the end position of the object that gives evidence of PK. In the experiment it is the p-value, but that is only a measure of the *end product of the motion*. The actual difference lies in the way the two operations are initiated. As already remarked, in experiments the experimenter initiates the process, usually, in dice experiments by releasing them to fall by gravity. In the spontaneous cases on the other hand the initial step itself presumably is caused by PK.

At this point it well may be that the peculiar aspect of PK with regard to stationary objects comes in. It may be connected with the fact often mentioned by those who report spontaneous effects, that no one *sees* the object when in motion. Even in poltergeist reports, this is usually true, and those set to observe —family members, police, investigators, and even if present when some object is moved—seldom see it when in motion, and even more rarely does anyone see an object *start* to move. It is possible that this is a meaningful fact. It could be tied up with the unconscious aspect of PK. Like some of Forwald's results, once attention is directed to them, they fail to occur.

Although the line of supposition is a thin one here, it may be that the reason attempts in the laboratory to move a static object directly have failed is just because they were direct. It may be that the situation is somewhat analogous to trying to develop film in daylight. If no images appear it would be, as one might say, because a necessary condition was lacking, in this case, darkness. In the PK situation, the condition lacking would be an unconscious mental state. Although frequent reports of movement of static objects without contact have come from the séance rooms of "physical mediums," none of them have ever been satisfactorily validated, and even if they had been it would be impossible now to tell what the actual mental state of the medium may have been.

One of the earliest claims of this kind on record was made by Sir William Crookes,[6] not in a séance room, but with the famous medium, D. D. Home. According to the account, an effect that could only be ascribed to PK (if the medium was controlled as well as the report states) was secured on an apparatus Crookes had made himself. No one who has tried it since has reported similar results. But no one else has had Home for his subject. Recognizing the possibility of "special subjects" for PK just as in ESP, where a few individuals have shown much greater natural ability than the average, W. E. Cox at a meeting of the Parapsychology Association in New York in 1960 presented a research brief urging that parapsychologists "keep a weather-eye out" for special PK subjects, who may have much greater ability than the average, but who have not had the opportunity of being formally tested. But to date no such individual has been reported.[7]

The situation seems to be either that only special subjects can initiate the PK process—natural PK subjects they would be—or that a technique still remains to be discovered, by which unselected subjects can do so.

The suggestion arises at this point that if one unselected subject alone cannot do so, perhaps many working together might succeed. The unfortunate fact, however, is that as far as tests have gone, it still is far from proven that in this, two or more are better than one. The only evidence that has been obtained thus far to show that the attempts of different subjects to produce a PK effect are additive comes from the Help-Hinder work of Betty Humphry which still needs confirmation (Chapter 9).

---

[6] Crookes, William, F. R. S., *Researches in the Phenomena of Spiritism* (West London: The Psychic Bookshop, 1926).

[7] Cox, W. E., "Physical Mediumship," Research Brief.

Since mental processes are different in different people it may be that group efforts operate at cross purposes. Possibly if they could be unified, the outcome might be different.

However, *supposing* is an indifferent tool in science. Unless it can lead to an experiment it is time wasted. But the supposing indulged in here should at least show that the question of the affect of PK on static objects is only opened and not by any means at a dead end.

It must be remembered, of course, that only in the laboratory research are the results on a reliable statistical basis. None of the results claimed by physical mediums have been established beyond dispute, and the idea that PK is involved in spontaneous cases like the examples given above is only an inference. However, both the inference and the claim are supported by logic at least, sufficiently to encourage the idea that further research on the topic may be successful. One particular line of investigation needs to be taken much farther than has yet been the case. That concerns the subjects, mainly, although possibly the conditions as well.

In laboratory research the implicit assumption has been that all persons may have potential PK ability. But only a comparatively few individuals have reported spontaneous experiences and only a few mediums have claimed the ability of physical mediumship. It is possible that, for reasons still to be determined, the ability to exert a PK effect on static objects is limited to certain individuals, circumscribed let us say, by characteristics that subjects in general do not possess or cannot exercise under prevailing conditions. This is a possibility that needs further investigation.

However, if the spontaneous kind of occurrence is ever to be taken at full value many questions of the *modus operandi* will be raised. How and why could such effects be produced? At the present time they seem part of the unresolved mystery of the ages which modern science seeks to dispel. But it will not be dispelled as long as an effect like PK exists but is not fitted into the recognized scheme of things.

# CHAPTER 15

# What Does It Mean?

✢

THE evidence is in. The case for PK has been presented, at least in outline. In experiment after experiment statistically significant scores were obtained. The objects used in the tests would not have behaved the way they did by chance alone. Unexpected as the verdict may be, the only reasonable explanation for the results of the tests was that they were affected by the will of the subjects.

The strength of the case does not depend on the work of a single or even only a few experimenters. Many different persons at a number of different places contributed to it. The initial experiment at Duke University by JBR was repeated with variations many times by persons under his direction. Then after nine years of this when the results that had accumulated were published, other persons at other places in the United States and abroad added their confirmations as they, too, secured results that were not explainable by chance or by defects of experimental procedure. After all this, it is clear that the idea of "mind over matter" that may have seemed just a science fiction concept is instead a true one.

However the fact that PK has been shown to be a reality settled one question only to raise others. Who has this ability? Is it a characteristic of only a few special persons, or is it general over the race? And still more important, what is this phenomenon by which will alone affects objective matter? What is the nature of PK? How does it fit into the personality?

The beginning of an answer to these questions is already possible from the research results that have accumulated. If seen in sufficient perspective the characteristics of PK stand out so that something of its general nature can be deduced.

### RESEARCH RESULTS IN PERSPECTIVE

Who has PK? Is it a widespread ability or something possessed by only a few persons? If only a few then its nature presumably might be different than if it is a general human characteristic. In the former circumstance it might be a "sport," a mutant, a peculiarity of a few that need not involve the race in general. But if it is something inherent in practically everyone, then it is of concern to everyone.

As it turns out, the answer to this question, as far as one is available is closely tied up with the answer to the second one, the nature of PK, as it is shown in the research results. From those results, and based on a survey of the persons who have been subjects in PK tests, it seems likely that PK is a universal human potentiality.

This impression comes first from the fact that the PK subjects have been unselected individuals, with no a priori reason to think that they could affect objects by will power. Except for the few in Gatling's contest they were not even successful gamblers who might have had a reason to think they could "do it." Instead they were mainly just persons who happened to be available. In a number of cases they were experimenter-subjects far from being convinced of their ability, but who used their own skepticism as a reason for a test.

This idea of the probable universality of the PK ability was supported when it began to be recognized that the person's mood and attitude affected his results. No subject succeeded all the time. Even such reliable ones as Margaret P., Lottie G., and Forwald scored mainly only on certain trials in the runs. This helped to give the impression that the ability was latent much of the time in these subjects. It presumably was latent in others, too, as more and more it was shown that the conditions of the test, as they affected the subject's attitude, decided the result. It was not the presence or absence of some inherent capacity that did it. Rather, the ability was shown as one which only operates under a narrow range of psychological conditions and is easily inhibited if those conditions are unfavorable. From that the deduction was natural that in most persons it is inhibited practically all the time.

The special conditions in the laboratory that seemed to be favorable involved normal mental states marked by interest, enthusiasm, personal involvement, strong desire or motivation, and freedom from distraction, doubt or inner conflict. Only if these psychological conditions were maintained did evidence of PK appear. It was the conditions, not the individual per se, that appeared to be the controlling factor.

The impression was strengthened still more by the evidence of psi-missing, wherein while some element of the test situation was unfavorable but still not bad enough to cause the PK ability to be entirely inhibited, a significant negative deviation resulted. It was this characteristic of sometimes yielding positive, sometimes negative deviations that showed that PK was not a constant ability that a person did or did not have but instead a process something like that in marksmanship. In that operation the person with his "sights" properly set may be able to hit the bull's eye. But if the sights should be inadvertently shifted a bit, then he must miss just as consistently as he hit before.

This characteristic of PK was thus shown as one more reason why the ability might be potential but not active in many persons. It was one more way in which the capacity might tend to cancel its own evidence and so remain unrecognized. In the laboratory this result was shown to be possible, for example, when decline effects were produced within sections of experiments in which positive deviations in one part were canceled by negative ones in another.

The realization that PK is a process that can operate to hit or to miss the target, quite drastically affects the concept of the nature of PK and shows it as a process that *needs to be directed.* This realization shows, too, that the psychological reaction of the subject to the conditions of the test determine the direction of the deviation. One can say that when conditions are favorable, positive deviations tend to result; when they are less so, negative ones; when they are entirely unfavorable, only chance scores will be produced. While these various indications do not finally prove that PK is latent in everyone, they give strong indication that such may be the case.

When the research was focused on the physical properties of the test objects, for instance when the size and number of dice were varied, then presumably the scores could have varied according to their mass. If a light and heavy ball should be thrown on a single toss, the light one would move farther than the heavy one and in inverse proportion to the mass of each.

But the PK results did not come out that way. The effect was greatest on the one the subject fancied most. In a test like Forwald's on the Bakelite and aluminum cubes in which he measured the actual dynes of force involved in the movement of the two kinds of cubes, he showed quite objectively that they did *not* react according to their mass relations. In his case his psychological attitude toward the two kinds of cubes is not reported, but in many other experiments by other investigators the scores generally followed the psychological rather than the physical factors involved.

However, at this point the results on the question of physical relations are not yet wholly definitive. They do not show whether the mass has no effect or whether they merely indicate that the psychological influence, within the physical ranges studied, is the more dominant one. Forwald's measurement was a beginning, and it gives encouragement to the idea that further attempts may yield more information. But thus far the physical range invest-igated is quite a restricted one. With dice the highest number released in a single throw in any reported test was 96. No great expenditure of energy would be required even if all of them had been affected, which was not the case. Instead, the rate of effect per cube was roughly the same as when smaller numbers were used.

In that connection, and as part of the finding that the results of experiments were not in proportion to the mass of the objects, it was found that when numbers of dice per throw were being compared most subjects failed to score above chance, when throwing one die at a time. Apparently it was because those tests were slow and boring. But when higher numbers were used no pronounced difference in average results *per die* was found. Lottie G. with six averaged a few tenths of a point per run above MCE and the rate was comparable still when 96 per throw were used as in some of the drug and hypnosis tests of Chapter 7. The deduction is that the entire amount of energy called out with the larger number must have been greater than with the smaller, but the level of success per run remained about the same. While results, say, with six dice might fluctuate from an average of 4.1 in some cases (when 4.0 was MCE) to 4.8 or 4.9 with a special subject like Woodruff at his best, the difference seemed to be personal and psychological and not one dependent on the number or size of the dice as such.

Observations like these make it unlikely that, because a small amount of energy would be required, microphysical particles should be better for PK tests than macrophysical ones. It is already clear that the limiting factor in PK tests with larger targets is not that the amount of force required is too great to be mustered. The limitation lies elsewhere, and to a large extent its nature still remains to be discovered.

The more puzzling question about the amount of energy involved in a PK experiment is that of how *great* rather than how small it can be. Although the range so far called for in experimental research is relatively small, that suggested by spontaneous cases is much larger. Of course the basis of reliability in the spontaneous area is still questionable, but if tentative credence be given to reports of poltergeist phenomena, and some of those from such physical mediums as D. D. Home, the one with whom Sir William Crookes made his test, fairly heavy objects like tables, chairs, and other furniture sometimes are moved. But even so, it is probably true that all movement reported would be within the physical strength of the person presumably involved so that the PK he shows could be the result of energy derived from his own physiological system.

As Owen remarked in his discussion of Virginia in the Sauchie poltergeist case (Chapter 14), none of the phenomena that occurred in connection with her would have been beyond the energy ability of a girl her size. But if an upper limit of this kind exists, it remains for future experimentation to demonstrate the fact.

However, if the energy utilized in PK is drawn from the physiological system of the human being involved, as seems a reasonable possibility, it is a kind of energy, or of energy transformation still unrecognized in the world of physical forces. It is a mental force that operates in the physical world as well, and is possibly not to be subsumed entirely under the laws of either one but it may have aspects of both. Much further study is surely necessary before even a tentative understanding on this point will be possible. At the present, however, it at least looks as if the limiting factors are within the psychological area. The magnitude of an individual's test result does not appear to be a constant one like the pressure of water in a tap, but instead something regulated by the human purpose involved. Thus it is that the attempt to understand PK continues to be centered mainly on the mental processes involved even while they must be inferred and measured indirectly by way of the physical effects.

### PK AS A MENTAL PROCESS

The most distinctive aspect of the mental process involved in PK is that it goes on without introspective awareness. In sight or hearing, or in performing a motor act, the person normally knows he does it, but he has no such evidence when psi occurs.

In experiences in real life that seem to involve PK, as when pictures fall or clocks stop at the time of the death of a distant friend, the individuals so entirely lack any awareness of their own part in it that they spontaneously think the other person (perhaps dying at the time) was somehow enabled to do it; the religious, perhaps may think that it was "a sign from God." But it does not suggest to anyone that he himself may have been the one responsible.

In the laboratory the situation is a bit different superficially because there the person makes a conscious effort to affect the target object. But he is just as unable to know introspectively whether or not he did so, as the person in the spontaneous situation. This is something that every subject has many opportunities to test, because in every subject's record of a run of PK trials both hits and misses occur. PK and ESP records are a bit different on this matter for on a few occasions a subject has succeeded in making a perfect score in an ESP run (25 trials), but no PK subject has ever achieved a perfect run (24 trials). Just why this is so is a matter of conjecture, but at least the lack of perfect runs means that subjects always have the opportunity to distinguish hits from misses. Yet all that each one knows is that he wants to get a given result, but until he gets objective information about it, he does not know whether he was successful.

If a subject is successful on a given trial, he still does not know if it was just a hit made by chance or if he exercised the force that produced it. If the total results of a run of tests show that PK probably was involved, he knows no more about how he managed to accomplish the feat than he would know just how he guided his muscles to hit a tennis ball. The PK ability thus appears to be as unlearned as any physiological process.

The fact that the mental side of PK falls in the area of unconscious processes is no doubt responsible for its late discovery and also for the relative difficulty of finding the conditions that control it. Unconscious mental processes can only be studied indirectly, and in this particular area, no guidelines had yet been laid when PK research began. For in the field of psychology, technically the one concerned with all aspects of mental life, the study of consciousness itself has been an unpopular one, and unconscious mental processes, too, have largely been neglected. Parapsychologists, therefore, did not have the way made easy for them. In the study of this unconscious process they have had to make their way without the help of already established psychological rules.

However, successful results in PK research show that at least a slight degree of conscious control of the unconscious process can be attained. The conscious and unconscious levels of mentality involved are not entirely separate. Thanks to that fact, PK experiments have succeeded to statistically significant degrees, even though never perfectly. Even fairly complicated tasks have yielded a measure of success, as for instance Betty H.'s attempt to secure high and low results on two kinds of dice at once (Chapter 8); or Cox's when he secured a significant discrimination between place and face targets in one of his experiments (Chapter 11). As far as such initial experiments can go to do so they indicate considerable control even of fairly complex operations.

The situation in the laboratory, however, is necessarily an artificial one with its demand that an unconscious process respond to conscious intention. The spontaneous experiences that appear to be instances of PK in life situations, have no conscious aspect whatever. But most of them do involve emotional crises, so that on both counts the laboratory and the spontaneous circumstances are different.

Still, in a few spontaneous cases, the level of emotional involvement may be relatively slight. This at least means that whether or not PK may be more likely to occur under strong emotion, it is not entirely limited thereby. It appears that in laboratory situations strong conscious motivation can replace it. This fact probably explains why it has been possible to get results in the laboratory where the emotional aspect is practically nonexistent. However, it should be noticed that in successful experiments the subjects did attain a degree of interest and involvement and this perhaps was a substitute at least for the mental state present in the spontaneous cases that involved only a slight emotional element. This level may not have been the optimum, but still was great enough that extra-chance scoring could occur. Even so, however, as Pratt's analysis showed, the areas were limited in which circumstances were sufficiently favorable that the scoring could reach an extra-chance level. Those places were usually at the beginnings of runs or the first runs of a set or page of records. In Forwald's later case the likelihood of outstanding evidence of PK was circumscribed even more and frequently occurred mainly on his first throws for the A-side sets.

What is different about the beginning? For one thing it has novelty. In this context novelty apparently means a more nearly uncluttered mind, an openness that could permit a breakthrough from unconscious into conscious levels. It may also mean that the subject is then most clearly aware of his own objective; that just then his will is more definitely directed. In the laboratory the emotional concomitant of spontaneous experiences is apparently to be translated into strong motivation to succeed. At the start of each new test unit, the subject usually has a fuller realization of that objective than later when it is progressively more difficult to keep the full force of determination necessary while he remembers the target (an artificial objective of course), remembers his just previous score, is somewhat aware—marginally —of the entire test situation and is also struggling to keep out extraneous thoughts of other competing interests. That the situation then tends to choke off his ability to get evidence of PK may not be much to wonder about. Instead it could seem a marvel that he sometimes succeeds in scoring successfully. And also the reason can be appreciated that laboratory experiments have not given more nearly perfect results. Since they are attempts to mobilize an unconscious ability by conscious desire, discovering the way to do it has been a little like learning to operate an intricate machine without a chart or directions and even, in the beginning, without an appreciation of just the type of machine it is. However, now that discovery has been made and the unconscious nature of the process recognized. In the Parapsychology Laboratory that recognition was hastened because of the similarity that was early seen between ESP and PK.

### THE RELATIONSHIP OF ESP AND PK

Since the research on ESP was well along when that on PK began, similarities were quickly recognized. Even though superficially the two were very different, ESP being a way of getting information without the senses and PK a way of affecting objects without material contact, still it was almost expected that a relationship between the two effects would be found, for one aspect of their historical background was similar, and suggested a relationship even before the first dice tests had been undertaken.

As already discussed, the possibility that there could be such an effect as that of mind over matter had been suggested by certain kinds of spontaneous happenings, that had been occasionally reported over the ages, just as had some that suggested ESP. They were both taken as message bearers, bringing information about some distant or otherwise unknown event. One mother, for instance, might "just know," or have a vivid dream that, and when, her son was stricken on a distant battlefield, presumably an ESP experience; another might find her son's picture unaccountably fallen from the wall at the critical time—probably a spontaneous PK effect. Thus both forms served the purpose of bringing information. A close relationship between the two had thus become something of a traditional assumption, and both, in popular terms, were considered "psychic" experiences.

As research on both topics proceeded, the fundamental similarities were remarked again and again, and the question raised thereby whether they were actually different or simply two aspects of one basic mental process. In fact, as was pointed out in the very first report (Chapter 2), it seemed necessary to assume ESP in order to explain the PK effect, for it obviously has an intelligent aspect, too, and requires the recognition of the proper die face, which would have to be by extrasensory perception. The discovery of PK, then, seemed to be in effect a further confirmation of ESP ability. As far as the basic process was concerned PK was too closely related to ESP to be considered as a separate function.

In that first report, JBR went on to say that if this relation between PK and ESP does in fact exist, then "there will likely be found in the research of the future many common properties and reactions." He continued, that the decline effect recently discovered in the PK data (in the 1942 analysis) was very similar to decline effects in ESP data; this experimental result already strongly suggested a relationship.

A few years later, in 1947, in his book *The Reach of the Mind*, mentioned in Chapter 8, JBR practically assumed the unity of the two processes, and as the research proceeded, further tests did confirm the earlier impression. The test conditions that gave the best results were shown to be practically the same for PK as for ESP. In both a certain mental state that seemed to be a peculiar but definite combination of motivation and enthusiastic interest—almost a gamelike spirit—appeared to be the best. And in both, too, the psi-missing effect occurred, and similar position effects in runs of tests.

Then came several experiments with "blind" targets, the actual target hidden, and only available by ESP: Thouless first, and then Osis, Fisk, McConnell, and Forwald—each by slightly different techniques showing that ESP too must have functioned to produce the PK results. After all of these demonstrations the point was fairly well established that ESP and PK both were basically unconscious mental processes that operated either to hit or miss their targets according to the circumstances, and also that both probably were part of the potential capacity of all individuals.

The latter seemed just as likely to be true of PK as of ESP and for practically the same reasons.

Long before this it had been clear in the ESP research, that the various types of ESP effects—the telepathic, the clairvoyant, and the precognitive—occurred as though they were all manifestations of a single process. The differences between them concerned only the kind of information they brought. In clairvoyance it was about things, in telepathy about thoughts in other people's minds, in precognition about future events. But the fundamental ESP process appeared to be the same regardless of these differences in kind of target. It simply was one of getting information about the environment without using the senses. The working assumption, that ESP is a single process, had already been made before it began to be considered likely that PK too was part of the same process. But as the evidence accumulated, including that from blind targets, it became more and more logical to consider that psi is a single many-sided ability.

As the psi research has progressed it seems more and more as if the experimenter is actually dealing only *with the unconscious processes by which psi comes into expression, and that in essence ESP and PK are deeper-lying realities with which the experimental methods of the present do not yet deal directly.* However, it seems clear at least that psi serves the purpose of directly relating the mental side of life to the physical world. A few theories about this and attempts to fit ESP into the scheme of things have been advanced by persons philosophically inclined, but very few indeed have yet attempted the ESP–PK combination.

### THEORIES ABOUT THE NATURE OF PK

Just as the present still marks an early stage in the experimental investigation of PK, so is it likewise with the development of theories about it. To the world in general very little about the PK research is known. The discovery of PK has come about so quietly that it has been easy to overlook or ignore it, and even if known the idea that there could actually be such an ability has been so generally unsuspected that reports of it have had little impact.

Actually, too, the emphasis of a new field like that of parapsychology must properly be empirical. It must be first of all a search for facts. The majority of parapsychologists have been too busy in this search to spend much time on speculation. They have tacitly realized it would seem, that the first necessity is a body of facts with which a theory could concern itself, or else the theory might go off wildly into the blue and be a hindrance rather than a help to succeeding experimenters. Thus, though they have had reasons for making the tests they made, speculative theories on a comprehensive scale have had only a secondary place.

However, even though parapsychologists have not done much theorizing they have thought about the meaning of their phenomena and have questioned how and where they fit into the scheme of the universe. While few have recorded their queries both JBR and Thouless have some of theirs on record. But neither one considered the meaning of PK alone. For both of them, the first assumption made, or deduction from known experimental facts, was that ESP and PK are closely related and must be considered together.

Because of McDougall's death before the PK investigation was scarcely started the thinking he would have done, or perhaps already had done, as to the meaning of psi and its place in the human personality never was recorded.

While a very few persons not within the field of parapsychology have advanced possible explanations as to the place of psi, their ideas are usually highly theoretical and hardly on a plane that can lead to actual tests. Most of them too, take into consideration ESP alone. The following one however includes PK as well.

## A *Psychiatrist-Psychologist Looks at Psi*

Dr. J. R. Smythies, an Edinburgh psychiatrist, in 1952 published an article that began by noting that experiments in parapsychology do not fit into current scientific theory.[1] He therefore considered it necessary that the fundamental assumptions of natural science be revised, and suggests some alternatives under which the parapsychological data could be included.

The fact that current theory will not accommodate the parapsychological data stems, Smythies said, from a fundamental error in outlook on the world. This error, a little like that of the ancient common sense assumption that the world is flat, is the one that presumes that the world of reality, the physical universe, is what it seems to the senses to be. But the psychological picture of the world and the actual physics of it are very different. Briefly stated, Smythies' argument is that the space-time system of the mind has been built up on the basis of this error. The system therefore is an illusion. In reality the three-dimensional world concept it has engendered is not necessarily true, or rather it is not necessarily complete. The three recognized dimensions may not be the only ones.

Smythies then postulated a seven-dimensional universe, of which the familiar three-dimensional one is only a part. The psyche (his word for mind), he said, may consist of "an organized *material* entity located in higher dimensional space. [A definition of material, however, is not given.] As such it could abstract information from the brain; or through another part of the mechanism could control its action."

Still, even with the psyche on a higher dimension than the brain Smythies found a gap between the psi phenomena and any organization by which liaison with the physical world could occur.

[1] Smythies, J. R., "The Extension of Mind." *J. Amer. Soc. psych. Res.*, 1951, 36, pp. 415–425.

But, he said, he thinks it must be realized that things may be invisible not because they are immaterial "but because they may be on the other side of a dimensional interface." He felt however that further experimentation can close this gap.

The result of his paper was a series of comments from a number of authors, mainly philosophers. One of the commentators, however, was Thouless who while questioning some of Smythies' ideas still felt that it was a theory that should stimulate experimental inquiry. Thus far, however, no report has indicated that it did so. In the field of parapsychology at least it seems that experimental investigation has usually been undertaken in the first place because of an observation or actual experience that raised a question and that therefore needed to be investigated. From there inquiry went on to the succeeding questions that the answer to the first one raised.

Within the field of parapsychology both JBR and Thouless have attempted to fit the psi-complex into the scheme of the personality. As a matter of fact, and as far as they go, the reflections of JBR and Thouless on the place of psi do offer a theory that deserves more consideration than it has had. While the two men did their thinking separately, the similarities in their general lines of thought far outweigh any differences. This may be testimony to the correctness of their general view of psi and its place in nature.

## Where PK Fits In—JBR

As far back as an editorial in the *Journal of Parapsychology* in June 1943, JBR suggested a way that ESP–PK, or psi, could fit into the already known attributes of mind. It might fit in most easily, he said, by supposing first of all a return to the common sense idea of the relation of the mind to the body, which is also the traditional and religious view. It is that man consists of a nonphysical mind and a physical body and that the mind exercises an active influence on the physical system. As such it constantly controls and guides the muscles. PK, with its combination of thought and action, would be the routine method by which the control is exercised, and in this view PK would be no extraneous process whatever.

Taking the same idea further in a later discussion[2] JBR went on more specifically:

Belief in such a capacity of the mind (as PK) is probably as old as the distinction of mind and body itself. It is one of those familiar, taken-for-granted concepts that are no longer noticed in our intellectual life. Some sort of psychokinetic action obviously has to occur every time our thinking initiates neuromuscular activity. This psychophysical effect evidently produces certain electrochemical and other physical changes in the brain, and starts a train of physical reaction in the nerves and muscles of the body.

Still later[3] he discussed his view of the relation of mind and body by making clear that he intended no such final basic division of nature as is embodied in traditional dualism. He felt that a unifying continuity of exchange between thought and matter was real and necessary too. For him, an inclusive energy concept served to integrate the two areas of nature, thought and matter. PK as demonstrated in the laboratory represented volitional interaction of mind with matter and suggested a parallelism with the mind-body relationship.

So it could be for him that, on the assumption that it takes energy to direct energy, the path of action would be that mental energy directs nervous energy. Nervous energy directs muscular energy. Muscular energy moves physical objects. In this formulation mental energy therefore was implicit and to be taken for granted in all discussions of the relation of body and mind.

[2] Rhine, J. B., *The Reach of the Mind* (New York: William Sloan Associates, 1947), p. 87.

[3] Rhine, J. B., *New World of the Mind* (New York: William Sloane Associates, 1953), p. 202.

The main difference between PK of this ongoing everyday kind and that which is displayed in the experimental situation, or in spontaneous instances involving it, would be that in these latter situations it goes on outside of the organism and moves external objects. If considered in this light, the idea of PK is not quite so strange as at first it seemed. To JBR a chain or pathway of energy like this was brought to reality by the discovery in PK experiments that the mind has *real* and *demonstrable force.* Mental energy was no longer just an untested hypothetical term but a useful working concept like energy in any physical system even though in this application it was newer and still in need of thorough exploratory study.

The important point in this natural science approach, was that it could be put to controllable quantitative test. Unlike many purely hypothetical approaches, this one could be kept in mind as tests proceeded. Already it seemed that some of the basic criteria of the known physical world did not apply here. But JBR felt that any final decision as to the energetic relations of psi processes with the physical world could and must await the results of future research. For him it was much less urgent to decide just where PK fits into the scheme of the universe, than to get more data about it so that a more intelligent theory of where it fits can in time be formulated.

However, he felt that the first step in that direction had already been taken. The results of research on ESP had shown that the mind is not limited like the body is to the immediate place and time.

## ESP AND SPACE AND TIME

ESP experiments over space, the "distance tests," developed in the early 1930s from tests of telepathy and clairvoyance in which the subject and the target material were near each other. Using for his subjects volunteer college students mainly, in the early 1930s JBR had tested their clairvoyant ability by asking them to identify the symbols on a concealed deck of cards. The ESP deck, developed for the purpose, consisted of 25 cards of five each of the symbols $+$, $\bigcirc$, $\square$, $\approx$, $\star$, in which the number of hits expected by chance alone, on the average, was five per run through the deck.

After a number of subjects had demonstrated their ability to identify the cards when near them tests were made with the cards at greater distances. These too succeeded to an equally significant degree, so it appeared that, at least over the ranges studied the distance had had no appreciable effect.

Whether or not the ESP ability is entirely unaffected by distance, has been the subject of further tests by Osis, the same experimenter who (Chapter 8) carried out a blind target PK experiment. He has reported slight effects, but his tests are still inconclusive. Whatever the outcome of them may eventually be, the question becomes somewhat academic in view of the much more extensive tests of precognition (prophecy) that have been made, beginning in 1933 right after the distance tests showed that proximity of test cards to the subject is not an important factor in ESP.

For these precognition tests only a simple change in technique from that used in clairvoyance tests was necessary. Subjects were asked to write down in a vertical column the order in which they thought the symbols in the deck would be *later*, after the deck was shuffled.

One of the first subjects to be tried out on this was Hubert Pearce, an early subject of JBR's who in large numbers of clairvoyance tests had scored an average of seven per 25 (MCE = 5), when close to the cards. Now in 106 runs in which the cards were shuffled *after* he had made his calls his average was practically the same, 7.1 per run. The same kind of tests were tried with 15 other subjects. Between 1934 and 1937 they together scored above MCE sufficiently to produce on 4,523 runs a deviation of 614, CR = 4.5; p = millions to one.[4]

[4] Rhine, J. B., "Experiments Bearing on the Precognition Hypothesis." *J. of Parapsychol.*, 1938, pp. 238–254.

All of these early precognition tests however, were only exploratory efforts on the topic. Later, methods of testing were refined (especially that of randomizing the targets) and varied, but the evidence that precognition can be demonstrated was already introduced by these simple early trials. Even by the time the PK work began, JBR had already launched the precognition research and had positive indication that time is not a barrier to ESP. Accordingly, since space and time are the main criteria of physicality, it was a breakthrough to find a mental ability that was not bound by them. It meant that the operations of mental life are at least in some degree free from the restrictions of the physical world. This was to demonstrate that mind has a nonphysical element; that it includes an aspect that seems profoundly different from that of the physical world, even while it is all part of a single universe.

Adding now the results of the PK experiments, which showed that the mind also has *real force* and can exert actual agency, JBR felt that sound support was given to the hypothesis that the mental aspect of the human being has some control over his physical aspect. Even though it seemed to mean only a relative dualism, at least the results of the psi experiments seemed to sustain a workable view of the relation of mind and body, a kind of diversity within a relative unity. The new element was only that PK had shown that mental influences could operate *beyond* the sensory-motor system as well as within it.

In addition was the fact already mentioned that ESP had been recognized as an ability that operated below the level of consciousness. It had no organ for its expression like the senses did. Even its spontaneous manifestations did not come in forms of their own. That was one reason they were difficult to identify. They came in the same forms used in other mental processes not connected with ESP, which were dreams, intuitions, and occasionally even hallucinatory experiences. And now, PK, too, had shown itself to be basically a quite unconscious process, and one which could only be recognized by its effect on the physical object it influenced.

All of these characteristics were well established by 1957 when in another general summing up, JBR discussed still further the possible genesis of psi and its place in nature as he glimpsed it.[5] He felt that the fact the psi operations were both nonphysical and unconscious elements of personality suggested that psi may have originated far back in evolution; that as primitive organisms met more specialized physical elements of their environment and were modified accordingly, and as the sense organs developed and helped them to adjust to those conditions, consciousness may have developed along with them. It could well have come about then, that over the ages, the more elementary and probably even primordial psi function became submerged, fell into comparative disuse as the sensory-motor systems began to function. It thus seemed possible to him that the psi processes "may constitute a more fundamental aspect of the organism than do consciousness and sense experience. These," he concluded, "are at this stage tentative lines of thought suggested by the facts."

## Where PK Fits In—Thouless

The thinking of Dr. Thouless regarding the place and explanation of PK runs parallel with that of JBR and fills in certain areas that JBR did not touch upon in his printed articles.

Thouless too accepted the close relationship and probable unity of ESP and PK. In 1946, with his collaborator, Dr. Wiesner, he wrote an article about the nature of psi phenomena as he could interpret it, in which he considered primarily the probable evolutionary origin of ESP and PK.[6]

The discussion began by a recognition of the fact that the several forms of ESP are probably all manifestations of a single ability, or in other words that ESP is a single process, whether

---

[5] Rhine, J. B., and J. G. Pratt, Parapsychology, Frontier Science of the Mind (Springfield, Ill.: Thomas 1957), p. 88.
[6] Thouless, R. H., and Wiesner, B. P., "On the Nature of Psi Phenomena." J. Parapsychol., 1946, 10, pp. 107–119.

occuring as clairvoyance, telepathy or precognition. He then went on to consider the way the mind makes contact with or learns about the world. The basic fact of course is that items in the outside world do become known to the person, or in Thouless' psychological terminology, "some part of the universe is projected by some means on the behavioral system of the organism." He named the two ways by which this "projecting" occurs; by sense perception and by ESP. The common way, by means of the senses he spoke of as "perceptually controlled," and, as he observed, this might have been the only way. But in fact another way too exists and that one, without the senses, he called "psi-determined." In the perceptually controlled type, only the part of the universe within sensory range is projected, but in the psi-determined type the area projected may be anywhere and at any time.

However, and this is where his theory about psi really begins, he drew attention to the confusion that would be caused if an organism were open to projections from the universe "at any place and any time." No organism so "bombarded" by the facts of the world could function effectively. It would *know too much.* Some degree of restriction would have to be imposed so that necessary interaction between the organism and the local surroundings could occur.

Thouless' idea, then, complementing that of JBR, was that nature may have accomplished this screening service by causing to be developed the more specific—and more restricted—sensory system, which confines the area to be projected to that of light and air waves and contacts through touch and chemical exchange; these avenues then become the ones through which organisms come to "sense" their environment.

When the idea of PK was added to that of ESP, Thouless supposed that in the primitive organism the PK ability also may have been unrestricted and potentially able to affect external matter. But as evolution occurred, here too more specific or more restricted application of the ability was needed, and nature responded with the development of the sensory-motor nervous system. With that, the free range of the PK effect became limited *within* the confines of the organism. This, of course, would be the ordinary PK by which supposedly the mind controls the body, as had been supposed too by JBR who also had thought of psi as being more primitive than the sensory-motor system.

As Thouless was to observe later, if the sensory and motor systems had in evolution come to be superimposed on the more primitive psi abilities then one of the curious facts of experimental psi might be explainable. This fact was that strong effort to succeed in psi tests often seemed to defeat its purpose (as had seemed to occur in several of his experiments), while in ordinary perception and motor activity, the greater the effort (within limits) the more effective the result is likely to be. This could mean that conscious voluntary effort tends to be channeled into the sensory-motor system, thus preventing the desired contact with the underlying psi system.

As Thouless closed this discussion he commented on the fact that despite an attempt like his to explain the possible place of the psi processes in the organism, they still do not fit into the general body of present day scientific theory. This is because that theory has been constructed only to cover the already known processes in sense perception and in movement controlled by nerves, and glands; each of which depends on a well-recognized type of "continuity" (i.e., physical intermediation) between the organism and the environment. But in the psi-processes such energetic continuity in any presently recognizable form is lacking. This, however, does not necessarily mean that no kind of causal continuity exists in these. It seems logical to suppose rather that here too a connection or continuity between mind and the physical universe must exist, but it is a type that has not yet been discovered. It is here that in JBR's formulation psi energy plays its part. It supplies the connecting link.

In a later article Thouless returned to the question of the nature of psi.[7] The findings of parapsychology, he said, reminded him

[7] Thouless, R. H., and Wiesner, B. F., "The Psi Process in Normal and 'Paranormal' Psychology." *Proc. Soc. psych. Res.*, 1947, 48, Part 174.

of scattered pieces of a jigsaw puzzle that did not seem to fit into the larger pattern of scientific psychology. He wanted to see to what extent they could be put together and whether a place for them could be found in the current pattern of scientific thought. However, he knew beforehand that it could only be found if changes were made in that thought, too.

The current pattern of scientific thought, however, was entirely mechanistic, so he began by marshaling the parapsychological facts of ESP and PK and dressing them up in behavioristic terminology. He drew attention once again to the fact (translated here from the imposed phraseology) that the two kinds of perception (the "perceptually-controlled" and the "psi-determined") differ only in that material, or content received by the senses, is used in one kind but not in the other. He showed again and in greater detail that the basic process in the two is the same as far as the brain and nervous system are concerned and that both ESP and PK are but *unfamiliar* forms of everyday sense perception and habitual motor activity.[8]

But Thouless could not stay within the set pattern any farther. When trying to explain *how* these "paranormal" forms could occur he could not do so without breaking out of the restrictions imposed by the current psychological concept of the mind-body relationship. If, according to the accepted view in psychology, biology, and physiology, consciousness is merely a reflection of the way the organism responds to the activity of the brain, then there is indeed no place for the psi process.

At this point, therefore, Thouless gave up the job of trying to fit psi into the psychological thought pattern. He boldly pre-

---

[8] NOTE: In his own words, after a short discussion of the viewpoint on the mind-body problem of an earlier century he expresses his idea thus: "There is no such venerable ancestry for the other part of our hypothesis that extrasensory perception, psychokinesis, . . . are exosomatic examples of processes familiar to us in their endosomatic forms as normal perception, normal volition . . . respectively. Indeed such an hypothesis could not have been formulated until, in comparatively recent times, psychical research had demonstrated the reality of these "paranormal" processes."

sumed instead that in control of the brain an entity must exist that is distinct from it, just as according to the older viewpoint the mind was held to be. He needed a term for it, but the word "mind," was inexact and psychologists had therefore practically ceased using it; the word "soul" could have been substituted, but that had religious overtones that were irrelevant to his purpose. He therefore coined his own term or rather selected one that had no preformed connotations. It was a letter from the Hebrew alphabet, *shin*. He used it to signify the element in personality that is in control, or in other words as the "I" that exercises the will guiding the personality and that also learns about the external world by the perceptual processes, whether it be with the senses as in sense perception or without them as in ESP.

Thouless knew of course that this idea would not be accepted by orthodox scientists, unless they could "break the barrier" of current ways of thinking. But psi had been shown to be a fact and it had to be accommodated. This idea of mind, or *shin*, rather, seemed to him to be indicated by the kind of phenomena the experiments had shown ESP and PK to be.

He closed by observing that although the greater part of the interaction of *shin* and the material world is restricted to its own organism thus making psi the *un*usual kind of process, this may just be an accidental circumstance of the world we live in. For all anyone can know it might just as easily have been the other way around. Then psi would have been the usual kind, and sense perception and volition the unusual.

## A Place For PK in Neurophysiology—Eccles

As far as what could be called theoretical "working models" of psi are concerned, those of JBR and Thouless stand practically alone. But some years after Thouless' paper, in a field quite different from parapsychology the same model was assumed when a place was found in which PK seemed to be a necessity. It was pointed out in a study of the relation of mind and brain by an Australian neurophysiologist, Professor John Eccles, later Sir John Eccles.[9] That even a discussion of the mind-body problem should have come in the field of neurophysiology was unexpected, for neurophysiologists, like most biologists, were as mechanistic in outlook as behaviorists. In fact, all of the life sciences had long been endeavoring to be as objective as the physical branches, which of course depend for their raw data upon measurements that are made by *sensory* observations.

By the 1950s when Eccles' book appeared few voices were heard in any biological field showing any but a physicalistic viewpoint. JBR and Thouless in their theories of psi were definitely swimming against the stream when they called for a mind-controlled instead of a brain-controlled human being, and of course any biologist who did so was similarly running counter to the orthodox view in his own professional field. Therefore Eccles' was venturing out of line, both in his own special field and in biology in general.

The scope of Eccles' book was plainly stated in the preface as covering the entire field of neurophysiology from the reaction of a single nerve or muscle fiber to those of the cerebral cortex and finally to the relationship of the brain to the mind. It was an attempt he said to see to what extent the advance of knowledge of the nervous system could help in the understanding of the brain and how the interaction between the brain and mind could occur.

By definition Eccles restricted his usage of the word "mind" to conscious mental states, and the final chapter of his book was devoted to the mind-body problem—the one that for decades had been ignored even by psychologists, for whom, as already mentioned, no mind-body problem existed. Eccles, on the other hand, maintained that mental events have just as much validity as do data that can be objectively measured. For example, even though

[9] Eccles, John Carew, *The Neurophysiological Basis of Mind* (Oxford: The Clarendon Press, 1953).

muscular movement can be produced as the result of artificial stimulation of the motor cortex and the fact commonly given a mechanistic interpretation, he found that subjects reported a significant difference between such acts and willed ones. They report that the two do not *feel* the same. Also there is reason to believe that each exercise of will, each percept, even each memory, is accomplished by a specific pattern of neuronal activity in the brain.

He pointed out, too, that the study of the amazingly complex neuronal structure of the brain shows that any influence that initially causes the discharge of even one neuron could be passed on, as it were, "stepped up," so that it could affect countless numbers of other neurones. Thus, the initial influence of the will might be very slight in terms of actual energy and yet be effective over the entire organ.

Eccles thus found mental states and brain activity so closely linked on every count, that he saw no problem in assuming that the will influences the related brain activity. Thus like JBR and Thouless he attributed causal action to the mind.

The question then was: How does this action of the mind on brain occur? The concept of PK was still quite new in 1953 when Eccles' book was published, but he noted that "extensive reports of well-controlled experiments . . . give evidence . . . that there is a two-way traffic between mind and the matter-energy system. Of particular significance for the above hypothesis of mind influence on the brain, are the psychokinetic experiments." The fact that the PK effect as measured on falling dice was so small that it could only be detected by statistical measurement was no argument against its place in Eccles' theory, because he had shown that the brain is a mechanism susceptible to very slight influences.

It was in order to accommodate ESP as well as PK that Eccles recognized that the liaison between brain and mind is a two-way system and that in perception, material from the brain, such as that from sense impressions (and without them as in ESP) can be transferred to the mind.

Speaking then of his hypothesis in general in which all the machinery of brain and nervous system is guided by the will, he observes that it is not a simple machine of ropes and pulleys but a system of "ten thousand million neurones . . . momentarily posed close to a just-threshold level of excitability." It is the kind of a machine, according to him, "that a 'ghost' could operate, if by ghost we mean in the first place an 'agent' whose action has escaped detection even by the most delicate physical instruments." The description could very well fit the psi process.

The several attempts to account for psi and fit it into the natural world agree almost entirely as far as they cover the same points. None of the authors is able to construct a theory within the limits of a mechanistic framework. The three that take up the point (Smythies does not) agree that PK appears to be the connecting link by which the normal interaction of mind and body is made. In JBR's terminology it is the energy or force of mind that initiates brain action. In man's attempt to understand himself this is a function the necessity of which has been heretofore unrecognized. And because it has been, one might interpolate, the relationship between mind and body has been such a difficult question, the answer being tossed back and forth as it were, from period to period depending on the prevailing viewpoint.

However, the theorizing of the persons as outlined above shows, not only that each one found a place for PK in the normal interaction of mind and body within the organism, but that each one found it necessary, in order to make that interaction reasonable, to suppose the action originating in the mind rather than in the brain. The falling dice did not cause the person to feel that he had willed the target face to come up, but he willed the way they should fall, and this is mind-over-matter action.

An objective of the PK research was to find the answer to the question of the relation of mind and body, but the answer it gives makes it necessary to "break the barrier" of current trends of thinking. After all, however, the barrier is not a fact of nature. It is just one *put up* rather recently in western thought especially.

It has been put up because the analytic, reductionist processes of science have made it look that way. But looks can be deceptive. The earth looked flat, but when it was so considered, there too many little observational discrepancies were found that did not fit in, and which were indications that the prevailing concept was imperfect.

The mechanistic trend of thought today also has its items that do not fit in. For one thing none of the spontaneous cases fit the pattern. Occurrences like a picture falling from the wall at a time particularly meaningful to an individual, which could only be taken as a coincidence before, now with the discovery of psi can at least be given a tentative explanation. Such an occurrence could mean that just then the person's PK energy was affecting an object external to its own organism within which ordinarily it was confined, and that it affected some object (preferably perhaps, one that was associated with the person in crisis) and affected it physically. Such a situation would be one in which PK would function suddenly and momentarily. Possibly it might be dimly analogous to the startle reaction of a person to an unexpected noise. This might be the quick spontaneous—even though unconscious—response to the news of crisis presumably supplied by ESP. It would be an unconscious response ending almost as quickly as it started, marking in an external way an essentially blocked ESP awareness.

In recurrent situations, however, it might be a more prolonged effect. In poltergeist cases, for instance, granting that some of them may be genuine, possibly because of some unusual and continuing emotional situation the PK ability again affects an object other than its own organism, and does so repeatedly, over an indefinite period of time. One feature in the majority of such cases is that the individual suspected of being involved is in a state of relatively chronic emotional unrest, which could result in repeated PK effects. Presumably the individual involved is just as unaware of his part in the occurrences as is the subject in a test. In neither case does he have introspective awareness of his own involvement. Something like this could be the explanation of these types of physical effects.

The above suggestion is a suggestion only. No studies have yet been made to confirm it, or to show a better explanation. Even so, however, it seems clear enough that with the addition of the concept of psi, these items too, would find a logical place in the scheme of things. As long as they were just isolated individual reports of occurrences that did not fit the pattern, they could be ignored. However, now that the psi research has given its results in the legal tender of science—statistical significance and confirmation—those results can take their place in the orderly processes of nature too. However, the fitting in of certain spontaneous experiences would only be one result and, on the whole, a minor one that should follow when psi is recognized as an adjunct of personality.

Just when that recognition will come is a good question, for the PK energy, as foregoing pages show is one so hidden, so subtle that even up to 1969 no need for it has been felt in philosophical theory nor has its occurrence been suspected in general science. Also its effects in nature have fitted in too smoothly to have been noticed, except for the few persons in parapsychology who were sufficiently arrested by the inexplicable reports of seeming mental influence on matter to take up the question and investigate it. And even now the finding probably must be exposed in the scientific market place for an appreciable length of time before the customers will buy it. A cursory glimpse rather than a serious study of the data may well give the impression that it is something quite peripheral, if not extraneous to the natural order. However, that it is instead a force inherent, necessary, vital, turns out to be the case.

In Chapter 1, before the data had been presented, there seemed little point in considering in any detail the effect on the thought and outlook of the present if PK were taken seriously. Now that the evidence is in, it is clear that first of all the integration of the fact of psi into the conceptual picture of the personality means a complete reversal in the current theory of the mind-body relation. The implications resulting from a reversal from a brain-dominated (cerebrocentric) concept to a mind-dominated (psychocentric) one each person can envisage for himself. With JBR's intimate contact with the idea of PK and with the experimental data from the inception of research in 1934, until the present, his outlook on the meaning of PK is the following:

"It staggers my imagination to conceive all the implications that follow now that it has been shown that the mind, by some means, as unknown as the mind itself, has the ability directly to affect material operations in the world around it. Let us look clear-eyed and fearlessly at what this means, first in the three areas that are the most directly affected, physics, biology, and psychology.

"In physics, a change must come no matter how soon or late, for that science certainly cannot consider itself unaffected by such findings as these. The known physical energies that of course operate in a PK test interact with an unknown causal influence, a mental force that is as yet entirely unrecognized in any of the physical sciences.

"In biology too the orthodox viewpoint long has been that no causal influence operates in the living organism that does not consist of some combination of essentially physical principles. In consequence it will probably be long before psi will be considered an acceptable component of the living system. But when the time comes biology will have a new type of causality to consider and incorporate. Then a new problem area too will be added, that of the role of psi as a biological determinant. It is true that thus far only the ESP side of the psi process has been studied actively in animals, but there has been on the part of laymen a long and deep-seated interest in the question of what mind can do to the living organism, to its functions and to its health. Beginning researches have already been made (and reviewed herein) on the PK effect on living targets, plant and animal, in health and disease, but the acceptance of the full significance of PK in the living system has an even more profound bearing; it raises many questions that will long be awaiting answers. For instance, what has been the role of psi back at the stage of evolution when rudimentary mental urges must have stirred in the primitive organism? In other words, what must have been the role of PK in evolutionary progress? The point of greatest importance here is not that the establishment of psi offers a new theoretical solution to these great problems of the origin of organisms but that it offers a firm exploratory empirical method of finding the possible facts and thereby ruling out some of the speculations with which men have too long been satisfied; speculations ruling out a possible psychical force or agency in the individual. Now as this PK story shows, the psi factor exists at least in *man's* nature, and with considerable evidence that it extends beyond the species.

"But to the psychologist PK is a gift of territory it had not dared to claim for lack of the kind of evidence it could easily demonstrate in the laboratory. But now with the findings of parapsychology, psychology will have to become a broader field once it recognizes that the mind has real agency and real existence. For one thing now a real psychophysics can be recognized. For the first time a distinctive psychical factor can be seen as influencing a physical operation. In general psychology in the past no one could ever tell from all the phenomena labeled psychophysics whether the *psycho* actually was causing the action of the neuromuscular system. But now a new department of energetic relations is indicated. The evidence of PK along with that of ESP establishes the case for the reality of mind, based upon more than mere clinical observation as is much of the present field of psychology. The reality of psi is an oft-repeated demonstrated experimental fact.

"These consequences of the findings of parapsychology however are not limited just to these pure sciences of physics, biology, and psychology. Other immediate effects also follow. Now for the first time mind is what the man-in-the-street thought it was all along—something of a force in itself; something that gave him some kind of special volitional freedom. He could not have been very certain of it, but after all he was intuitively right in following the heritage of the common sense of the race, that the mind was real in spite of the fact that a couple of generations of psychologists had been trying to discourage the idea and supplant it with a model of mechanistic behaviorism.

"Further it is not just the man in the street who was intuitively right on this point. The man in the pulpit too was right in preaching that the human spirit is something more than the material of his body and brain. For the first time science offered a little support to his view although necessarily limited, as yet. Now much of the seeming miraculous on which the church has depended for its special view of man's nature is shown to be the result of principles hitherto overlooked by the sciences: principles that make that "miraculous" possible, even though making the explanations natural ones.

"These practical effects on the man in the street, and in the church, will affect all the areas where it is important to know what a man really is, as in education and even more clearly in psychotherapy, areas in which it matters greatly if people are machines—or persons.

"But there may be a long wait for all these implications and bearings and meanings to be appreciated. The power of conservatism is strong. But the inevitability of change in intellectual climate is stronger still, however slow moving that change may seem."

From JBR's viewpoint and even from the mere accumulation of PK data, it is clear that the story of PK and of the entire psi development is far from finished. It has only just begun. It throws out too many challenges not to be carried further.

With a rising generation, hopefully less tradition bound than the older ones, and clamoring for new problems, new causes, new objectives to pursue, the challenges of psi research should not for long go unaccepted. On that account, a further chapter in the story of PK may confidently be expected.

*Index of Names and Topics*

# Index of Names and Topics

❧

Akolkar, V. V., 246–47

Alcohol, use of in PK tests; *see under* Physiological variables

American Society for Physical Research, 180, 185, 300

Animals, use of in experiments
mice, 317
paramecia, 312–15

Anxiety, effect of on PK; *see under* Psychological variables

Apparitions; *see* Physical effects

Attitude and PK test scoring, 14, 64, 103, 151–52, 173, 176, 180–84, 187, 195
comparison of men vs. women, 179–80

Australian aborigines as subjects, 173–77

Automatic recording, 113, 185, 211, 286

Automatic writing, 300

Averill, Richard, 117–20, 120–21

Baer, George, 50–53

Bailey, Wilbur E., 137–38

Barry, Jean, 323–25

Behaviorism, 5–6

Beloff, John, 156–58

Binski, S. R., 138–41

"Blockage," 203–04

Blunden, J., 214–16

Brugmanns, H. J. F. W., 5

Cadoret, Remi J., 316–17

Cambridge University, 132

Carington, Whately, 67–68

Carpenter, James C., 247

Chauvin, Rémy, 160–61

Children as subjects, 133–37, 161, 200–04

Clairvoyance, 6, 7, 186, 302, 370, 375–76

Communications from the deceased; *see* Spontaneous PK

Conscious attention, effect of on PK tests, 261–62, 273, 275, 366–67

Controls
against skillful throwing, 81–83
increased during second stage of research, 73
in early dice tests, 18
on dice bias, 76–77

Control series
in PK tests, 59, 253–54, 260, 267–69, 276, 314
to determine dice bias, 89–92, 112